# PLAYING THROUGH

PLAYING

# THROUGH

Modern Golf's Most Iconic Players
and Moments · JIM MORIARTY

UNIVERSITY OF NEBRASKA PRESS · LINCOLN AND LONDON

Library of Congress Cataloging-in-Publication Data
Names: Moriarty, Jim.
Title: Playing through: modern golf's most iconic players
and moments / Jim Moriarty.
Description: Lincoln: University of Nebraska Press, 2016.
Identifiers: LCCN 2016011020
ISBN 9780803278653 (hardback: alk. paper)
ISBN 9780803295452 (epub)
ISBN 9780803295469 (mobi)
ISBN 9780803295476 (pdf)
Subjects: LCSH: Golf—History. | Golfers—Biography. | BISAC:
SPORTS & RECREATION / Golf.
Classification: LCC GV963 .M67 2016 | DDC 796.352—dc23
LC record available at https://lccn.loc.gov/2016011020

Set in ITC New Baskerville by M. Scheer.

For Maya and Hayley

# Contents

# Acknowledgments

This book would not have been possible without relying on the work I did over a thirty-five-year period for *Golf Digest* and *Golf World*, and for that, I'm deeply grateful. I'm especially thankful and privileged to have had the opportunity to do it in the first place. These days the number of resources available with a keystroke or two is vast, but some works are especially valuable. The series of annuals created for International Management Group and Mark H. McCormack by the late, great Bev Norwood—with contributing writers too numerous, and sometimes too anonymous, to mention—is worth every inch it occupies on the bookshelves. The biographies of Greg Norman and Seve Ballesteros by Lauren St. John and Melanie Hauser's book with Ben Crenshaw are timeless resources, as are the autobiographies of Nick Faldo and Jack Nicklaus, the latter written with Ken Bowden. *Sports Illustrated*'s "Vault" is a deep well of knowledge produced by a long list of great writers, from Dan Jenkins to Jaime Diaz. The interviews compiled and archived by ASAP Sports Transcripts are as rich a vein of primary material as exists in the game. The exquisite "My Shot" series, written by Guy Yocom for *Golf Digest,* is the finest compilation of interviews ever produced in the sport and the source of countless nuggets. And, when it comes to the history of golf, Bill Fields is nothing short of a divining rod.

# PLAYING THROUGH

# Introduction

In 1982 the Pebble Beach Golf Links on the Monterey Peninsula hosted the U.S. Open Championship and played to 6,815 yards and a par of seventy-two. In 2015, in the second round of the U.S. Open, Chambers Bay Golf Course on Puget Sound played to 7,695 yards and a par of seventy. Perhaps never in the six-hundred-plus-year history of golf has the game changed as much as it has in its last thirty or so years. If you need to find a fall guy, blame the computer chip.

No doubt there has been golf instruction since one Scottish shepherd wielded a crook more proficiently than another. From H. B. Farnie's book in 1857 to Bobby Jones's newsreels to high-speed photographic sequences and videotape, the golf swing has been as dissected as any single athletic move. Now, launch monitors can tell you everything about the flight of a golf ball except whether the eyes of the person who hit it are blue or brown. In 1982 drivers were polished persimmon, almost works of art. Now, they're outsized laboratory experiments the size of small pumpkins fashioned out of titanium with a measurable coefficient of restitution—something that guys in 1982 would have thought was the time it took to get rid of a hangover. Today, golf balls are engineered. In 1982 some guys carried little steel rings to make sure they were round. Back then golfers didn't travel with instructors or sit in the dark with sports psychologists or get their menus from nutritionists or have their backs pulverized by chiropractors or their abs ripped by personal trainers. If you saw an agent at all, it was because someone needed to fill the field in the Philippines in November and was prepared to pay handsomely, maybe several thousand dollars, to do it. These days every player has his or her "team."

Are golfers more fit now? Sure, but how much clean and jerk is too much? Are they mentally more able to compete at the highest level? Well, that depends on whom you're talking about and whether you think you can buy self-belief or, at the very least, rent it for a while. Has stretching championship venues like Gumby made the game better or just more expensive to maintain? Have sports psychologists slowed play with preshot routines and visualization? Are drivers that cost as much as the used vw beetle I bought right out of college in the early '70s worth the price, or have they priced the game out of reach? Those weren't even considerations thirty years ago.

Nostalgia, however, is a losing bet. Distance, time, cost, metadata, all the things that are right or wrong about the modern game, failed to do one thing—change it fundamentally. During my time covering golf, most of my colleagues and virtually all of the players were introduced to the game as children. I came to it as a sportswriter covering a beat no one else wanted and grew to understand that golf tests an athlete's insides like no other sport. To be able to perform as if that performance meant nothing more than stopping at the corner convenience store when it actually means all the world is an immeasurable talent some seem born into, while others forge it in failure. The essays that follow are about my people, the players I saw revealing the best of themselves in the biggest moments. Whatever it is that made Jack versus Tom great in 1982 hasn't been altered one whit. The fundamental things still apply, as time goes by.

# 1

## Last Tango in Pebble Beach

Whenever television cameras peer down from a blimp swimming through the air like a floating dolphin above Pebble Beach capturing the scenery of the Monterey Peninsula, some network wag will invariable trot out the old line attributed to Robert Louis Stevenson describing this stretch of majestic coastline as "the most felicitous meeting of land and sea in creation." Stevenson must have made up his mind fast.

The author of adventures like *Treasure Island* and *Kidnapped* shipped out of Scotland on the *Devonia* in August 1879 in hot pursuit of a married woman, Fanny Osbourne, whose husband was a crackerjack philanderer himself. After arriving in New York and journeying across North America by rail, Stevenson caught up with Fanny in Monterey, the capital of Alta California before the Mexican-American War. The tiny town with its heavy Spanish and Mexican influence had three streets with wooden walkways and, according to the haggard and nearly penniless writer, a "population . . . about that of a dissenting chapel on a wet Sunday in a strong church neighborhood." He was not greeted warmly by Fanny, who had yet to actually set her divorce from her debauched husband into motion. So, the sickly, impoverished, and love-stricken Stevenson took a horse and pack and headed off into the unfamiliar pine-covered hills above Carmel, where he became delirious and nearly died before being rescued by a couple of goat ranchers, one a seventy-two-year-old Mexican War veteran and the other an Indian named Tom. Nursed back to what passed for health in a man who always appeared, if not on death's door, to have a foot on its welcome mat, Stevenson moved into Monterey and took a job writing for the *Monterey Californian*, the state's first newspaper, earning the munificent sum of two dollars a week. Fanny left Monterey for Oakland by mid-October, and Stevenson followed her by the end of December, so the quote that is the Monterey Peninsula tradition like no other was penned by a freelance vagabond and quasi-vagrant Scottish émigré who spent less than three months there, some of it hallucinating and the rest of it wandering the beaches looking at bleached whale bones. How utterly Left Coast.

In 1982 the U.S. Open was returning to Pebble Beach's felicitous meeting of land and sea ten years after it hosted its first National Open, won spectacularly by the best player in golf at the time, maybe of all time, Jack Nicklaus. By '72 Nicklaus had already won two U.S. Opens, two Open Championships, two Professional Golfers' Association (PGA) Championships, and four Masters, including his most recent wire-to-wire victory that April, the first Masters following the death of Augusta National founder Bobby Jones and the first Masters reprieve for Jack Whitaker, the television announcer who had been banished from the CBS broadcast team for likening Augusta's spectators (the club refers to them as patrons) to a mob. More on him later. On the all-time list of winners of professional major championships, in '72 Nicklaus was one behind Jones's rival Walter Hagen, and if you included his U.S. Amateur titles for the purposes of comparing him with Jones (and that was the mark that meant everything to him), Nicklaus was one behind there, too. In short, he was the man to beat and had been for the better part of ten years. The only golfers with career résumés more glittering than his were dead.

Nicklaus was thirty-two then, confidently in his prime as golf's force majeure. After his opening round of 71, he led or shared the lead every day. On Sunday the wind blew so hard off the Pacific Ocean that a sailing regatta of small boats off Carmel Bay had to be canceled, and no one was able to shoot in the 60s. As a side note, Tom Watson was playing in his first U.S. Open and shot a 76 that day. So difficult were the conditions, his four-over par score passed thirty players. Arnold Palmer, Nicklaus's first professional rival who hadn't won a major championship in eight years, crept up on Jack's lead, but when Arnold failed to make an eight-foot birdie putt on the par-five fourteenth that would have tied him with Nicklaus, he went sideways, following it up with bogeys on the next two holes to drop away. After Nicklaus made a three on the par-four fifteenth, he put an exclamation point on the championship when his one-iron into the harsh wind on the seventeenth took one bounce, hit the flagstick, and stopped inches from the cup. Even more astounding than the dramatic shot itself was that, at the top of his swing, Nicklaus's club had gotten a little too far inside the line and slightly closed. Sensing it was out of position, he made an adjustment in the milliseconds of the downswing, resulting in the near-perfect strike. Nicklaus's one-iron was the first of the transcendent feats the seventeenth would witness.

Ten years later Jack was no longer the man to beat, even by his own estimation. That man was Thomas Sturges Watson. After a horrific, for him, 1979 season, Nicklaus had rededicated himself. "That's the first year I hadn't won a golf tournament," said Nicklaus.

I got away from it. From the time I finished in the first part of August until January, I touched a club three times. So, when I went back to Jack Grout [his teacher] in the first of January, I said, okay, J. Grout, I've been away from it a long time. My bad habits are gone. Let's start over. We started with grip, stance, posture, everything. That was a real revamp. I went from being very upright to moving my hands probably a foot behind me, which changed my whole angle of attack. I was so bad that I needed to get away from it to get rid of the bad habits so I could go back fresh and have the energy and desire to go do it. That's what I did. Competition always motivated me. I love the game of golf, but the game of golf was my vehicle to the competition. In '79,

I lost my vehicle. I had to get energized and away from it so I could go back and get my vehicle back. Once I won in '80, I'll have to say that I didn't have a lot of motivation after that for a while. I really liked to play golf, but I knew the game wasn't quite at the level it was.

If his poor showing in '79 was the motivation that spurred Nicklaus to his major victories of 1980 in the U.S. Open at Baltusrol and the PGA Championship at Oak Hill, his determination to take on the finest player of the next generation, Watson, kept him at it. In his autobiography, Nicklaus writes, "If Arnold Palmer hadn't been there when I turned pro, or Johnny Miller or Lee Trevino or Tom Watson hadn't come along and whipped me as often as they did, I'm certain my record would have been a shadow of what I'm proud to have achieved." Had Watson not kept Nicklaus's fires at the very least smoldering, would Jack have won the 1986 Masters at the age of forty-six? And had it not been for the presence of the greatest collector of major golf titles the game has ever known to measure himself against, would Watson have won five British Opens and hung around long enough to nearly win a sixth at the age of fifty-nine? It was no coincidence that, as they aged, the two rivals became the best of friends, deeply appreciative of the greatness each was able to draw out of the other.

Nicklaus had announced his dominance in 1962 when he won the U.S. Open in a playoff against the game's reigning king, Arnold Palmer, at Oakmont when he was just twenty-two years old. While Palmer always wondered what might have been had he been able to hold off the young Ohioan's ascendance for a year or two or three, forced him to taste disappointment instead of success, it didn't happen that way. Nicklaus unapologetically stepped right to the head of the line. Tiger Woods would do exactly the same thing thirty-five years later. For most players who eventually succeed in the biggest moments, however, there is a learning curve, and the curve has a warning sign that says, "Choking Ahead." It certainly was that way for Watson.

Growing up in Kansas City, Missouri, Watson's father, Ray, knew everything there was to know about the U.S. Open. He could recite all the winners back to 1895 and how they got there. An insurance salesman who was a good-enough player to have been the club champion at Kansas City Country Club (CC), an A. W. Tillinghast–designed course built in 1925 for a club originally founded in the 1890s on land owned by a businessman who made a fortune outfitting settlers departing on the Oregon Trail, the elder Watson and his friends called young Tom "Flytrap," after Flytrap Finnegan, a wisecracking caddie in a Depression Era comic strip, *Toonerville Folks*, a.k.a. *The Toonerville Trolley*. The name stuck not because the gap-toothed boy was glib. It was just the opposite. He was deadly determined on a golf course, as serious as his father was about the primacy of the National Open.

As a student at Stanford University, Tom would drive down U.S. 101 from Palo Alto to the Monterey Peninsula on Saturdays to play Pebble Beach, leaving at five in the morning so he could be there by six thirty, stopping only for a dozen bite-size glazed donuts and a carton of milk for breakfast. He became friends with the starter, who would put him off before the first tee time, and when he got to the last four holes Watson would pretend he needed four pars to win the U.S. Open. "Never did it," he recalled.

Watson played in the '72 U.S. Open at Pebble Beach, his first major, and tied for twenty-ninth. Two years later in the '74 U.S. Open at Winged Foot and again in the '75 championship at Medinah, Watson put himself in position to win the national title he coveted most but backed away both times. After losing the fifty-four-hole lead at Winged Foot, he was approached in the locker room of the Tudor-style clubhouse by Byron Nelson, a five-time major champion who was then working for CBS, and the two forged a lifetime friendship that would help Watson control both his swing and his nerve. It wasn't until '75 in the British Open at Carnoustie, Watson's first Open Championship, that he broke through in a major, beating Jack Newton, a gifted and fun-loving Australian, in a playoff. Eight years later Newton would suffer horrific injuries, losing an arm and an eye and suffering severe internal trauma, when he walked into the spinning propeller of a Cessna at Sydney Airport after spending the day watching an Australian Rules football match between Sydney and Melbourne.

That Watson bounced back so quickly in '75 from his disappointment at Medinah to win at Carnoustie was the first sign he'd learned to perform under the most intense pressure. But it wasn't until he went head-to-head against Nicklaus, and bested the best, that Watson's competitive soul was vindicated. The first of their battles was in the '77 Masters when it came down to the two of them at the end, with Watson making a birdie on the seventeenth. The roar forced Nicklaus into a mental error, choosing an easy six-iron instead of a hard seven and hitting his approach to the eighteenth fat. It was a mistake Nicklaus never really got over, mostly because his mind was better under pressure than probably any golfer who ever picked up a club with the possible exception of his idol, Jones. Physical mistakes were one thing. Everyone hits bad shots. But this? It was just the sort of miscalculation he could never forgive himself. Their second head-to-head confrontation was at Turnberry the same year, when the two champions went eyeball-to-eyeball for two days, leaving the rest of the Open Championship field, literally, in their dust. On that weekend on the Firth of Clyde, Nicklaus shot 65-66, while Watson turned in 65-65. So superb was their golf, Nicklaus was ten shots better than third place. Watson had now won three major championships, two staring straight into the blue eyes of one of the greatest champions who ever lived. No one would ever again question his resolve. In 1981 Watson won his second Masters, beating Johnny Miller and Nicklaus, again, by two shots.

"We had some pretty good contests, yes we did," says Watson.

And we wanted to beat each other. I wanted to beat Jack Nicklaus because Jack Nicklaus was the best in the game. I wasn't afraid of him but I certainly had tremendous respect for him. Trying to play and beat the best at the game, that's what I was out there to do. He was the best there was. Any time you played in a tournament, if neither of you won, you always compared yourself to Jack. Did I beat Jack that week or did he beat me? First and foremost, you're there to win a golf tournament but if it happens to be against the best, that's the ideal situation you want to be in. The more you beat heads against each other, the more you get to know each other even better. You have stories to tell each other, share with each other. Nobody owned Jack. I was fortunate to beat him in some pretty exciting contests. But you look at Jack's record, he ran circles around my record. When all is said and done, you look at the record. He beat me more than I beat him.

But not in 1982.

The Pebble Beach Golf Links opened in 1919, forty years after Robert Louis Stevenson's ride-by. It was designed largely by Jack Neville, as good an amateur as the state of California had to offer at the time but a complete novice when it came to routing and building golf courses. He'd been picked for the job by Samuel F. B. Morse, a Yale man who recognized an opportunity when he saw it, and instead of disposing of land on the Monterey Peninsula owned by his employer, a division of the Southern Pacific Railroad, as he had been hired to do, he formed his own business, the Del Monte Properties Company, and acquired it himself. Positioning eight holes on the cliffs that look out over the ocean was the single act of genius that gave Pebble Beach a cachet enjoyed by few courses anywhere in the world and, among major championship venues, rivaled in its rough beauty only, perhaps, by Turnberry, where Watson and Nicklaus had already faced off.

In the building of Pebble Beach, one majestic hole got away, an error rectified nearly eighty years later. One of Morse's first acts in 1915 was to sell off a five-acre tract looking out across Stillwater Cove. When Neville set about laying out his golf course, he had to build around William Beatty's spectacular parcel. His solution was to transition from the fourth green perched on the cliff above Stillwater Cove to the par-five sixth hole that plays directly toward the Pacific Ocean, with Stillwater Cove now positioned to the right of the landing area, by means of a blind, uphill one-shotter, the old par-three fifth. It was the mud in the eye of one of the most glorious stretches of golf holes ever created. The Beatty land changed hands in 1944, and in 1995 the estate of the then current owner, Mimi Jenkins, sold the land back to the Pebble Beach Company for $8.75 million. Jack Nicklaus was hired to construct the current par-three fifth on the cliff above the cove, undoubtedly the single most expensive golf hole ever built, which opened in the fall of 1998.

In 1981 Nicklaus had experienced another winless season, thanks in some measure to the recognition he was no longer the player he had once been and, one supposes, also to Watson's play thwarting him in the Masters that April. Both Watson and Nicklaus, however, had been winners on the PGA Tour before the U.S. Open made its reappearance at Pebble Beach in June 1982. Nicklaus had won the Colonial National Invitation at Colonial CC in Fort Worth, Texas, Ben Hogan's old club, while Watson had won two tournaments in playoffs, the first against Johnny Miller, who was still some years away from his second career as an NBC commentator, at Riviera CC in Los Angeles and the second at the Harbour Town Golf Links, a South Carolina low-country golf course on Hilton Head Island that Nicklaus had a small hand in designing in conjunction with Pete Dye, who actually did the work.

The week of the U.S. Open in 1982, the weather was typically cold and dreary, with low, thick clouds hanging over Pebble Beach. This "June Gloom," as it's called, is the product of a temperature inversion that takes place when the cold water pulled south from British Columbia by the California Current mixes with the summer's inland heat. It's a condition diagnosed by Mark Twain: "The coldest winter I ever spent was a summer in San Francisco," except, of course, Twain never said it. The cold and damp part up and down Northern California's coastline is, however, completely accurate. Fireplaces, mostly gas but some wood burning, are to the Monterey Peninsula what peat fires are to classic Irish pubs. In nearby Carmel one of the best-known hangouts was the Hog's Breath, a bar and restaurant down a narrow walkway off San Carlos Street with a large courtyard filled with gas fireplaces and fairy-tale white lights strung in the tree branches above. About the only way you knew the place existed was because the entrance was marked at the street with a gas lamp. It didn't hurt business that the owner was movie star and director Clint Eastwood, also a frequent patron. Eastwood, who had done a stretch as Carmel's mayor, would become part of an investment group that purchased Pebble Beach in 1999.

The old saying is that you can't win a golf tournament on Thursday, but you can surely lose it, much as Watson had done in the Masters that April when, as the defending champion, he opened with a 77 and still finished three strokes out of the eventual playoff. At Pebble Beach Watson could have lost the U.S. Open before he got to the weekend. During his early career his problems under pressure were often mistakenly attributed to how quick his swing was. The tempo of a golf swing, though, is as individualistic as a thumbprint. What is most important is that it always be the same, and Watson's was always fast, regardless of the situation. It wouldn't be until 1994 that he would discover what he came to think of as his personal holy grail, that his shoulder plane was too steep on the downswing. After he adjusted it he never again struggled for long with his ball striking. In 1982, however, the driver, in particular, could give him fits, and it did on Thursday and Friday. There was another characteristic to his game then, too. It was called the "Watson Par." Through a combination of superb midrange putting and a magical assortment of shots around the green, with the lone exception of Spaniard Seve Ballesteros, no one in golf was Watson's equal at keeping disaster at arm's length.

"I was hitting it awful," Watson has said. "I gave myself no chance to win the tournament at the beginning of the week." On Thursday he was three over par with four holes to play and made three birdies coming in, including the seventeenth and eighteenth to finish at even (par was seventy-two in those days), two shots behind the leaders, Bill Rogers, who had won the Open Championship the year before at Royal St. George's, and Bruce Devlin, a forty-four-year-old Australian better known for his commentary on NBC than he was for his eight victories in the 1960s and '70s on the PGA Tour. Watson's ability to stave off disaster was put to the test again in the second round. "I shot a 77 and scored 72," he said afterward.

He had driven the ball so poorly for two days that, by his own account, he had "gotten away with murder." At even par Watson was five shots behind Devlin, who seemed unlikely to stand up, but only one behind the two players who had won a major championship, Rogers and Andy North, who captured the U.S. Open at Cherry

Hills CC in Denver four years earlier but had done nothing at all since. North, by the way, would win the U.S. Open again, walking with a soaking-wet white towel draped over his head in bitter cold and drenching rain at Oakland Hills CC near Detroit. Because he won only three events in his career, two of them National Opens, North is often overlooked as a top-rank player. That's a mistake. A close friend of Watson (Tom named him as a vice captain for the 2014 Ryder Cup), North's career was plagued by injuries, but when healthy, the tall, lanky player from Madison, Wisconsin, was both steely and formidable.

Going into the weekend, Watson was surely more concerned with his poor driving than the players ahead of him, but he was also tied with Nicklaus, and Jack never escaped anyone's notice. Softened by some overnight rain, Saturday was the best scoring of the week. On the range after Friday's round Watson found something in his golf swing (he thought it had gotten a bit too upright) and began hitting the ball more crisply. Commonly acknowledged as one of the finest links golfers ever, Watson's success in winning the claret jug five times during his career was more than just a pure affinity for a style of golf that can be played along the ground. A well-struck shot is always less impacted by wind than the poorly hit one, and when Tom Watson was on, few players ever hit the ball more squarely in the center of the clubface than he did. He began doing just that on the weekend at Pebble Beach.

With the benign conditions Watson fashioned a four-under-par 68 to tie Rogers at the top of the leader board. Devlin, as many had expected, had gone in the other direction with a 75, but he was still tied for second with Scott Simpson, who would keep Watson from a second U.S. Open title five years later at the Olympic Club in San Francisco. They were tied with George Burns and David Graham. The last two had battled down the stretch in the National Open at Merion Golf Club (GC) outside Philadelphia one year earlier, with Graham winning, thanks partially to Burns's poor finish but mostly because Graham, a hard-nosed Australian who had known more of life's rough than its smooth, turned in one of the finest final rounds ever played in a U.S. Open. Nicklaus was a shot further back, tied with Calvin Peete, one of the few black players on the U.S. tour.

Peete was known for three things, the diamond chips in his front tooth, his crooked left arm (he'd fractured the elbow in three places in a childhood accident), and the fact that he could hit a half dozen drives off any tee and when you got to the balls, invariably in the middle of the fairway, it seemed like you could cover them with a handkerchief. Peete took up the game at twenty-six when he was in Rochester, New York, selling goods out of the back of his car to migrant farmworkers. The diamonds were his calling card.

Killing time on a Sunday morning when you're going to try to win a national championship in the afternoon is never easy. Watson spent it with his two-year-old daughter, Meg, and the Sunday papers, reading about a 7.2 earthquake in El Salvador, while his Kansas City Royals were losing to the Seattle Mariners back on the sports pages. Nicklaus and Peete teed off together just past noon on the cool, overcast day. Nicklaus had family with him, too. His twenty-year-old son, Jack II, who was a student at the University of North Carolina, was carrying the golf bag. He'd done it before, as early as the '76 British Open at Royal Birkdale, but it was still a novelty. He would be there again in '86 when his father won the Masters at the age of forty-six.

Jackie is considerably taller than his father (even before Jack's collapsing vertebrae turned him into the incredible shrinking man as he aged), and when the two lined up putts together, the photographers credentialed by various news outlets covering the U.S. Open couldn't get enough of the picture. Even after four days, when Jackie would lean over Jack, crouched behind his ball on the putting green, sizing up the line, first one photographer would snap a frame, then another, and then, as if they were all afraid this particular picture would be somehow different from all the others they'd taken that week, they would all hit the button. Cameras weren't the digital computers of today with a soft click engineered into them just so the person pushing the button will know when the picture has been made. No, 35-millimeter-film cameras back then made an audible *thwack* as the mirror flipped out of the way to allow light to pass through the shutter, so when the Nicklauses would survey a putt, it sounded like the rhythm section of a Rio samba school. It got so even Jack and Jackie laughed at it. Until things got serious, that is.

Watson was out last with Rogers, but it wasn't long before they had Nicklaus ringing in their ears. The book on Pebble Beach has always been pretty simple, depending on the weather, of course. The opening stretch, through the tiny downhill seventh, is where a player makes his score. After that, whatever strokes you've managed to bank serve as a cushion all the way to the finish. If the Masters doesn't begin until the back nine on Sunday, Pebble Beach doesn't start until the eighth tee. Nicklaus didn't have the best of beginnings, missing the green at the first for bogey and then failing to birdie the second, a par five (played as a par four now) reachable in two shots. Then, as he often seemed to be able to will himself to do on the Sunday of a championship, Nicklaus produced his best golf of the week. He made putts of just under and then just over twenty feet on the third and fourth holes for birdies and on the blind, uphill fifth hit a six-iron two feet from the hole. On the sixth Nicklaus drove to the bottom of the hill and then hit a towering one-iron on the blind second shot, lofting it over the one-hundred-foot climb from the fairway to the green and two-putting for yet another birdie. From a similar spot in the rough eighteen years later, Tiger Woods would reach the green with a seven-iron. Nicklaus's sand wedge on the 110-yard seventh left him an eleven-foot putt for his fifth birdie in a row. When he made it he was tied for the lead with Rogers, two holes and four twosomes behind him. Then, as often happens at Pebble Beach, he began to give shots back. He bogeyed the eighth when he missed the green and chipped poorly and three-putted the eleventh.

Behind him Watson was playing even-par stuff, despite a mistake on the tiny seventh. Pebble Beach's Poa annua greens are devilish things, and missing short putts on them is never much of a shock. The surfaces get bumpy as the day goes on, and putts have to be struck firmly to hold their line. Watson's two-footer at the seventh hit the left edge and sailed on. His reaction to the miss explained as much about his character as Nicklaus's soaring one-iron did about his game. Watson told himself, "I'm one of best putters in the world. Why should I let one missed putt convince me otherwise?" The notion was reinforced when he holed a crucial seven-footer at the eighth for a par.

The club that had been his nemesis for the first two days was one of Watson's best weapons on Sunday. He was driving the ball enormous distances and hitting all the fairways. His length appeared even more impressive than it actually was because he was paired with Rogers, who, a fader of the ball and never particularly long, wasn't at the top of his game. Taller than Watson and thinner, Rogers had the anxious demeanor of a nervous Boy Scout caught out after curfew. Brilliant the year before at Royal St. George's, in the aftermath of his Open Championship victory Rogers had traveled the world too much, played too often for appearance money, and lost his appetite for the game at the highest level. His desire to be home in Texarkana, Texas, and his skills were moving in opposite directions. Meanwhile, Watson was driving it like thunder. On the tenth he was a full forty yards by Rogers.

It was the first of the holes that ultimately decided the championship and the first of what Rogers, who became the spectator with the best view in the house after his bogeys at the ninth, tenth, and twelfth, called Watson's Three Miracles. From a perfect spot in the fairway, Watson lost his seven-iron approach right of the green. Luckily for him, the ball hung up in deep grass on the side of the cliff. A little bit farther right and it would have ended up on the beach with the joggers and the dog walkers strolling to and from Carmel. Nicklaus, cruising along in '72, had put his drive on the same hole on the beach and made a double-bogey six that could have cost him dearly but didn't. Watson avoided his own disaster, popping the ball onto the fringe of the green and making a twenty-footer to stay even par for the day and four under, a stroke ahead of Nicklaus.

On the next hole Watson again drove it miles beyond Rogers and then put his pitching wedge on the green, leaving himself a twenty-foot sidehill slider. He made it to take a two-shot lead over Nicklaus again but gave it right back on the twelfth. A difficult downhill par three under the best of circumstances, the twelfth green is wide but shallow, and holding it can be a chore. Watson missed it in the right bunker and didn't get up and down. The lead was a single stroke again.

Nicklaus was far from finished. A roar from his gallery cut through the heavy air and the Monterey pines when he made another birdie up ahead at the fifteenth, tying him with Watson again at four under. The dogleg-right par-five fourteenth is the longest of Pebble Beach's long holes. The green is tiny, sitting behind a deep, steep-faced bunker. The bit of green visible from the fairway to the right of the bunker is all false front. The left side is protected by an overhanging oak tree, and anything that misses left trundles even farther left down the hill, where the only things that thrive are double and triple bogeys. Watson's wedge shot to the fourteenth carried to the back-right portion of the green, much deeper than he wanted but a safe play that left him as far from the front-left pin as it was possible to get and still be on the fringe of the green. "Humans three-putt from there," said Rogers.

This was the second of the Three Miracles. Watson holed the putt, something in the range of forty feet, dead in the heart. A shot in front once again, he wagged his finger at the cup as he walked toward the hole, the harbinger of a gesture he would make a few minutes later to his friend and caddie, Bruce Edwards. Nicklaus had chances from inside twenty feet for birdie on each of the last three holes but couldn't get any of them to drop. He was asked about taking three-wood off the eighteenth tee rather than challenging the hole, but without a trailing wind and with the pin hidden behind the large bunker in the front right of the green, he'd done what he always had under pressure (except for the eighteenth at Augusta in '77) and stuck to his plan. It was in Watson's hands now.

After a safe par at the fifteenth, Watson missed his only fairway of the day at the sixteenth. Two bunkers are positioned exactly at the crook in the dogleg-right hole. From there the fairway turns right and runs downhill, then comes back up slightly to the green. Before the first U.S. Open in '72, Jack Neville had suggested the bunkers over time were proving less of a hazard than he intended. In preparation for the Open's return in '82, Frank "Sandy" Tatum, a San Francisco attorney, former president of the United States Golf Association (USGA), a Stanford alum who won the National Collegiate Athletic Association (NCAA) Tournament individual title when he was there, and, last but surely not least, a close friend and mentor to Watson, took Neville's suggestion to heart and deepened the second bunker, adding a couple feet of sod to the face. Watson found it.

His only missed tee shot of the day couldn't have come at a worse time. There was no option but to come out sideways. He did and played a pitching wedge that barely held the green, once again finding himself about as far away from the hole as it was possible to get. The severe back-to-front slope of the green made it an even bigger challenge than the putt he'd holed on the fourteenth. Watson cold-bloodedly lagged it to within inches and went to the seventeenth tied once again with Nicklaus, who was posting his number on the eighteenth.

Pebble Beach's seventeenth has an hourglass-shaped green positioned kitty-corner to the tee so that the front right of the hourglass can be two clubs less than the back left of it. A ridge in the neck of the hourglass makes it imperative to get on the right portion of the green. Watson picked a two-iron for the shot at the left pin and overcooked it, turning the ball perilously toward Stillwater Cove. The ball missed the green, settling between two bunkers on the left, in the deep grass that had been grown up especially for the U.S. Open as both a hazard and a highlight of Pebble Beach's wild seaside mien. As soon as he hit it, Watson yelled, "Down!" Had the course been groomed as it usually was for the PGA Tour's event hosted for so many years by Bing Crosby, the shot likely would have kicked left onto the rocks and into the cove. Instead, he would be faced with what he immediately assumed would be an unlikely up and down. Ahead at the eighteenth, as Nicklaus tended to his card, he certainly thought it was. It looked very much as though Watson was about to make back-to-back bogeys to give away the championship he coveted more than any other. Watson believed then, as he does now, that no American player's résumé, no matter how glittering, could be considered complete without winning his own national championship.

"Well, that's dead," he said to his longtime caddie, flipping the club to him as they left the tee box. Bruce Edwards began working for Watson in 1973 at the St. Louis Children's Hospital Classic when he was just seventeen, and with the exception of one brief stint with Greg Norman, he stayed on Watson's bag until he succumbed to amyotrophic lateral sclerosis (ALS) in 2004. Their last appearance together was in the 2003 U.S. Open at Olympia Fields, where Watson produced an opening round 65 that shared the lead. It was as if the round had been a gift just for Bruce, who was, by then, suffering so badly from the disease he could hardly form a word. At various points in their relationship, Watson was keen for Edwards to get a college degree (he'd gone only through high school, graduating from Marianapolis Preparatory School in Connecticut before hooking up with Watson), but Edwards, invariably a glass-half-full kind of character, was happy with the job he had. If Eastwood's hangout in Carmel was his own Hog's Breath, Edwards fancied Jack London's more caddie-friendly milieu. So it wasn't much of a surprise that, coming off the tee right after Watson had delivered the shot that was going to cost him the championship, Edwards simply said, "Let's get this up and down." Rogers would have a chance to witness Miracle No. 3.

When Watson missed the green at the seventeenth, Whitaker, now employed by ABC instead of CBS, was dispatched to interview Nicklaus, who seemed destined to win his fifth U.S. Open Championship, one more than Willie Anderson, Bobby Jones, or Ben Hogan. At the scoring tent by the eighteenth green, Nicklaus beamed, confident he was going to have at least a spot in a playoff, if not an outright victory. When he finished the interview, he turned back to his scorecard.

By the time they got thirty or so yards from the green, both Edwards and Watson knew they had reason for hope. They could see the top of the ball. Had it settled to the bottom, Watson surely would have been dead. Now, there was a chance. "Get it close," Edwards told him. "Get it close?" Watson replied. "I'm gonna sink it." He opened the face of his sand iron, a Wilson model he'd liberated from David Graham's workshop, and flipped the ball onto the downslope. Watson crouched slightly as he watched it roll, hit the pin with force, and disappear. When it dropped he exploded, running to his left, then wheeling around and pointing at Edwards as if to say, "I told you so," when no words could ever have been heard above the screaming crowd.

That cheer, loud enough to make dogs bark at Point Lobos, forced Nicklaus, pencil in hand, to look up from his card and swing around in his chair. He thought perhaps Watson had gotten it close. Then he saw on the television monitor exactly how close. He sagged visibly but recovered just as fast. "I can't believe it," Nicklaus said. He might just as well have been saying it to Bobby or Ben or Willie as to anyone in the scoring tent.

Watson played the par-five eighteenth like a man with a one-shot lead. It was three-wood off the tee, a seven-iron lay up, and a nine-iron on. When the twenty-footer went in for a closing birdie, it gave him a two-shot victory and a reason to reach his arms to the sky before embracing the caddie and friend he would lose too soon. Nicklaus met Watson as he came off the eighteenth green. "You little son of a bitch," he said. "You're something else. I'm proud of you." And he was, too. No champion ever took more pride in the contest than Nicklaus. "Regardless of the outcome, the actual doing of it had been tremendous fun," he had written of their duel at Turnberry. This was more of the same.

Beneath Pebble Beach's gray skies with its nooks and crannies kept cozy with gas fires and the noise of the crowd still echoing up and down Robert Louis Stevenson's coastline, it was hard to imagine golf changing. How could it be any better than this? But the year before at the Michelob-Houston Open, a journeyman professional from Tulsa, Oklahoma, Ron Streck, had become the first player to win on the PGA Tour with a metal wood, beating Hale Irwin and Jerry Pate by three shots. Golf was about to embark on a technological revolution, while the USGA and the Royal and Ancient (R&A) looked the other way.

One thing didn't change, however. Playing with wooden clubs, steel shafts, and forged irons, two of the game's all-time great champions, Jack Nicklaus and Tom Watson, took each other's measure one final time. For more than thirty years nothing in golf could compare with the two of them head-to-head.

# 2

## El Momento and Mr. Ryder's Cup

The word *champion* had a sacred meaning to Severiano Ballesteros. Not a religious man in any formal sense, that single word encapsulated the bedrock of his ethos. "When I got up and down on the last hole of the Ryder Cup in '95 at Oak Hill, Seve was balling and he comes down and puts his arms around me and tells me, 'You're a great champion. You're a great champion,'" said Englishman Nick Faldo, who was born the same year as Seve. Between them they won six British Opens and five Masters, though they rarely found themselves blocking each other's competitive paths. "It's funny, in all the emotion of it and all the noise, it took me three days to learn what he actually said to me. I was so taken aback by it, I wrote him and said to him, that is the biggest compliment I ever had in my life."

To liken the dark-haired, tempestuous Ballesteros to a matador would be the commonest of nationalistic stereotypes, the most banal, ordinary cliché imaginable, unless, of course, it had been written by Ernest Hemingway, which, in a curious way, it was. There is a passage in *The Sun Also Rises* where Jake, the narrator, looks across the crowd in the *plaza de toros* after the nineteen-year-old

Pedro Romero kills his first bull and exchanges a look with his friend Montoya, the hotel owner and fellow aficionado. "Montoya caught my eye and nodded his head," Hemingway wrote. "This was a real one. There had not been a real one for a long time." So it was with Ballesteros. To be a champion was to be a real one, and they are rare. From the time Ballesteros called José Maria Olazábal when Ollie was just fifteen and invited him to play a match at Real Golf Club de Pedrena, Seve knew the young boy was one of the real ones, and they remained brothers in kind to the end of Seve's life. This was not the experience of another, even younger, Spanish star, Sergio Garcia. The difference between the two comes as close to explaining what, to Seve, was the cornerstone of his faith. And the sacraments were the big moments.

Seve was born and died in Pedrena on the north coast of Spain. He became the best golfer on the planet but, in many ways, never really escaped the two-story whitewashed house with the wood-burning stove where he grew up. He had three older brothers, four if you count the first child of Baldomero (his father) and Carmen (his mother), who died at the age of two. It was a life of hard labor but not destitution. His father farmed and dug for clams and caddied at the Real Golf Club de Pedrena where Seve's uncle Ramon Sota was the well-known and respected pro. One of the best courses in the North of Spain, Royal Pedrena was designed by Harry Colt, the architect of Sunningdale and Wentworth. It opened in 1928 and was dubbed "royal" almost immediately by Alfonso XIII, the king of Spain, an avid player, who was forced to flee the country three years later with the arrival of the Second Spanish Republic. After being court-martialed by the Republicans, Seve's father served in the army of General Francisco Franco until the end of the Spanish Civil War in '39. Pablo Picasso's iconic painting *Guernica* depicts the horrors of the bombing of a Basque village just over eighty miles from Pedrena. After the war Baldomero and Carmen settled on their land near Santander Bay. He became famous locally as a powerful oarsman in a fourteen-man boat, competing for the town in a three-mile race around the bay and won it five times, the same number of major championship titles his youngest son would have.

Seve was given his first golf club, the head of an old three-iron, at the age of seven. He fashioned his own wooden shafts, soaked them for a tight fit in the hosel, and hit shots on the beach, substituting rocks for golf balls. By the time he was eight he, too, was caddying at Royal Pedrena and sneaking out on the golf course close to dark to play. By twelve he was winning competitions, and at fourteen already able to beat his brother Manuel, also a professional golfer, he abandoned any pretense of formal education. By sixteen Seve passed a test administered by the Spanish PGA and turned professional, and just days before his seventeenth birthday, with the financial backing of a doctor in Madrid, he was off to play in the Portuguese Open. But it wasn't until the Open Championship at Royal Birkdale, at just nineteen years of age, the same as the fictional Pedro Romero, that Ballesteros arrived in the ring.

The dashing young phenom, trying to become the youngest winner of the claret jug since before they even played for a claret jug, led the 1976 Open Championship by two shots over Johnny Miller going into the final round. Just the week before he'd been working alongside his father bailing hay on the farm in Pedrena. Ballesteros's wizardry, his ability to create shots and save strokes—sometimes even shave them—from the most preposterous places on the golf course, in the end couldn't hold up against the impressive ball striking of Miller, whose signature career event had been his final-round 63 to win the U.S. Open at Oakmont three years before. Miller shot 66 in the final round to tie what was, at the time, Birkdale's course record and finished six shots clear of Ballesteros and Jack Nicklaus, the blond to whom Miller was so often compared. Seve double-bogeyed the sixth hole and tripled the eleventh but clawed back strokes down the stretch to finish with a 74.

"He was so very bold," Miller said then about the young Spaniard. "If Seve had played a one-iron off the tee more often, he would have been the champion. He has the ability around the greens to be a great player some day. I think this tournament is a plus for him, not a minus. It would have been very hard on him being the Open Champion at age 19."

Ballesteros finished eagle-birdie to tie Nicklaus for second. "On the last hole, after missing the green with his approach shot, he got my attention with one of the best shots I've ever seen," Miller has written. "He played a delicate chip that ran between two bunkers and trickled close to the hole for a tap-in birdie. The crowd went wild." This was a crowd of links golf aficionados who understood the degree of difficulty in a simple pitch with a nine-iron to four feet, knowing it could be as perilous as walking a tightrope strung from one tower of the London Bridge to the other. They also knew they were watching a player who understood no other way to master a golf course than by dragging the wetted bottom of his cape through the dirt and stomping his feet in the dust. A month later Ballesteros would win his first tournament on the European circuit, the Dutch Open.

In '78 Seve won the Greater Greensboro Open in America. After Ballesteros's victory in a PGA Tour event, commissioner Deane Beman tried to persuade him to become a full-time member of the U.S. tour. In the end all his overture accomplished was to begin a long-running feud. Ballesteros wanted to play in America when he wanted to play in America and not necessarily as often as the tour required of its members, fifteen events a year. The by-laws made an allowance for foreign-born players to skip tour tournaments when competing in opposing events in their homeland. In Seve's case Beman defined that as Spain. Ballesteros defined it as Europe. In Ballesteros's universe if you didn't see things as he saw them, not only were you patently wrong, but you were heaping the most dastardly of insults upon his character as well. Writer Peter Dobereiner described this trait, or flaw, this way: "He is hypersensitive to a slight or injury and cherishes his grudges like a miser gloating over his hoard of gold pieces." At one time or another, Seve's enemies list included Beman, the U.S. tour, virtually all the caddies who ever worked for him, American players in general, some European players in particular, the European Tour, Ed Barner (his first manager, who also represented Johnny Miller), the government of Spain, and the thick rough at any and all U.S. Opens, if not the U.S. Open itself.

The week after his North Carolina victory, playing in just his second Masters, Ballesteros found himself paired in the final round with Gary Player. They had met six years before in the South of

Spain. Ballesteros was traveling with a group of fellow caddies from Royal Pedrena. "Manos de plata. That's what we called him," Ballesteros told Sarah Ballard of *si*. "Silver hands. He was the first champion I ever met." It says something, does it not, that he doesn't include his uncle Ramon Sota, who in the '60s finished in the top ten in both a Masters and a British Open, in that lineage. On that final day in '78 at Augusta, Ballesteros went out in 40 and was a nonfactor. Player, on the other hand, birdied seven of his final ten holes and shot 64 to come from seven shots behind and win his third Masters. While Player tends to be the hero of most of his own stories (after all, when you win nine major championships, you're entitled to top billing in at least a few of them), his reminiscence of Ballesteros has the ring of truth. "On the 11th hole some patrons said that I was so far behind that it was not worth following our group," Player posted on his website after Ballesteros's death.

I told them not to leave because I was going to win. Seve looked at me and asked if I really thought that I could and I told him that one can never give up and to always believe. I think he was surprised to hear me say that and was not really sure I believed what I was saying. When I holed that last putt, Seve was as excited as I was and that really shows what kind of a person he was. Afterwards Seve told me that I showed him how to win the Masters and just two years later he did it.

The kinship between the two was strong. "I admire him very much because he came from a modest family, he went through tough things and because of the way he fights," Ballesteros said of the man who was twenty-two years his senior. "He never gives up. I am like Gary Player. The more the crowd is against me, the more I want to prove something."

He proved it from a car park the following year at Royal Lytham and St. Annes. Ballesteros played the final thirty-six holes alongside Hale Irwin, who a month earlier had won his second U.S. Open at Inverness GC in Toledo, Ohio, to go along with his victory in the Massacre at Winged Foot five years before that. Irwin, generally acknowledged to be one of the game's most precise long-iron players, would win a third National Open eleven years later at Medinah CC near Chicago and go on to become the most prolific winner in the history of senior golf, capturing forty-five titles both before and after the PGA Tour rebranded it as the Champions Tour. But steady and competent proved no match for the mercurial brilliance of Ballesteros at Lytham.

Going into the last day two shots off the pace, Ballesteros overtook Irwin, who struggled at the start, in just two holes. The remainder of the day, his closest challengers were Australian Rodger Davis, who was playing in just his third major championship, and American Ben Crenshaw, who had tied for second in the Open Championship the year before when Jack Nicklaus drove to a second victory on the Old Course at St. Andrews. Once again Ballesteros was playing the golf course as he found it, and he found pretty much every part of it. Irwin remembers him hitting just three fairways in the final round, and he averaged fewer than that in the previous fifty-four holes. Ballesteros made birdie at the short thirteenth, chipped in for par on the fifteenth, and then on the sixteenth drove it wide right underneath a car in a temporary car park that had not been marked as out-of-bounds (OB). He got the relief to which he was entitled, and the angle from the car park toward the hole was perfect. He played a sand-wedge approach to fifteen feet and made birdie. Coupled with Crenshaw's double bogey at the seventeenth up ahead, Ballesteros became the Champion Golfer of the Year, as the winner is traditionally introduced at every prize giving. "I can't understand how anyone can drive as badly as that and still win an Open Championship," Irwin said. To the Americans it was luck; to the Europeans it was genius. And as if the two constituted a hybrid engine, Ballesteros's golf was able to run at high speeds on both luck and genius.

The next April he would win the first of his two Masters titles, adding to his reputation for wildness during the second round by hitting a drive off the seventeenth tee that landed inside David Graham's ball on the seventh green. After Graham putted out Ballesteros took a drop and still made birdie. Paired with Australian Jack Newton on Sunday, Ballesteros began with a seven-shot lead and stretched it to double digits by the time they reached the tenth tee. On his way to becoming the youngest Masters champion to that point (Nicklaus held the distinction before him), he began to give back shots. A three-putt at the tenth. A tee shot into Rae's Creek at the twelfth. A fat three-iron (a precursor of his four-iron at the fifteenth in '86?) into the winding tributary in front of the thirteenth green. By the time he reached the fourteenth, his lead was just three. He thought of Player, who had left a note in his locker earlier in the day saying, "Buena suerte. I'm pulling for you," and of the South African's charge in '78. "I say to myself, you stupid," said Ballesteros. "You have comfortable lead and now you lead by three. You must try very hard."

Ballesteros would win a third major championship, his second Masters, in 1983. Going into the final round at Augusta National a shot behind Raymond Floyd and Craig Stadler, both Masters champions, and a shot ahead of another, Tom Watson, Ballesteros delivered an early knockout when he played the first four holes four under par. Roughly 2,300 miles away, in California, a few months shy of his thirteenth birthday, Phil Mickelson was watching intently. "I was just watching on TV, watching him stroll up 18, giving it the fist pump and chipping in on the last hole," said Mickelson. That year, uncharacteristically, the Sunday pin location on the eighteenth was just about as deep into the green as it's possible to cut a cup. Ballesteros's third shot carried beyond the pin, into the back fringe, and he holed out from there for a four. "I remember saying to my Mom, I want to win the Masters. I want to do that like Seve did it. I want to be like that." Given the control, or lack thereof, Mickelson would display with the driver during his career and the assortment of otherworldly shots he possessed around the greens, Phil may have gotten closer to Seve than anyone.

Watson played alongside Ballesteros as Seve won that second Masters, and they played together again in June down the stretch in the U.S. Open at Oakmont. Watson, too, was prone to flights of wildness and had his own well-deserved reputation for being able to recover from difficult spots, but in Ballesteros he had come up against someone able to out-Watson even Watson when it came to scrambling. Already a seven-time major champion and considered the best player in the world, Watson finally got his nose out in front of Ballesteros at Oakmont, only to have Larry Nelson snatch the title away from him when they finished the weather-delayed championship on Monday morning. Watson would successfully defend his Open Championship crown a month later at Royal Birkdale, his last victory in a major. It was against this backdrop that in 1984 Ballesteros stood on the eighteenth green of the Old Course at St. Andrews, gesturing with his fist at nearly every point of the compass, turning to acknowledge the crowd—his crowd—on the ground, on the porches, in the windows, like a great actor performing the role of a lifetime in the round.

There is no place on earth quite like St. Andrews. Every sport should have one. You could, one supposes, build a case for Yankee Stadium in baseball or the Boston Garden in basketball or the Coliseum in Rome—for either the lions or the Christians, depending on your betting interest—but they pale in comparison to St. Andrews, where they've been doing the same thing in the same place for six hundred years or thereabouts. You might as well start hanging championship banners with William the Conqueror. It is said that, with the lone exception of Ben Hogan, every great champion who ever played the game has walked across the Swilcan Bridge. To cross it on the way to becoming the Champion Golfer of the Year is the Mount Everest of every player's bucket list. It happened twice to Jack Nicklaus, who was given an honorary doctorate by the University of St. Andrews prior to the championship in '84. "Nowhere on earth have I been received more warmly, more affectionately or with greater understanding than by the people of this country," Nicklaus said. "As I have said many times before, this is my favorite place in all of the golfing world." It would be Ballesteros's, too.

Already a five-time champion, Watson came into St. Andrews trying to become the first player since Peter Thomson to win three consecutive Open Championships. A sixth title would tie him with Harry Vardon for the most ever, something Watson would come desperately close to doing once again twenty-five years later at the age of fifty-nine. Though he had won at Birkdale in '83, he didn't win a tournament in America that year. His runner-up finish to Ben Crenshaw in the Masters in April, however, was proof enough he still had it in the big moments. That, at thirty-four, Watson might already be in decline seemed as innocently quaint and farfetched a notion as having air-conditioning in Rusacks Hotel. He was still the man to beat.

Going into the final round, Watson was tied for the lead with Ian Baker-Finch, two shots ahead of Ballesteros and German Bernard Langer, who had already conquered the putting yips once in his life and would do so twice more. Baker-Finch, who won the championship seven years later at Birkdale, would experience one of the most dispiriting things that ever happened to a championship-caliber player on the first tee of the Old Course when the championship returned in '95. The amiable Aussie who became a respected TV announcer for CBS had by then contracted the worst disease a professional golfer can have—the driver yips. As Langer proved in winning the Masters twice, it's possible to find a work-around for a twitchy putter. When a tournament player stands on a tee box with no earthly idea whether the ball is going to go left or right, he's as cooked as a curried vindaloo. In '95 Baker-Finch was buffeted on the first tee by a gust of wind just as he was playing his opening shot, lifting his visor off his head as he duck-hooked his fairway metal, sending the ball scuttling across the eighteenth fairway and out-of-bounds, an almost impossibly bad result for any decent player. That was not the Baker-Finch of '84, however. That player was twenty-three years old, tall, dark, handsome, and formidable. Just not ready to win a major championship, yet. On Sunday he was four over par through six holes on his way to an outward nine of 41 and relegated to watching one of the greatest duels in golf. Langer struggled on the greens and shot 37 going out, as the day quickly devolved into a match between Ballesteros and Watson, with Seve one a hole ahead.

After number 5, the two were tied, and Ballesteros took the lead for the first time all week with a birdie on the eighth. As they made their way through the Loop, Watson birdied the tenth to tie Ballesteros and then took the lead again when Seve dropped a shot at the eleventh. Watson gave it right back when he drove into the gorse on the twelfth and was forced to take an unplayable. A birdie on the thirteenth nudged Watson back ahead, but Ballesteros caught him with a birdie of his own on the fourteenth. After pars on the fifteenth and sixteenth, first Ballesteros, then Watson, came to the Road Hole, the most famous hole on the most famous course, tied.

When Ballesteros first turned professional, he spoke almost no English. Pushed to learn the language by his agent, Ed Barner, Seve became so adept at it he could be playfully witty in his second language. Once, in 1988, when asked how he could four-putt the sixteenth at Augusta National, he replied simply, "I miss. I miss. I miss. I make." In '84 at St. Andrews he'd made bogey on the seventeenth in each of the first three rounds. After he finished on Saturday, Seve said, "If I don't par No. 17 tomorrow, I will come back Monday." His four on the treacherous 461-yard Road Hole turned out to be the most important par of his life.

First, there's the drive over the corner of the Old Course Hotel (it used to be railway sheds) to a fairway that doglegs left to right. Ballesteros's tee shot found the wispy rough through the fairway on the left. Staring at the fearsome Road Hole Bunker, the deliverer of horrors (Tommy Nakajima took four to get out in '78, and so did David Duval in 2000) that protects the front of the shallow but wide green, Ballesteros played a magnificent six-iron from 193 yards onto the green and two-putted for his four.

Behind him Watson had driven perfectly into the middle of the fairway. First pulling a three-iron, the American changed his mind and took one more club. It turned out to be one too many. His approach was thirty yards right of where he was aiming. It hit a corner of the green, bounded across the gravel road that works up the right side of the hole and crosses behind the green, and stopped eighteen inches from the stone wall, stone dead. In practice rounds Watson had fiddled around with playing a bank shot off the wall, but he chose instead to take a choked-down seven-iron and chop down sharply on the ball, getting it to pop up on the green, still thirty feet away from the hole. Up ahead Ballesteros had driven in the eighteenth fairway and played his wedge shot over the Valley of Sin to fifteen feet. As Watson took the measure of the lengthy putt he knew he needed to make, the roar of Ballesteros's birdie echoed off the old buildings along the Links, across Grannie Clark's Wynd, over the Swilcan Bridge, past the Jigger Inn, and all the way to Leuchars Air Force Base, stomping on Watson's heart as it went.

When Seve's right-to-left putt toppled over the edge, Ballesteros clenched his fist and punched across his body in exaltation. With a catlike bounce he turned and did it again, over and over. Pump, turn, repeat. Pump, turn, repeat. El Momento. "It told me what I had to do, in spades," said Watson. The claret jug was Ballesteros's.

Seve would return to the site of his first Open Championship triumph, Royal Lytham and St. Annes, to win his fifth, and last, major in 1988. His championship career lasted a decade. Watson won his majors in nine years. Hogan captured all of his in eight. Palmer in seven. In '88 Ballesteros would rise to become the number-one-ranked player in the world, a position he held off and on for 61 weeks during his career. Nick Faldo was number one a total of 97 weeks, while Greg Norman, who never approached either Ballesteros's or Faldo's record in the four majors, held the top spot for 331 weeks. While he was raising the Ryder Cup up by its golden bootstraps throughout the '80s, when it came to the majors, the time between El Momento in '84 and Lytham in '88 (when Ballesteros played one of his finest final rounds, a near-flawless 65), he was defined largely by two anguished images from Augusta National.

It's a good bet there have been as many words written about the 1986 Masters as any single golf tournament. In March of that year Ballesteros's father passed away. It was the year he'd had his membership on the PGA Tour revoked for failing to play in the required number of events. For Seve there was much to prove at Augusta National. When he got to the fifteenth hole on Masters Sunday in '86, he held a two-shot lead. Jack Nicklaus, at forty-six, was well on his way to fashioning a back nine of 30. Ballesteros had a four-iron in his hands and 210 yards, downhill to the green. He'd already eagled the thirteenth and barely missed a birdie at the fourteenth. Yet another eagle, even a birdie four, on the other par five on Augusta National's back nine would surely put the tournament away, Nicklaus or no Nicklaus. What followed was one of the worst swings Ballesteros ever made in the heat of competition until he'd lost his game toward the end. He hit it so fat, the ball barely reached the water hazard. If it's possible for a single swing to demoralize a golfer, that one did. "It was destino," Seve said. "It took a long time before I was confident with my 4-iron again. I lost my confidence, no question." In some ways he never got over it.

In the very next Masters, however, Ballesteros found himself in a playoff with Norman and Augusta, Georgia, native Larry Mize. On the first hole of sudden death, Ballesteros's approach on the tenth settled in the fringe on the back right of the green. His first putt was deadly fast and ran four feet by. Needing to hole out to stay alive, he missed the comebacker on the left edge. Ballesteros shook the hands of both Norman and Mize, who would hole a remarkable 140-foot pitch on the eleventh to deliver yet more heartbreak to the Australian, and then made the steep climb back up the tenth fairway, a forlorn figure with his caddie and a single official. Two years running he'd been devastated at Augusta National. On the long walk back he cried inconsolably. While Ballesteros would win more tournaments after his triumph at Lytham in '88—his last victory was the Spanish Open in '95—the downward slide had begun. Genius became harder and harder to find.

While it was Jack Nicklaus who first suggested that the Great Britain and Ireland team in the Ryder Cup be expanded to include all of Europe, it was Seve Ballesteros who turned the matches into his personal cause célèbre. For someone who would become the heart and soul of the European side for the better part of two decades, Ballesteros's (and Europe's) Ryder Cup debut in '79 at the Greenbrier was particularly inauspicious, getting drummed four times by Larry Nelson, including in singles, and leaving the West Virginia mountains with a 1-4-0 record.

The diminutive and dogged Nelson was an amazing 5-0-0 in the matches at White Sulphur Springs. A Vietnam War combat veteran, Nelson didn't even take up the game until he was twenty-one, learning the basics by reading Ben Hogan's *Five Lessons: The Modern Fundamentals of Golf.* A member of the World Golf Hall of Fame, during the '80s he would win two PGA Championships and one U.S. Open and, rather remarkably, be passed over as a Ryder Cup captain despite having played on three U.S. teams with an amazing record of 9-0-0 in his first two. Of all the players who should have been given the honor of a captaincy, on both sides of the Atlantic, and weren't, Larry Nelson stands at the front of the line.

The European side didn't fare any better when the matches were played two years later at Walton Heath in Surrey, England. In fact, the drubbing was even worse. The result of eighteen and a half to nine and a half remains the worst outcome for any European team. Seve didn't play, having been voted off the side because of yet another of his raging disputes, this one with the European Tour involving appearance money. Coincidentally, Tony Jacklin was also passed over as a potential captain's pick, and this double slight of Ballesteros and Jacklin would give them a unique bond they called upon during Jacklin's four Ryder Cup captaincies, three of which resulted in Europe either winning outright or tying and retaining the cup, which is every bit as good.

The turning point in Europe's fortunes came in '83 at West Palm Beach at PGA National. Jack Nicklaus was the U.S. captain for the first time, and Jacklin debuted in that role for Europe. They had shared one of the finer moments of sportsmanship in the history of the matches in 1969 when Nicklaus conceded a short putt to Jacklin to end the final-afternoon singles match in a draw. Jacklin, by the way, had beaten Nicklaus in the morning singles, 4 and 3. The draw meant the team score would be tied, with the United States retaining the cup. While it was a fine sporting gesture, Nicklaus, himself, has always maintained Jacklin would never have missed the putt anyway. With little on the line, why force the issue?

When Jacklin accepted the captaincy of the European side, he did so with conditions. No expense would be spared in the treatment of his team. Everything was to be first class, including transportation on the supersonic airliner Concorde. The next step was Seve. "I knew I couldn't do it without him, so we met. He felt slighted and hurt by what had happened, and boy was he angry," Jacklin said. "I said, 'I can't do it without you and it's as simple as that—as far as I'm concerned you're the best player in the world.'

I think he had the same opinion as me that the Americans weren't any better than us, given a level playing field, so he agreed to come on board and, by God, did he help."

Coming down the eighteenth all square against his singles opponent, Fuzzy Zoeller, Ballesteros delivered what many still think is the single most remarkable shot ever played in a Ryder Cup. After driving badly into deep Bermuda rough on the embankment of a bunker and hacking out a wedge only as far as the next fairway bunker up, still 245 yards from the green, Ballesteros took out his three-wood. Zoeller, who still had a two-iron to the green himself, couldn't believe it. This was no small bunker. The shot would have to clear a three- or four-foot lip. "I was licking my chops thinking, 'What the hell is he doing?'" Zoeller said. Ballesteros's high, arcing cut out of the bunker finished on the fringe of the green, where he got up and down to gain a halve with the American. "One of the greatest shots I have ever seen," said Nicklaus. As the lightning flashed in the distance, Lanny Wadkins played a wedge tight to the pin on the eighteenth to seal the victory for the United States, fourteen and a half to thirteen and a half, but the earth had shifted under the Americans' feet.

The real approaching storm was Ballesteros. The nucleus of Europe's success to come—Sandy Lyle, Ian Woosnam, Nick Faldo, Bernhard Langer, Sam Torrance, Bernard Gallacher—was disconsolate. "When Seve walked into the team room after we lost by one shot, wow," says Faldo. "We'd given all that. Seve comes in. 'We must celebrate!' He was waving his fist. 'This is a victory for us!' He was right. In that era, it's fair to say, six of the team thought we could win, the other six weren't so sure. From that moment on, we were really inspired."

Two years later the Europeans won at The Belfry. "After '85, we were singing, 'We're going to win in America! We're going to win in America!' to the tune from *West Side Story*," Faldo recalled. Two years later, for the first time ever on American soil, at Jack Nicklaus's Muirfield Village in Ohio, no less, they did.

Billy Foster, who has been one of the world's top caddies for twenty years, was on Ballesteros's bag that week. It was the Yorkshireman's first Ryder Cup. It was José Maria Olazábal's first Ryder

Cup, too. "Going to the first tee, Seve puts his arm round José," Foster says. "'José, you are a fantastic champion, eh, my friend? One of the best golfers in the world, rookie of the year last year. You just concentrate on your game. I will take care of these sons of my bitches.'" The confidence the European team had in Ballesteros and Olazábal knew no bounds. "Seve and Ollie," says Faldo. "Sending them out, that was like sending out your 50-mm guns. You literally knew they were going to come back with a win. That was very powerful."

David Feherty, famous as the neurotic, scatological, witty, goateed, bike-riding CBS, then NBC, roving reporter and Golf Channel's version of Barbara Walters, played on one Ryder Cup team with Ballesteros in '91 at Kiawah Island. The War by the Shore. "I remember looking at Seve, he was running around the team room," says Feherty.

There were five rookies on that team. I felt this pair of hands on my neck, rubbing my shoulder. I hear this voice, "Are you nervous?" This guy doesn't talk to me any other week of the year. I said, "Yeah, I'm nervous." He said, "Me, too. I shit myself at this event." I said, well, cool. He got all the rookies together. He made us feel like we were one of his friends, which was a special thing to us. Of course, the next week, he called me Doug. I remember looking at him that week and I thought, he seems smaller than I remember. It was only weeks afterwards that I looked back and, it wasn't that he seemed smaller, it was that he made me feel bigger. He did that because he loved the event so much. That one event, the Ryder Cup, which he transformed singlehandedly.

But just as the memory of a fat four-iron or a long, lonely uphill walk lingered at Augusta, so did his last appearance as a player in '95 at Oak Hill CC. Two years later Seve would be the captain of the European team in Spain at Valderrama. In his last match as a competitor, he played with all the heart but none of the skill that had once seemed his birthright. Whether it was his back, which had troubled him all his life, or just the erosion of time, he was like Paul Newman in *Cool Hand Luke* fighting George Kennedy. He kept coming at Tom Lehman with a hand full of nothin'. "We saw him gutted at Oak Hill," Faldo says. "His game was off by then." In the first singles match on the course, wild doesn't begin to describe Ballesteros's lack of control. He didn't hit a single fairway in his first nine holes. "Seve was playing just as badly as you can play," said Ken Brown, a Ryder Cup player who had disgraced himself with his behavior in '79 so much so that he'd nearly been sent packing by his own captain and who, later, became a Sky TV commentator. "He really didn't know where the ball was going." At one point Ballesteros made Lehman, who had putted out of turn, replay his tap-in. It was the dispirited echo of all the accusations of gamesmanship he'd been accused of by numerous Americans, in particular Paul Azinger. They had run-ins in '89 and '91, and of course, there was that persistent cough Ballesteros always seemed to contract every other September.

If Azinger didn't always get the best of Ballesteros, he did beat him at cancer. Just months after winning the PGA Championship in a sudden-death playoff against Greg Norman at Inverness Golf Club, Azinger was diagnosed with non–Hodgkin's lymphoma in '93. Radiation and chemotherapy sent it into remission. Azinger would come back to captain the successful U.S. Ryder Cup team at Valhalla GC in 2008.

By '95 Ballesteros had begun working with Mac O'Grady, an ambidextrous former player who shared Seve's profound distaste for by-then former PGA Tour commissioner Deane Beman. O'Grady was an eccentric swing coach who once took Ballesteros out into the desert near Palm Springs to bury tapes of the Spaniard's old golf swing. O'Grady was just one of the instructors Ballesteros consulted in an effort to find some way to strike the ball soundly again. After Phil McGleno, the name O'Grady had been born with in Minneapolis, Minnesota, it was Butch Harmon, and before O'Grady it had been David Leadbetter. But, in golf, there is no Band-Aid for genius.

"I never played with anybody like him," says Feherty.

There was sort of a feline grace to everything he did, kind of an animal-like quality. You felt like he could change the weather with his mood. He would be thunderous one minute, his face would be purple. When he smiled, the world lit up. He was too beautiful to be bad but he *was* bad. He was a villain. He was really special. His imagination, apart from anything else. I remember his driving a 4-iron—he was about 35 feet from the hole—into the revetted face of a bunker. There's no chance, downwind, downhill, tight lie, fuckin' full 4-iron, just thooook!, into the bank and it came out dead and just rolled down to the hole. I remember standing there going, who the fuckin' hell thinks of that? Really?

As the captain at Valderrama, two years after he couldn't keep a golf ball on the face of the earth, Ballesteros seemed to be everywhere at once, orbiting the Americans in his golf cart as Europe won the cup again, fourteen and a half to thirteen and a half. Ten years later at Carnoustie, already having suffered a minor heart episode, Ballesteros would announce his retirement from the game at fifty, having tried one tournament on the PGA Tour's Senior Tour and deciding it wasn't for him. Ballesteros began his farewell in a most un-Seve-like way. "Obviously, I feel very, very lucky, personally, and I'm very, very grateful for these things that really happened over those 30 years. I want to make one remark," he said, "that whatever I say or I did something that hurt somebody else's feeling or whatever, I apologize."

A year later going through Madrid's Barajas Airport, Ballesteros collapsed. A stranger, a woman, came to his aid. "I told her to bloody well leave me alone," Ballesteros said later. "People were saying, 'Bloody hell, it's Seve Ballesteros' and I said to her, 'Christ, can't you see what a fuss you're causing?' She started calling me rude. I haven't seen or heard from her. I would like to see her now and give her a hug." That was after Ballesteros left the airport with his nephew Ivan to meet his son Miguel for lunch. He collapsed again at the door of the restaurant and was taken immediately to Madrid's LaPaz Hospital. A brain scan revealed an oligoastrocytoma tumor. After three separate surgeries chemotherapy and radiation had left a diagonal scar across his head, partial paralysis on his left side, and the vision in his left eye nearly gone. Ballesteros died on May 7, 2011, at the age of fifty-four. Toward the end he granted a few interviews in his house in Pedrena, the front door decorated with a brass plate of El Momento. In the beginning he'd been quick to anger. In the end he was quick to tears.

José Maria Olazábal was the captain of the European Ryder Cup team at Medinah in 2012. It was Olazábal who was standing on the seventeenth green, across the street from Francis Ouimet's home, at The Country Club in '99 when Justin Leonard rolled in an enormous putt from the front of the green, setting off an unrestrained celebration by the Americans, who thoughtlessly ran across the green to embrace Leonard. Olazábal stood stone-faced, still with a putt to halve the hole. He missed, and the United States completed what was, at the time, the biggest comeback in the history of the Ryder Cup. In suburban Chicago in 2012, the Europeans flipped that record on its head.

Going into the Sunday singles behind 10–6, wearing blue sweaters with the figure of Ballesteros's moment stitched on their arms, with an airplane skywriting the words *Do It for Seve—Go Europe* above them, Ollie's team equaled the biggest comeback the matches had ever seen, and they did it on American soil. "Yeah, we carried Seve on the arm for Sunday for a reason," said Ian Poulter, who had pulled Europe back from the abyss on Saturday. "For that team to know that we're going out today in blue and white, you know, it's unbelievable. We won it for Seve."

In the European team room there was a picture of Olazábal leaping up behind Ballesteros, his hands on his shoulders, trying to get a glimpse of something in the distance. Looking at it made Ollie tear up. In the European celebration on the eighteenth green, someone asked Olazábal what it meant to him. He couldn't get through the answer. "It means everything," he said, turning away. "For him and for me, yes, everything."

At Carnoustie, in his farewell to competition, Seve said, "Life is like a dream. I don't know if that's a good translation, but we say that in Spain. Life is a dream. You go to bed and you wake up with age. That's exactly what happened." The dream of a champion.

# 3

## The Shark and Sir Nick

Born two years apart on opposite sides of the world, Greg Norman and Nick Faldo seemed to have destinies governed by different planets altogether. One was a blond, charismatic Australian who lost major championships in every conceivable way—and some no one would or could have imagined—while the other was a dark-haired, aloof Englishman who seemed to stand on golf's toniest street corners gracefully accepting major titles as others blithely cast them off like wadded-up candy wrappers. Faldo won three Open Championships and three Masters, the most titles of consequence of any of his contemporaries. Norman won two Open Championships but will be remembered more for losing all four in playoffs and whiffing on a handful of others when he had them in his sights. They were the dominant players of their generation, with Faldo spending 97 weeks as the world number one, while Norman, who won more but not as importantly, spent 331 weeks in the top spot, second only to Tiger Woods since the ranking system began. They would become fishing buddies and television commentators for different networks but will be forever linked by a rivalry that culminated in the most bizarre Masters Sunday Augusta National ever witnessed.

Faldo grew up in Welwyn Garden City, an easy drive up the A1 from central London. He honed his game on the miniaturized practice ground of the Welwyn Garden City Golf Club after he quit school at sixteen, having announced to his parents his intention to become a professional golfer. If you go to the club's website today, you'll find a passing mention of his connection to the place. An only child, Faldo was the favorite son of George and Joyce and virtually no one else, though his early instruction from the club's head professional, Ian Connelly, would be pivotal. He was driven, determined, and a loner. When the young Faldo came to America to enroll at the University of Houston, he decided classes would interfere with the time he wanted to spend on his golf, a complaint almost singular among anyone who ever teed it up in Cougar red. Let's just say Fred Couples, to name just one, never found their academic pursuits too rigorous. Faldo lasted a mere ten weeks in Texas. When he reached adulthood, the six-foot-three Faldo had the muscular build of a Dallas Cowboys tight end, but throughout his career he drove the ball with the authority, and precision, of a hairdresser.

Two years older and 9,400 miles away, Norman was born in Mount Isa in Queensland and grew up in Townsville, on the coast near the Great Barrier Reef, later moving to Brisbane. His father, Merv, was a stern, disciplined man, an engineer's engineer. His mother, Toini, was the athlete who introduced her son to golf at Virginia GC in Brisbane. Norman loathed school, choosing to spend his time outdoors, riding horses on the beach, diving and surfing or sailing with his sister, Janis. Outside of his obvious athletic skills—he played Australian Rules football and golf at Aspley High—the young boy showed no inclination to make anything of himself. He disappointed his despotic father, first by showing neither an aptitude for nor any interest in engineering, then by walking out of a recruiter's office rather than enlist in the Australian Air Force to learn to fly fighter jets. It wasn't that he lacked direction; it was that his direction took him to the beach at Noosa to camp out and do nothing. Well, what seemed like nothing to his father. Whether it was because he was tossed about in a frightening experience in the surf one day, as he has claimed, or if Norman just finally grew up, he eventually decided he could play golf for a living, a notion his father found as preposterous as any other Greg had had. Norman took a job in a warehouse for Precision Golf Forgings and began practicing fanatically. He entered the Australian Open. He became an assistant pro in Sydney, then returned to Royal Queensland to work for and, more important, with Charlie Earp. At twenty-one he won the West Lakes Classic. No less than David Graham finished second. Norman became an instant star, and in five years the Great White Shark would leap from the pages of an American newspaper.

Faldo joined the European Tour in 1976, a year before Norman, who arrived from Australia with the good looks and marquee billing of a leading man. Norman won the Martini International in his first season. Faldo was a year behind, taking the Colgate PGA Championship the following year. Norman led the Order of Merit in '82, Faldo in '83. The cracks in Faldo's game started to appear about the time he was moving on from wife number one, Melanie, to wife number two, Gill, in 1984. After having faded on the weekend in the Open Championship the year before at Royal Birkdale, Faldo was in the mix in the '84 Masters, playing in the next-to-last pair with the eventual winner, Ben Crenshaw. He shot 76, and the British tabloids dubbed him "El Foldo." Between the all too public knowledge of his marital life and his struggles in the big events, Faldo's disdain for the media blossomed like the wisteria clinging to Augusta's pines. His golf, however, was in incipient decline. In position to challenge at the Old Course in '84, he shot 76 in the third round to become a nonfactor yet again, left to watch as Seve Ballesteros delivered El Momento on the eighteenth green. Faldo's feud with the British press, which liked nothing better than lacerating painful personal wounds, the fresher the torment the better, scaled new heights.

After leaving Connelly behind in '82, Faldo spoke with a number of instructors to try to find his golf swing, including John Jacobs, Bob Torrance, and a Rhodesian (Rhodesia is now Zimbabwe) named David Leadbetter, a lanky character who resembled the Disney depiction of Ichabod Crane and was the little-known instructor advising Nick Price and a handful of other South Africans. After a poor start to the '85 season, then watching his boyhood nemesis, the impressive and likable Scot Sandy Lyle, win the Open Championship at Royal St. George's while the best he could manage were rounds of 73, 73, 75, and 74, Faldo jumped off the proverbial cliff. He told Leadbetter to throw the book at him. Thus began what Faldo has always referred to as his wilderness years.

This wilderness was no paradise, even if it was in Florida. Visiting Leadbetter at the Greenlefe Resort in Orlando, where he had his first American-based school, Faldo hit bucket upon bucket upon bucket of balls, sometimes 1,500 a day until his hands bled. It wasn't a tweak; it was a complete rebuild from the crankshaft to the pistons, the spark plugs to the cylinder heads. Even the belts and hoses needed tightening. Set up. Backswing. Leg action. Downswing. Follow through. The lot. It would click; then it would misfire. Faldo stayed with it. In for a penny, in for a pound. He suffered like Job, sometimes frustrated, at other times angry, doubting his own judgment and Leadbetter's advice. Instead of Monty Python's Ministry of Silly Walks, was he enrolled in the Ministry of Silly Drills? Had the whole thing been a colossal mistake, a waste of a year and a half?

Of all places the path out of the wilderness went smack through Mississippi. Hattiesburg, where the also-rans play while the focus of the golfing world is on Augusta, is a little more than five hundred miles from Magnolia Lane, but the week of the Masters it's as close as the dark side of the moon. In 1987, without an invitation to play in the one tournament in April every golfer wants to be in, Faldo was headed to Hattiesburg, far better known as the home of the University of Southern Mississippi, where both Brett Favre and Jimmy Buffett matriculated, than it is the town where Nick Faldo finally found his mojo. Fifteen years later Hattiesburg would become the place Tiger Woods went to lose his, retreating to a clinic there to address his "sexual addiction." Whatever that last tumbler to click into place is, whether it's confidence or acceptance or something more tangible, it happened to Faldo that week in Hattiesburg. He finished second in the Deposit Guaranty Golf Classic behind David Ogrin. The last nubbin had been resolved. He knew he was ready to win again, and a month later in Spain he did.

The Open Championship that July was at Muirfield, the Honourable Company of Edinburgh Golfers, in Gullane. The defending champion was Norman, who'd won by five shots at Turnberry the year before, putting to rest for the time being a gaggle of his own demons. Muirfield is probably the least quirky of all the links in the championship rota, but with the exception of the early times on Thursday, that week it was an amalgam of pelting rain, heavy winds—particularly on Saturday—and a thick Scottish haar that rolled in off the Firth of Forth to blanket the course the final day. Faldo began the last round, the day after his thirtieth birthday, one stroke behind American Paul Azinger, who led after both thirty-six and fifty-four holes, though he was playing a tournament on a links course for the first time. Azinger seemed determined to seize control early in his round, going out in 34. Playing in the twosome just in front of the American (who would be his opposing Ryder Cup captain twenty-one years later at Valhalla GC in Kentucky), the best Faldo could manage was nine straight pars, missing birdie chances on the first five holes, to trail by three. Within its stone-fence boundary Muirfield is, essentially, two circles, one clockwise, the other counterclockwise, with the first nine the outside holes and the finishing nine on the inside. Coming home, Faldo missed birdie chances on the fifteenth and sixteenth, the last from just five feet. Australian Rodger Davis, who liked to wear plus fours with his name embroidered on the socks, finished strongly to post four under par, a shot behind Faldo, two in back of Azinger. Knowing he needed at least one more birdie down the stretch, Faldo managed just a par five into the wind at the seventeenth and a solid four at the last for a round of 71, turning in a card composed of eighteen straight uninspired-looking pars. It was one better than Davis but still one behind Azinger. It looked as though he had let another chance at the claret jug go begging.

Azinger, a sinewy twenty-seven-year-old who was at that moment six years and a few months away from being diagnosed with non–Hodgkin's lymphoma, had made back-to-back bogeys at the tenth and eleventh but was stubbornly holding tight to his one-shot lead. Like Faldo, he had his birdie chances but also couldn't convert. On the seventeenth he made the mistake that cost him the championship. Taking his driver off the tee instead of a one-iron, he reached a deep fairway bunker and was forced to come out sideways. The best he could manage was a bogey that dropped him into a tie with Faldo. The American drove beautifully with his one-iron at the last, but his five-iron approach found the greenside bunker left. Enough of the crowd cheered that the deputy secretary of the R&A was moved to apologize for the unsportsmanlike display at the prize giving afterward. Facing a difficult lie, with one foot in and one out of the bunker, Azinger's explosion shot came up well short, and the putt to tie Faldo never got to the hole. A great player's breakthrough in major championships never seems to lack for defining qualities, but in Faldo's case, this one grew to symbolize the man himself. Making eighteen straight pars was like coasting along in the Indianapolis 500 under the caution flag, then winning after the leader blows a tire and crashes into the wall in turn four. As time went on, however, the metaphor of the first of his two Open Championships at Muirfield took on a truer meaning. Faldo could compete. The man they dubbed El Foldo was, in fact, nothing of the sort. He was no chocolate fireman. When the heat was on, he wasn't going to melt. Faldo might be beaten, but he wasn't going to beat himself. And what great champion hadn't, at one time or another, relied on the kindness of strangers?

One of the curiosities of Faldo's curriculum vitae is that he wasn't a factor more often in the U.S. Open. After all, one would have imagined that a man who could win a major on Sunday with all pars would have been something of a natural in the championship in which "par" is the benchmark. For whatever reason, however, it seldom happened. At Medinah CC in 1990, Faldo missed the playoff by a shot between Mike Donald and Hale Irwin who, at forty-five, would become the oldest-ever U.S. Open champion after sinking a forty-five-foot birdie putt at the eighteenth in regulation and running around high-fiving the spectators lining the right side of the hole. And, in 1992, Faldo went into Sunday at Pebble Beach Golf Links with a chance but shot 77 on a day when the wind blew so hard players on the tiny par-three seventh were taking their seven-irons and bumping tee shots onto the cart path to let the ball roll down the hill rather than risk hitting it up in the air. Tom Kite, the bespectacled Texas rival of Ben Crenshaw who spent more time on a practice ground in one week than Ben would in an entire season, shot even-par 72 that day, good for a two-shot victory and his lone major title.

Faldo's best chance in America's National Open came a year after his breakthrough at Muirfield in an eighteen-hole playoff against Curtis Strange at The Country Club in Brookline, Massachusetts, the course where the twenty-year-old Francis Ouimet held off the British challenge of the great Harry Vardon and Ted Ray in their 1913 U.S. Open playoff. In an era dominated by the Europeans, Australians, and South Africans, Strange, a Virginian who was the son of a golf professional, was the best America had to offer. He won back-to-back U.S. Opens, the first time it had been done since Ben Hogan in 1950–51 and made a solid run at a three-peat at Medinah when Irwin edged Donald. Strange and Faldo, though not friendly, had a lot in common. A powerful driver of the golf ball as a young man, Strange retooled his swing, sacrificing length in favor of accuracy. "He was out to be the best he could be and there's not one thing wrong with that," Strange says of Faldo's work. "As far as personalities and the way we went about playing, during the playoff there wasn't one word said other than, 'Good luck,' and, on the last green, 'Congratulations.' What were we going to say to each other? How are the wife and kids? I don't care at this point how your wife and kids are. I don't care how mine are right now. I'm playing for the U.S. Open. I got one round to play for the trophy. I thought it was a great exhibition. I thought we went about it very professionally." Forced to press at the end, Faldo bogeyed three of his last four holes and lost, 75 to 71.

For whatever reason, Faldo's chances in the PGA Championship turned out not to be any better than in the U.S. Open. Slightly worse, in fact. In twenty-two appearances, he had four top fives, tying for second once, in 1992, three shots behind Nick Price. In that other American major, the Masters, it was quite a different story, though the narrative, fairly or not, remained much the same as it had for the Open Championship at Muirfield—someone gave it to him.

It's indisputable that Scott Hoch, a Raleigh, North Carolina, native who played golf at four-time Masters champion Arnold Palmer's alma mater, Wake Forest University, missed a two-foot putt on the first hole of sudden death that would have made him the 1989 Masters champion. What is often overlooked is that Faldo forced sudden death when he birdied the fifteenth, sixteenth, and seventeenth holes for a final round of 65 on a cold, gloomy day, at the end of a windy, cold, and gloomy week, after beginning the final round five shots behind the fifty-four-hole leader, Crenshaw. Faldo's birdie on the par-three sixteenth was particularly noteworthy, making a putt from the back fringe with eight or ten feet of break and mud on the golf ball. Norman and Crenshaw both had chances to join the playoff, and each bogeyed the eighteenth, Norman when his five-iron landed on the front fringe and rolled back off the green and Crenshaw when his five-iron approach found the front-left bunker. Neither could get up and down to save par.

Hoch spent so much time looking over his putt at the tenth, it was like he was reading *Atlas Shrugged* instead of a two-footer. When he missed, the momentum clearly belonged to Faldo. The Englishman hit a perfect drive down the eleventh and a stellar three-iron to within twenty-five feet. Hoch missed the green to the right. Unlike Augusta-born Larry Mize, who had snatched victory from Norman's jaws two years before from slightly closer range, Hoch's third didn't find the cup. It didn't matter, though, because Faldo's birdie putt did. In near darkness—the tee times had been pushed back to accommodate television, something that would become commonplace—Faldo raised his arms over his head. He was a multiple major winner and, in an even more delicious moment, would have the green jacket placed on him by the defending champ, his boyhood rival, Lyle, whose game was already hell-bent for oblivion after reaching its apex the previous year when his stunning seven-iron from the fairway bunker on the eighteenth allowed him to add a green jacket to the claret jug he won in '85 at Royal St. George's. It wasn't just a passing of the jacket; it was the baton, too, from the affable Scot to the loner from England. For the first time the Masters had back-to-back foreign winners.

For some reason Faldo always seemed to drive the golf ball more powerfully at Augusta National than anywhere else. It wasn't that he turbocharged his clubs or somehow magically found another five miles per hour of clubhead speed in the trunk of his courtesy car careening down Magnolia Lane. What Faldo was able to do was place his low, raking draws to take maximum advantage of Augusta's slopes. Added to that was an iron game as bang on as any in modern golf. He knew exactly where he needed to leave the ball on the green and within a three-foot radius where he needed to land his approach to create that result. All of this was overlooked once again the following year at Augusta when Faldo became just the second player—Jack Nicklaus was the first—to successfully defend a Masters title when he was accused, once again, of choosing the right opponent at the right time.

With six holes to play in the 1990 Masters, forty-seven-year-old Raymond Floyd, who had won four major championships and lacked only a claret jug in the trophy case to complete the career Slam, had a four-shot lead over Faldo. Known as one of the toughest competitors in all of golf, after two fallow years devoted to captaining the American Ryder Cup team of '89, Floyd looked to be on the verge of becoming the oldest Masters winner ever. He previously won the Masters by eight in 1976 when he five-wooded the field into submission. Playing just in front of Floyd, Faldo birdied the thirteenth, but Floyd couldn't match him. The same thing happened at the par-five fifteenth, and the lead was cut in half. Another birdie by Faldo at the sixteenth, as Floyd looked on from the fifteenth green, halved it yet again. As Faldo was sizing up his putt from the back of the eighteenth green, Floyd three-putted the seventeenth, and they were tied. If not for Floyd's scrambling four at the last, getting up and down from both the fairway and the greenside bunkers, Faldo would have won it outright.

Just like the previous year in sudden death, Faldo hit his second shot on the tenth into the bunker short and right of the green, but this time he got up and down. Even so, Floyd had a chance to win but missed his fifteen-foot birdie attempt. After they both found the fairway on the eleventh, Floyd pulled his seven-iron from a hanging lie into the pond front and left of the green. Ignoring both the groans of the patrons and the fate of the old warrior Floyd, Faldo deftly placed his eight-iron safely on and two-putted. In a year in which the blooms had already come and gone on Augusta National, so had the hopes of Floyd. The naysayers, however, remained unconvinced. Faldo, they claimed, was the luckiest man who ever wore green. "When you face a shot over the bloomin' pond left at eleven at Augusta, if you haven't got 100 percent commitment, you cannot hit that ball on that green," said Faldo. "It doesn't happen by accident, does it?" He would silence those critics a few months later at the home of golf.

"I think people think Nick was a little bit lucky to have won majors because a lot of people had thrown strokes away over the last few holes and Nick had sort of gratefully received it," says Bernard Gallacher, who played on eight European Ryder Cup teams and captained another three.

In 1990 when he won the Masters he was playing one of America's toughest players. Faldo's a difficult person to play against in match play and it really became a match play situation when you went into a playoff for the Masters. I don't think there's a better match play player than Faldo. He would realize that everybody would be rooting for Floyd but it wouldn't matter to him. I don't think players on the other side can actually get to Nick Faldo. He's in his own world. You can't put him off. Nick was never going to collapse. He will never collapse under pressure. The Open Championship at St. Andrews, when he won there, he really had the bit between the teeth. He was in the ascendency all week.

The tabs that had delighted in calling him Nick "Foldo" took just as much pleasure in reminding him that, despite having won three major championships, he hadn't done anything special to merit any of them other than hang around like a vagrant on a lamppost. Those eighteen straight pars had burned themselves into the media's psyche. It was as though he kept winning hands at a high-stakes blackjack table because the dealer busted over and over again. That ended on Saturday on the Old Course at St. Andrews.

"I was a man on a mission that week," Faldo says of St. Andrews. "The only guy I ever felt I had to beat that week was Greg. I thought, right, he's the one. He was on form, as well. That was a good, old match play within a stroke play event. Two guys who really can win it right there."

After thirty-six holes in benign conditions on the most hallowed ground the game knows, Faldo and Norman were tied at twelve under par, four shots clear of Payne Stewart and the stoutly built Australian Craig Parry. The prospects for a dramatic weekend were drawing comparisons with the way Watson and Nicklaus had separated themselves from the field at Turnberry in '77 to stage a *mano y mano* contest between the game's two best players. This one didn't last long. Faldo delivered the coup de grâce in one afternoon. Jumping quickly ahead of Norman, the Australian seemed to abandon his previous strategy and began playing too boldly. The book on St. Andrews has one inviolable rule: whether you lay up short of the bunkers or fly over them, one way or another, you avoid them. Norman didn't. Out in a pedestrian 36, Norman bogeyed the twelfth, thirteenth, fifteenth, and sixteenth holes to come home in 40, while Faldo posted a tidy 67. The nine-shot swing was two less than the one six years later at Augusta National.

Faldo's manhandling of Norman was so impressive, the bookies, always active during an Open Championship, stopped taking bets on him. With just one round to play, he had a five-shot lead over another Australian, Ian Baker-Finch (who, like Faldo, would become an announcer for CBS), and Stewart, who showed up on the first tee on Sunday wearing his patriotic Stars and Stripes, or, as Raymond Jacobs of the *Glasgow Herald* described it, "dressed for burial at sea."

By then Leadbetter was teaching both Faldo and Baker-Finch. "One thing I do recall," says Leadbetter, "was saying to Ian, listen, do not expect Nick to even recognize the fact that you're there today." And he didn't. That was the Faldo way. "It was like, I'm getting on with it. This is how I operate on a golf course, get completely focused in it and get on with it," says Faldo. "I had that intensity, that focus. And I finished it off."

Stewart was the only one to apply any pressure, closing the gap to two shots at one point. Fanny Sunneson, who would later become the coach of her Swedish countryman Henrik Stenson, was in her first season as Faldo's caddie. "We were going down 14 and she recognized things were tightening," said Faldo. "Between the tee shot and the second shot, she come along behind and says, completely out of the blue, 'Are you thinking about getting a dog?' This is her effort to take my mind off things. I was always actually the opposite. I don't mind talking golf when we're on the golf course. But she's got it in the back of her yardage book—pressure release lines. Things to ask. It was very sweet." Faldo ended the day as he had begun it, with a comfortable five-shot lead. The demonstration squadron, the Red Arrows, flew up the eighteenth from the nearby air station at Leuchars, streaming red, white, and blue smoke, altering the scene below with shades of color. This time no one had given Faldo anything. He had seized his fourth major championship by the throat.

Back at Muirfield two years later with Baker-Finch now the defending Open champion after winning at Royal Birkdale, Faldo would stake himself to another large lead, this time four shots over Americans Steve Pate and John Cook, going into Sunday. "I don't know anyone I would want to give a four-stroke lead going into the final round of a British Open and Nick Faldo probably the least of all," said Pate. The Englishman had shown signs of vulnerability that year, however, surrendering big leads in both the Irish and the French Opens. It looked like it was going to happen again at Muirfield.

With nine holes to play, Faldo was three shots clear of Pate and four on José Maria Olazábal, who was playing better than anyone that day, and Cook, who had snapped his drive out-of-bounds on the eighth to undo a lot of good work on the opening holes. Looking at a ten-footer for birdie on the tenth, Faldo could have thrown a headlock on the championship but missed. Then he began to throw away shots, with bogeys at the eleventh and thirteenth and again at the fourteenth. Meanwhile, Cook's form returned, applying pressure to the now grim-faced Faldo with birdies on the fourteenth, fifteenth, and sixteenth. Like flipping a switch, the American had gone from four behind to two in front in seven holes.

On the fifteenth tee Faldo told himself, "You had better play the best four holes of your life." He got one stroke back with a quick birdie. Cook, meanwhile, reached the par-five seventeenth in two. Surely a birdie there would give him the Open Championship. But that angel that had whispered so often in the ears of Faldo's opponents broke into song again. Cook barely missed the eagle try, then lipped out the two-footer for birdie. Faldo parred the sixteenth and then reached the seventeenth in two with a drive and four-iron to twenty feet. A birdie would tie him with Cook, who was going down the eighteenth.

After driving perfectly, Cook lost his two-iron approach right. It bounded through the metal fence and into the gallery. He got relief, of course, but couldn't salvage his par. Faldo's two-putt birdie coupled with Cook's bogey meant that he had recaptured the lead and needed only a four at the last to win his third Open Championship. His drive was perfect and his three-iron dead at the pin, but it rolled just off the back. He lagged his first putt to three feet. When he wiggled it in, Faldo staggered like a man getting off a roller coaster. He covered his face with his hands and wept, on the green and again in the scorer's cabin. The same man who didn't even know Ian Baker-Finch had been in his twosome two years before at St. Andrews showed himself to the world. At the prize giving, after he'd composed himself, Faldo couldn't resist taking a jab at the hated media. "I want to thank the press from the bottom of my heart—no, the heart of my bottom," he ad-libbed.

Though born in Ohio, John Cook was a product of Southern California, as was his close friend Mark O'Meara. Boyhood rivals, they each won the California Amateur and also won the U.S. Amateur in back-to-back years, with O'Meara beating Cook in the finals in 1979. Surprisingly, O'Meara would win his two major championships, the Masters and the Open Championship, at the age of forty-one, rejuvenated after playing friendly rounds with Tiger Woods at their home course, Isleworth, in Orlando. Cook, who also lived in Isleworth and often joined Woods and O'Meara, never got close again in the Open Championship and, though he had eleven victories on the PGA Tour, never was able to break through in the majors the way his lifelong friend would.

In 1983 when Faldo was doing his rebuild, Greg Norman had already won nine times on the European Tour, with a similar number of victories in Australia, and had his first win on American soil, an unofficial pro-am in Hawaii, the Kapalua International. He'd also participated in the writing of the first of his two autobiographies, *My Story*. In the foreword to *Down the Fairway*, Grantland Rice writes,

> About one person in every ten million might have an interesting autobiography to put out at the age of twenty-five. Bobby Jones in this respect is one among ten millions. . . . His golf record is remarkable. At the age of twenty-five he had won the United States Open twice, from the best professionals and the best amateurs. He had won the British Open. He had won the Amateur Championships of the United States twice. For a period of five years he had never finished lower than second place in the United States Open Championships, facing the best golfers in the game.

Norman, on the other hand, was twenty-eight when his biography appeared and hadn't done much more in the big moments than win a nickname when he was dubbed the "Great White Shark" by the *Augusta Chronicle* in his first Masters in 1981, finishing fourth behind Watson, Nicklaus, and Johnny Miller.

Norman's book alienated many of his European brethren, having basically called them lazy, though he took pains to exclude Lyle and Faldo from that assessment. Some players refused to talk to him. In the end it didn't matter that he had worn out his welcome on the European Tour. He was taking his high profile, his Rolls-Royces and fiery red Ferraris, his wide shoulders and thin waist, and his shock of white blond hair that made him look like a ring announcer for the World Wrestling Federation and heading for America, the tour he'd always wanted to play anyway. He was entitled to his opinions—and Norman has never shied away from sharing them—but where was the record to back it up? His detractors said he was, to spin the old Texas saying, all hat and no kangaroo. Certainly, Norman wouldn't have ranked highly on Grantland Rice's scale of the ten million. While the twenty-eight-year-old Australian may have seemed more notorious than notable to some of his European colleagues, no one underestimated his ability. Norman was widely thought to be the finest driver of the golf ball since Nicklaus. No other player came close to having the combination of power and accuracy that Norman could summon. It was such a potent weapon even the keenest of observers could be blinded to his flaws.

As impressive as his long game was, when the heat was on, something seemed to go missing. Perhaps it was the noticeable slide in his lower body, or perhaps the defect ran deeper. There had been at least one other player whose stars were as crossed as Norman's. Craig Wood was on the veranda at Augusta National receiving congratulations on winning Bobby Jones's second Augusta National Invitational at just about the moment Gene Sarazen made double eagle on the fifteenth hole in 1935. Wood would lose the playoff the next day. The previous year Wood had lost the inaugural Masters to Horton Smith by a shot. That same year he'd lost the PGA Championship to Paul Runyon in extra holes. In '33 he lost the Open Championship to Denny Shute at St. Andrews, again in a playoff, and he would lose the 1939 U.S. Open in a playoff with Byron Nelson. Wood did finally win two major championships, the same number as Norman. Like Mark O'Meara's sudden double in 1998, they came late in his career and in the same year, the 1941 Masters and U.S. Open. Regardless, the ground had been plowed for Greg Norman.

Running through Norman's litany of futility can feel a bit like wandering through the cemetery of a New England church reading gravestones. There is a melancholy aspect to his record as one imagines what might have been. Norman, himself, is quite happy to inform you he never does. If Doug Sanders is haunted by a ghost he met on the eighteenth green in St. Andrews in 1970, surely Norman could use an exorcism. You might as well take him at his word that he doesn't wake up at night in a cold sweat because, if he did, where would he begin?

Perhaps 1984, when he lost the U.S. Open to Fuzzy Zoeller. Norman made an unbelievably difficult putt from the back-left side of the eighteenth green, far longer but on much the same line as the twelve-footer Bobby Jones made there to get into the U.S. Open playoff he won over Al Espinosa in 1929. Back in the fairway, thinking Norman had made the putt for birdie, Zoeller, already a major champion, having won the 1979 Masters in his rookie appearance, took the white towel from his golf bag and waved it back and forth in surrender. Birdie to tie would be a tall order. Zoeller, who was, with the possible exception of Chick Evans, the best player the state of Indiana ever produced, thought he'd lost. Then, a USGA official informed him Norman's putt was for par. The Australian had hit his approach wide right into the spectator stands. Wide right would become something of a theme for Norman.

After Zoeller's four at the last forced a playoff, that evening he and Norman found themselves in the restaurant of the White Plains Hotel. Zoeller sent a bottle of wine over to Norman's rather large party. The next morning, in a playful move reminiscent of Lee Trevino producing a rubber snake in his U.S. Open playoff against Jack Nicklaus at Merion GC in 1971, Zoeller pulled the handset, with the wire attached, of the phone he'd appropriated from his hotel room and asked Norman if he wanted to make a last call. They both laughed, but it was Zoeller who had the last one, 67-75.

Or it could be 1986. Nicklaus had forced Ballesteros to crumble on the fifteenth, but behind him Norman was bravely undeterred. Playing alongside Nick Price, the Aussie birdied the fourteenth, fifteenth, sixteenth, and seventeenth holes in an attempt to hold history and the forty-six-year-old Nicklaus at arm's length. He'd gone from four back to tied for the lead. Norman's four-iron approach at the eighteenth sailed wide right, deep into the shoulder-to-shoulder patrons sitting on the side of the hill. He did well to get it to fifteen feet, but the putt that would have tied Nicklaus missed. Just shy of thirty years later, Jordan Spieth would make a crucial third-round up and down from very nearly the same spot on his way to winning his first major.

Of course, there were a lot of options in '86. That was the year of the Saturday Slam when Norman led every major championship going into the final round and won one. The Open Championship isn't exactly chopped haggis and mustn't go underappreciated, but more on that later. After the Masters Norman led the U.S. Open at Shinnecock Hills GC on Long Island after thirty-six and fifty-four holes. Following a double bogey on the thirteenth on Saturday, as Norman waited in the fourteenth fairway to play his approach, a heckler in the gallery—even if it was the Hamptons, this was still New York after all—yelled something about choking. After he hit his shot Norman walked straight over to the gallery rope and challenged the fan. "If you want to say something to me, say it to me after this round when I can do something about it," he said. Like an actor coming out of character when he forgets his lines during a performance, nothing much good can happen to a golfer who engages the crowd on their terms instead of his own. Worse even, the next day it was as though Norman's caddie, Pete Bender, had been directed in no uncertain terms to focus on crowd control. Bender spent so much time cautioning the crowd in a very loud and authoritative voice, it became hard to focus on what he and Norman were supposed to be doing. After a couple of early bogeys, Norman came back with a birdie at the seventh but then bogeyed five of the next eight holes on the way to a 75. The whole world passed him, with the forty-three-year-old Ray Floyd, who took only 1 1 1 putts in four days, shooting a brilliant 66 to win.

Or perhaps it was Inverness One. The Donald Ross masterpiece in Toledo, Ohio, was the site of weird goings-on in the U.S. Open won there by Hale Irwin in 1979 when the then amateur Bobby Clampett got pulled off the course by the USGA for excessive clowning (hitting shots off his knees just for the helluva it, among other things) and the blue coats planted a tree overnight—dubbed the Hinkle Tree—to prevent long-hitting Lon from taking a shortcut on the eighth hole by driving it down the seventeenth fairway. Those bizarre happenings paled in comparison to the finish of the 1986 PGA. Norman led by four shots after thirty-six and fifty-four holes. His closest pursuer to have previously won a major championship was Nicklaus, eight shots back. Paired with Bob Tway, who had been the first-round leader in the U.S. Open at Shinnecock in the worst weather that championship had seen in anyone's memory, the twosome barely reached the second fairway before play was halted because of storms. Resuming Monday morning, Tway briefly cut into the lead, but Norman was still four ahead with nine holes to go. That's when it came undone for him. After driving into a sand-filled divot and burying his next shot in a bunker, Norman double-bogeyed the eleventh. Tway shaved another shot off the lead with a birdie at the thirteenth, and Norman's bogey at the fourteenth meant they were tied. With both players saving pars down the stretch, they came to the short dogleg eighteenth.

Tway drove into the deep right rough. Norman's ball landed there but skipped out into the fairway. Tway's nine-iron second fell short into the greenside bunker. In those days Norman was playing a Spalding Tour Edition ball that spun more than most. His pitching-wedge approach landed on the green but went into full reverse, zipping back down the slope and into the fairway. Lee Trevino liked to say God didn't give great players everything. The golf ball aside, one of the voids in Norman's game was the kind of dead-handed shot that lands without spin, just the kind of shot, particularly with short irons, players need on waterlogged courses. Norman went after everything full bore. It was his nature. When Tway got to his ball in the bunker, he found a good lie on an upslope, the kind of bunker shot any tour player would think about making under less stressful circumstances. Nervous though he might be, he switched the controls to automatic talent. The twenty-seven-year-old Tway holed the bunker shot and began leaping up and down. Norman needed to chip in to equal his score. He couldn't. A final bogey gave him a back nine of 40.

The parade of haunting hole-outs continued in '87. The most memorable and improbable of all came at the Masters and deserves a special place in the pantheon of doom. Larry Mize, a twenty-eight-year-old born and raised in Augusta, Georgia, had birdied the eighteenth hole to post three under par. Seve Ballesteros and Greg Norman, who had held a slim one-shot lead going into Sunday, each birdied the seventeenth to join him, while Ben Crenshaw bogeyed there to miss what became a three-way playoff. On the first hole of sudden death, the cathedral of pines that is the tenth, all three players drove the ball well. Ballesteros went just over the green. Mize had the best chance at birdie, an uphill fifteen-footer. The Spaniard three-putted from above the hole, and Norman and Mize continued on as Seve walked back up the hill toward the clubhouse with tears in his eyes. Both Mize and Norman drove well at the eleventh, Norman considerably longer. Mize played a dreadful five-iron from 194 yards that hung far out to the right, a good 40 yards from the hole. Norman left his seven-iron on the right fringe. Mize pitched using his fifty-six-degree wedge. Norman watched carefully once the ball reached the green to gauge the break and looked on in stunned disbelief when it disappeared into the cup.

Amen Corner erupted. Sixty yards back up the fairway, sitting just inside the gallery rope (strictly verboten at the Masters), Mize's wife, Bonnie, was holding their infant son, David, in her arms. From the electric silence one moment to the sudden roar the next, the startled baby began to cry. Bonnie rocked him back and forth and said, "It's okay. It's okay. It's just Daddy." Norman, once again, would have to hole out for the tie. His forty-foot putt barely missed. "I didn't think Larry could get down in two from where he was," said Norman afterward, "and I was right." When fate put its thumb on the scales in favor of the local Augusta boy, it caused a tearful Shark to wash up on the beach in front of his Florida mansion later that night. In 1991 he confessed it had taken him four years to get over it. Ballesteros, who only saw Mize's pitch shot on television, said, "From that distance, it happens maybe once a century." But this century had Norman's name on it.

The nightmares continued in 1989. The first was the Masters when Norman closed with birdies on the tenth, thirteenth, fifteenth, sixteenth, and seventeenth holes only to come up short again on the eighteenth when he hit a one-iron off the tee (in other Masters he'd reached the fairway bunkers with his three-wood) only to deliver a poorly struck five-iron approach that finished below the green. The bogey and the dropped shot cost him a spot in the Faldo-Hoch playoff. Even worse, however, was the Open Championship at Royal Troon, where he wound up playing for the claret jug and never even finished.

Much like that April at Augusta, Norman made a bold charge to put himself in a position to win the Open Championship, beginning his round with six consecutive birdies. His only bogey came on the eighth, the Postage Stamp, and his inward 33 was good for a round of 64 and a thirteen-under-par total. It would be an hour and a half before the other contenders would finish. Mark Calcavecchia was the first to join Norman. Calcavecchia was a free-spirited, wisecracking American who had grown up in Florida after the family moved there from Nebraska. A rookie in '82, Calcavecchia drove from tournament to tournament with a pair of bowling balls in his car, looking for a bowling alley in every town. In one season he bowled more than two thousand games, keeping track of his score on every one. Never one to hide his emotions, he would blow a five-up lead against Colin Montgomerie in their Ryder Cup match on Kiawah Island's Ocean Course in 1991 and sit alone on the beach crying as the United States went on to defeat Europe. The third man in the playoff at Troon was the gap-toothed Australian Wayne Grady, who had gone into the final round with a one-shot lead over Tom Watson, who had come up just short in his attempt at a sixth Open Championship.

This was the first year of the aggregate playoff, and the threesome would go out on numbers one and two, cross over the sixteenth, and come home on the seventeenth and eighteenth. There was no set number of holes for an aggregate playoff, just what made sense on that particular course, and two out and two back was perfect at Royal Troon. Despite the long wait, Norman looked good early. (Where had we seen that before?) He played a little pitch-and-run to six feet on the first and birdied while the other two made pars. He added another birdie at the second, as did Calcavecchia. Norman was a shot ahead of the American and two up on his countryman. On the par-three seventeenth Norman hit his three-iron through the green and failed to get up and down. Grady also bogeyed, but Calcavecchia's par meant he and Norman were headed to the eighteenth 3-3-4 to 4-3-3. The American drove into the right rough. As he had every day, Norman took driver, too. This time his tee ball seemed utterly disinclined to cease rolling. It bounded into the fairway bunker 325 yards away, stopping almost up against the face. Dead. From 201 yards, Calcavecchia, who had gotten into the playoff with a stunning eight-iron out of the rough to four feet on the same hole, delivered a pure five-iron inside ten feet. "It was just so dry and dead. The shot I hit in the playoff actually did fly a little bit," says Calcavecchia. "I didn't think I could get a 5-iron there. There was OB over the green so I didn't want to take a 4-iron out in case it came out a little warm." His two approach shots on the home hole out of Troon's wispy rough would ignite a controversy over the square, or U-shaped, grooves in his Ping irons. A change in the rule covering grooves wouldn't be implemented until 2010, though an expensive three-way legal battle between the USGA, Ping, and the PGA Tour would erupt in the interim. With Calcavecchia in close, Norman needed a heroic shot but was able to advance the ball only as far as the bunker farther up the fairway. His next shot went through the green and stopped near the clubhouse, out-of-bounds. Calcavecchia would hole his putt, and Grady finished one over par for the playoff, three behind. Norman was in his pocket and retired to the locker room.

Or perhaps it's the twists and turns of Inverness Two. Once again Norman led going into the final round in Toledo, though this time it was by a shaky single shot in front of a highly deco-rated group that included Paul Azinger, Tom Watson, Vijay Singh, Lanny Wadkins, and Hale Irwin along with Texan Bob Estes. Faldo was another shot back. If this would wind up being just another garden-variety missed opportunity for Norman, it was something more for Watson. "This may be my last chance," said Watson, who was a few weeks shy of his forty-fourth birthday, of winning the PGA to complete the career Slam. Only five professionals have managed to win all four: Gene Sarazen, Ben Hogan, Gary Player, Jack Nicklaus, and Tiger Woods, with Woods and Nicklaus each accomplishing the feat three times over. Sam Snead lacked a U.S. Open. Watson and Arnold Palmer a PGA. So coveted is the achieve-ment that after Jeff Sluman won the PGA Championship, his lone major, in 1988, when Watson saw him in the locker room weeks later he jokingly said, "I'll give you two British Opens for it." If the pressure of the first chance is intense, the pressure of the last chance, weighed down with the gravity of time, is even worse. Watson couldn't summon enough of his old self and bogeyed three of his first five holes.

Norman fell three shots behind at one point, playing the sixth and seventh holes three over par. He recovered with birdies on the eighth, the eleventh, and another at the thirteenth. Azinger didn't make a birdie until the twelfth and then quickly added two more at the thirteenth and fourteenth. That surge drew him even with Norman, Singh, and Faldo, who played the steadiest golf of all the contenders with three birdies and fifteen pars. Neither he nor Singh could make anything happen over the closing holes, however. Norman hit a wedge two feet for a birdie on the sixteenth, while Azinger matched it with a birdie on the seventeenth, and they went to sudden death. Back on the short dogleg eighteenth where Norman had lost to Tway seven years earlier, both had good runs at birdie but missed. On the next extra hole, the tenth, which was just slightly longer than the eighteenth, both had little more than pitch shots to the green. Norman left his forty feet away, while Azinger stuck his to five feet. Norman's first putt came up four feet short. Azinger's putt for a winning three hit the lip and spun out. Norman had a chance to extend the playoff, but he, too, missed. Azinger tapped in to seal Norman's destiny as the second man to have lost all four major championships in playoffs. In the gift that keeps on giving, a mere twenty-three years later, after one season in the booth, Azinger would replace Norman as the color analyst for Fox.

It should be noted that lesser disappointments, like Robert Gamez holing a seven-iron on the eighteenth hole at Bay Hill in 1990 to pip Norman or David Frost making a fifty-foot bunker shot at English Turn in New Orleans the same year to do the same thing, served only to reinforce the narrative. Every player who ever weathered the storm near the top of a leader board with any consistency at all has had victory snatched from them by someone else's lightning bolt. What has been overlooked to this point are Norman's two Open Championships but not because his successes get in the way of an otherwise epic indictment. It's precisely because of his victories in 1986 at Turnberry and 1993 at Royal

St. George's that Norman can be viewed as an Ahab-like figure, with the important distinction that whereas the *Pequod*, Ahab's ship, was used to seek revenge rather than profit, Norman found revenge in the vast profits his business ventures would earn him.

The stars can align sufficiently for any accomplished player to stumble into a major championship. But you don't stumble into two. During his one-for-four major championship season in '86, it felt very much as though the only person who could beat Norman was Norman. It was just the second time the Open Championship had been to Turnberry, the first being the historic Watson-Nicklaus duel. The championship began in relentlessly dismal weather, cold with the wind cresting more than thirty miles an hour off the sea. The fourteenth hole was 440 yards right into the wind and was virtually unreachable in two. No one broke Turnberry's par of 70. Although the second day was better, the tourist board wouldn't have been sending out notices about it. The average score was 74.07. Fourteen players finally succeeded in breaking par. Norman, however, crushed it, joining the 63 club, tying for the lowest round ever in a major championship. And he did it with three bogeys. The round vaulted him into the lead, and he held it despite shooting 40 on the inward nine for a third round of 74. Pete Bender, who had been overzealous at Shinnecock, calmed Norman at Turnberry. At one point on the seventh Bender grabbed Norman by the back of the shirt as they were headed down the fairway after he'd hit a low, running hook off the tee, trying to slow him down. "I want you to walk at the same speed I am," Bender told him. Norman quickly calmed down and, on the eighth, hit a four-iron 5 feet from the hole. "When I hit that 4-iron in there, I said, 'All right, guys, that's it. I've shut the gate.'" And opened another.

*Validation* probably isn't the right word. Too much white water had gushed under the bridge by 1993. Maybe it was closer to an affirmation. Whatever it was, Norman proved unstoppable at Royal St. George's, the course where James Bond took Goldfinger's money in Ian Fleming's book. Wet and receptive after midweek rain, Norman went into the final round a shot off the pace of his nemesis, Nick Faldo, at that moment the number-one-ranked player in the world, and Corey Pavin, a tenacious Californian about the size of your basic middle school librarian who would win his only major championship two years later at Shinnecock Hills in the U.S. Open. Norman was tied with Bernhard Langer, the tough-as-tree-bark German who had overcome cases of the yips that would have ended many careers, not once but twice, to win the Masters in 1985 and, using a grip that held both the handle of the putter and his forearm, again that April. Augusta National is as likely to be played well by a golfer with the yips as Sandy Koufax was to give up a three-run homer to Alfred Hitchcock. Yet Langer had managed it twice. Norman and Langer were out just ahead of Faldo and Pavin, who fell out of contention early. Norman produced stunning stuff the last day. The course was scorable, as Payne Stewart's 63 showed and Faldo's own 63 in the second round attested. Norman caught Faldo by the third hole, and after the Englishman bogeyed the fourth he never led again. Norman went out in 31. When Langer hit his tee ball out-of-bounds on the fourteenth, not even a couple of birdies could get him back within reach of Norman, who shot a final-round 64. "I cannot say that ever in my career have I gone around a golf course and not missed a shot, but today I did," said Norman.

The worst, however, was yet to come.

"I don't wake up in the morning and go, 'Oh, shit,' 1996," Norman says. But for a while, everyone else did. Though undoubtedly someday someone will shoot a 62, or perhaps even better, in one of the four major championships, when Greg Norman opened the '96 Masters with a nine-birdie, no-bogey 63 he became the first player to have equaled the low score in a major championship twice. Everything had to go right, and it did. On the fourteenth he drove into the trees, and his ball dropped, still 220 yards from the flag. He hit a three-iron three feet from the hole. Norman was forty-one. He'd won on the Blue Monster at Doral, the resort near the Miami International Airport that would one day be purchased by Donald Trump, the first week in March and was on his game.

Nick Faldo hadn't done much since winning at Doral the year before—Norman had been the runner-up that week along with Peter Jacobsen—at least not on a golf course. Only once in a major championship in '95 had Faldo cracked the top 25 with a T24 in the Masters. His second marriage had ended when he began an affair with a twenty-year-old University of Arizona golfer, Brenna Cepelak, who had been a highly sought-after recruit from New Mexico. The affair would last three years, with Cepelak eventually taking a nine-iron to Faldo's Porsche 959 when he broke it off in favor of the woman who would become his third wife, Valerie Bercher. To be fair, Norman would eventually make some tabloid headlines of his own. An affair with Chris Evert, his subsequent divorce, and the fifteen-month marriage to the tennis Hall of Famer became all the rage in the Palm Beaches in 2006. In any event by April 1996 the turbulent seas of Faldo's personal life had temporarily, at least, settled to the degree to which the British press would allow. Augusta was his safe harbor.

A 67 in the second round got Faldo closer to Norman, but he was still four shots behind in second place. On a blustery, difficult third day with some tricky hole locations, when anything under par was a fine round of golf, Norman's one-under 71 stretched his lead to six over his English rival. It would be the first time they'd played together in a major championship since 1990 at St. Andrews. No one had ever held that kind of lead going into the final round of a major championship and lost.

At first it was drip, drip. Norman dropped a shot at number one but birdied the second. Not uncommon. Faldo's par-birdie cut the lead to five. Norman bogeyed the demanding fourth, the par three. No shame there. It might be the hardest par on the golf course. The lead was four. Faldo gave the shot back at the fifth anyway. At the downhill par-three sixth, Faldo hit his seven-iron inside five feet and made the birdie putt. The lead returned to four. On the uphill par-five eighth, Faldo made his four, and Norman couldn't match it after his second shot drifted left into the trees. It had been an aggressive play at the green. Not a horrible shot, just, perhaps, an unwise one. The lead was three. Norman's first mishit came on the ninth. You simply must carry the ball far enough over the false front to stay up on the green. He didn't, and the ball rolled back down the slope. Bogey for Norman, out in 38 to Faldo's 34, and the lead was two.

Heading downhill, the unraveling picked up speed. Nick Price, who had a 63 of his own at Augusta National ten years before, was watching the CBS broadcast in the clubhouse. "I feel sick to my stomach," he said. Norman bogeyed the tenth when he missed the green to the left. The lead was one. Norman three-putted the eleventh from just fifteen feet. The lead was gone. On the twelfth Norman's tee shot hit the bank and came back into the water. His double bogey put Faldo two ahead. From the ninth through the twelfth Faldo had produced nothing but pars but had gained five shots. "That's when it was mine to lose," Faldo said. They both birdied the thirteenth, parred the fourteenth, and birdied the fifteenth. At the 170-yard sixteenth Norman hooked his six-iron into the pond.

The back nine of Augusta National on a Masters Sunday is famous for its roars. That day it was infamous for its queasy silence. The Masters was the only one of the four major championships that had never been won by an Australian. The pain of Greg Norman was felt around breakfast tables on the other side of the earth. There was none of the usual cheering. If Faldo got applause, it was little more than polite. None of the rushing for vantage points. As Norman walked up the seventeenth and then the eighteenth fairways, you wanted to remove your hat and place it over your heart. He didn't need a caddie; he needed a caisson. After Faldo finished with a birdie for a turning-of-the-screw 67 and Norman a horrific 78, the man who would never go away put his arm around the neck of man who was always there and said, "Don't let the bastards get you down."

It was from that place of deep despair that seventeen years later Adam Scott, whose flagging confidence was bolstered when Norman picked him for the Presidents Cup team he captained in 2009, made a birdie putt on the same green and screamed so loud he could still be heard over the roaring patrons, "Come on, Aussie!" For Norman, Augusta was the pain that hurt so good. "Tom Watson always felt that Oakmont was his friend even though he never won around there," Norman says. "I always thought Augusta was my lover." It remained unrequited.

In 1996 Tiger Woods, a sophomore at Stanford University, shot 75-75 and missed the cut in his second Masters. The next year he would win it by twelve shots. The world was about to change.

# 4

## A Country Boy from Springfield

Springfield is a small town on the Ozark Plateau in a state that was red before anyone thought about color-coding them. It's the third-biggest city in Missouri, but if it was in California, it would barely crack the top thirty. The Trail of Tears passed through Springfield on what was once called the Military Road. The North and the South fought over it, and in 1865, three months after Lee surrendered to Grant, "Wild Bill" Hickok shot a man dead on its streets over a pocket watch. In the first decade of the twentieth century, three black men were hanged in the town square. Five decades later, in the post–World War II craze over a new medium, television, Springfield took country music nationwide with *The Ozark Jubilee*. A year later Chris Schenkel and Bud Palmer debuted on CBS at the Masters. Three men born in Springfield have won major golf championships, and two of them are in the World Golf Hall of Fame. St. Andrews might be the only small city east of Fort Worth to equal its output.

If Payne Stewart wasn't in uniform, knickers custom made from bolts of Italian cloth, silk stockings, gold- or silver-tipped spiked shoes, and an ivy cap in the Ben Hogan style, he was as unrecognizable in public as if a Maserati had been stripped down to a Dodge Dart. "He comes off as this real urbane, Great Gatsby type of guy," said his longtime swing coach, Chuck Cook, "but, really, he was a Missouri mule. Just a country boy from Springfield."

Back in the heyday of newspapers, when a sports star needed a nickname the way a clipper ship needs wind, Stewart was preceded as a major champion by Horton Smith, the Missouri Rover, and Herman Keiser, the Missouri Mortician, who won three Masters between them. According to Byron Nelson, Smith was the finest putter of his generation. He won the inaugural Augusta National Invitational when he holed a downhill four-footer at the last to pip Craig Wood, who would be victimized by Gene Sarazen's double eagle a year later. For good measure Smith took the title (it wasn't, after all, the championship of anything) back from Sarazen, overtaking Harry Cooper after being two strokes behind with four holes to play. A member of the World Golf Hall of Fame, Smith was the last man to beat Bobby Jones in tournament play before Jones's retirement from competition in 1930, and they remained lifelong friends. Dying from lung cancer and with the aid of a cart, Smith exercised his prerogative as a past champion to play his final Masters in '63, honoring his friend Jones, who was, himself, dying of syringomyelia. He shot 91-86.

Keiser spent thirty months at sea during his World War II naval service but earned his nickname on dry land for his funereal oncourse demeanor. In 1946 Ben Hogan and Byron Nelson were the prohibitive favorites in anything one or the other, or both, entered, but it was Keiser who built a five-stroke lead with one round to play in the Masters. Wobbly nines of 37-37 gave Hogan, who had yet to win a tournament of any real consequence, an opening. Not yet hardened into the champion he would soon become, all Hogan needed was to make a twelve-footer, downhill, to win, two putts to meet Keiser in an eighteen-hole playoff the next day. His first slid by just under three feet, and he missed coming back. Other than the '48 Masters, Keiser would never finish in the top ten in another major.

While Smith was eventually associated more closely with the Detroit Golf Club and Keiser with Firestone Country Club in Akron, for a time they were both at Hickory Hills Country Club in Springfield, where Keiser worked as Smith's shop assistant. Hickory Hills is where Stewart learned to play, as aware of the champions who came before him as he was of characters like Ky Laffoon, who favored sky-blue sweaters and socks as yellow as two daffodils and once hustled the young Stewart on its chipping green. While Springfield's other major champions both made their reputations in the Masters, Augusta was the big moment Stewart enjoyed least. Deeply patriotic, the National Open was above all others to him. At his father, Bill's, insistence, he always signed his U.S. Open entry with his full name, William Payne Stewart. He didn't like the Masters because he thought the little people were treated shabbily there, particularly the caddies. "He really felt uncomfortable," said Cook. "When we would go to Augusta, we'd always eat in the employee dining room instead of out front with everybody else." Before ugly false teeth became a Halloween cliché available at every party store in America, Stewart had a set custom made by a Springfield dentist, Dr. Kurt H'Doubler. He stuck them in his mouth frequently for effect, but took particular pleasure in wearing them in the Par-3 Contest at the Masters.

Even if he'd lived in the age of nicknames, Stewart was too complicated for that kind of lazy gimmick. He could be arrogant and thoughtless or generous and compassionate, sometimes in the same sentence. He was a devoted practitioner of the sporting jibe, what's mostly described now as trash talking, though it didn't always come in the form of talk. "He was an awful fan," said John Cook, a former U.S. Amateur champion who, like Stewart, lived in Orlando, Florida. "Just awful. I'd pick him up and we'd go to the Magic games. He'd be yelling at somebody the minute he got in the arena." Stewart's seats for the National Basketball Association (NBA) games were four rows behind the Magic bench, and he took great delight in ceaselessly taunting the head coach at the time, Matt Goukas. "Poor, old Matty," said Dr. Dick Coop, Stewart's sports psychologist. "Payne just lit him up every night." After only one season Stewart's seats were moved, not just from behind the bench, but to the other side of the arena.

Like Stewart, Ken Griffey Jr., a baseball star for the Seattle Mariners, had a home in the Isleworth subdivision in Orlando. Seattle was playing Tampa Bay, and Griffey was taking a helicopter back and forth. Stewart, John Cook, and Mark O'Meara, all Isleworth residents, decided to go to one of the games. "We've got these beautiful seats, right behind the Seattle dugout. Griffey is having the worst game of his life," says Cook. "He's struck out three times, looking. He's in the on-deck circle and Payne is absolutely hammering him." Griffey managed to ignore Stewart and coaxed a walk out of the pitcher. Edgar Martinez was batting behind Griffey, and the hit-and-run was on. Martinez swung and missed, and Griffey, caught in a rundown, was tagged out. "Payne gets the idea, let's go out to center field," said Cook. "We find these seats in the first row. As soon as Griffey gets out there, Payne is going, 'Juuuuunior. Juuuuunior. Does this look familiar?' And starts running back and forth across the bleachers. Griffey, it's like he's lost his mind, he's laughing so hard."

The canvas for Stewart's needlework included golf, and he didn't care whom he skewered. "Jack Nicklaus. Arnold Palmer. It did not matter," said his longtime caddie, Mike Hicks. "And you know what? A lot of guys didn't like it. Some guys didn't mind, and if they didn't mind, they liked Payne. But if they minded it, they didn't like him. If they all say they liked him, they're lying because he was tough, man. He would needle you and he would go overboard with it. He could take it, too. But he'd get under your skin if you let him."

Once when Stewart was visiting Jim Morris, an old family friend in LaQuinta, California, they arranged a money game with Donald Trump. The wealthy developer was five minutes late to the first tee, but Morris and Stewart didn't wait for him. By the time Trump pulled up in his golf cart, they were ahead on the first fairway. Stewart yelled back at him, "Trump, this ain't one of them corporate meetings. It's one o'clock and you're either here or you ain't here."

Dr. Coop, at the time a faculty member at the University of North Carolina at Chapel Hill, began working with Stewart the same year Hicks became his caddie, 1988. "The first day he came to see me," Coop said, "I told him what I'd heard about him very bluntly, very forthrightly. He calls Tracey (his wife) and she says,

'What did he say?' And Payne said, 'Well, he told me I was arrogant, cocky, brash, insensitive, etc.' She said, 'What did you say?' Payne said, 'Well, I told him he was probably right.' We started off that way."

Stewart grew up in a one-story house on Link Street with three women and a traveling salesman, which could be a joke if it wasn't true. His father, Bill, sold mattresses and box springs and was often on the road, leaving Payne with his sisters, Susan and Lora, and his mother, Bee, who was as rare a species in Springfield as a snow leopard—a staunch Democrat. In election season Bee filled the yard with political placards like dandelions. "He had a lot of girl in him," said Cook. "Ironed his own clothes. He loved to cook. He liked to dress up. Then, when he'd be with the boys, he'd be about as macho as anybody. He wasn't afraid to try to out-drink you or outplay you or anything else." Stewart made french toast on a local Springfield cooking show when he was three and reveled in making a breakfast of waffles and pancakes for his own children, Aaron and Chelsea, whenever he wasn't traveling to play golf.

In the late 1970s if you didn't make it through the PGA Tour's soulless meat grinder that was its qualifying tournament, your playing options were few. One was to go to Florida and join a mini tour where the prize money was the aggregate of the entry fees, less what the tour organizer skimmed off the top for himself. If they were unscrupulous, that included the prize money, too. You were essentially playing for your own cash, plus everyone else's. It was a hard lesson for even the best young former college star, being picked clean by local legends with garage-band swings who knew every blemish and blade of grass on the undistinguished courses they played. The other most commonly chosen option was the Far East, and that was where Stewart found himself after graduating from Southern Methodist University and failing to get his tour card.

Two of his traveling buddies in Asia were the Anton twins, Terry and Tom, who'd played at the University of Florida. Because of the springy way they stepped, with their heels off the ground, Stewart called them Tip Toe I and Tip Toe II. While Stewart's confidence in his golf game crossed the border of cockiness without clearing customs, it was actually more a case of the sum being greater than its parts. He swept the club back with a lag reminiscent of Bobby Jones and the hickory-shaft era. His tempo looked as effortless as the human eye wandering through a Cézanne still life, but he was neither a great driver of the ball nor the best iron player nor the best putter. In his prime, though, when it came to the short shots around the green, inside seventy-five yards or so, he had no peer. Some of that was learned from the hustlers in Springfield, but some of it was imported from Asia.

"We had a tremendous admiration for the Asian players' short games. All of us learned," said Tom Anton. "It was a great training ground. They showed us techniques around the greens, out of the bunkers, shots we'd never seen before. We'd bomb it by them but from 100 yards in, they were magicians." Besides a short game, the other significant acquisition Stewart made was in Kuala Lampur when he met a twenty-year-old Australian woman named Tracey Ferguson, who was at one time a draftsperson employed by Greg Norman's father at Mount Isa Mines. He fell in love with her the moment he saw her in a string bikini. Stewart succeeded in making it through the PGA Tour's spring qualifying school in June '81, the same month David Graham played a near-flawless final round at Merion Golf Club to become the first Australian to win the U.S. Open. He and Tracey were married that November.

While Stewart won twice in Asia and again at the '82 Quad Cities Open, the only tour tournament his father saw him win, his early reputation was that of a player who could come close but not finish it off at the end. He lost playoffs in '84, '85, '86, and '88. He compiled so many seconds his nickname was Avis. When he finally won the '87 Hertz Bay Hill Classic, he donated the winner's check to charity in honor of his father, who had passed away two years before with cancer. After finishing in a tie for twenty-fourth in the Masters in '89, Stewart won the next week at the Harbour Town Golf Links, an event played on a classic South Carolina low-country course designed by architect Pete Dye and known for the quality of its champions, a list that included Palmer and Nicklaus and Miller and Watson. Stewart would become the first player to successfully defend that title. It was in August '89 at a Chicago suburban course named for an insurance company, Kemper Lakes, where Stewart captured his first major championship in typically controversial style.

By August '89 it felt like most of the big stuff had already been done. Nick Faldo won the first of his three Masters on the second hole of sudden death when Scott Hoch agonized over, and then missed, a two-foot sidehill wobbler on Augusta National's tenth. The big story of the year was Curtis Strange, who took advantage of Tom Kite's final-round 78 to become the first player since Ben Hogan to win back-to-back National Opens. "Move over, Ben," said Strange, who'd made a fist-pumping climb up the steep embankment of Oak Hill's eighteenth, the same spot where, six years later, he would lose to Faldo one up in singles as the American collapse handed the Ryder Cup back to Europe. In the wake of the Open Championship, all the conversation was about how star-crossed Greg Norman let yet another major championship elude him. Mark Calcavecchia won at Royal Troon, defeating Australians Wayne Grady and Norman, who couldn't even post a score in the four-hole aggregate playoff. Calcavecchia's shot out of the rough on the eighteenth with his Ping eight-iron ignited the growing controversy over square-shaped or U grooves.

Stewart had played progressively better in each of the year's majors, going into the final round at Royal Troon just two shots behind Grady, one better than Calcavecchia. After closing with a 74, however, he was nothing more than an afterthought at what would become storm-ravaged Kemper Lakes, especially since he'd shot 75-76 in Memphis the weekend before the PGA. It was Mike Reid, a product of Brigham Young University, slender as a cattail stalk whose reverse-C finish was so pronounced it made grown men wince, who took command almost from the outset. Reid, nicknamed "Radar" because his drives, though short, tracked the center of what seemed like every fairway, was tied for the lead after the first round and alone at the top after thirty-six and fifty-four holes. Stewart, dressed as he did every Sunday in the colors of the local National Football League (NFL) team, this time the Bears, went into the final round a full six shots off the pace.

A five-birdie back nine of 31 pulled Stewart within two of Reid's lead and gave him reason to stick around. In April Reid had led the Masters after thirteen holes on Sunday and didn't finish well, but that disappointment was nothing compared to what happened at Kemper Lakes. He bogeyed the sixteenth to lose half his lead and then smothered a lob shot from just off the seventeenth green and double-bogeyed, shockingly dropping a shot behind. Stewart couldn't be still in the scoring area, pacing back and forth, even mugging for the camera. Reid had a chance to birdie the eighteenth to tie him but missed a seven-footer. Stewart's glee was demonstrable. He emerged from the scoring tent slapping high fives with anyone he saw, and that, unfortunately, included Reid as he came off the course. Stewart's pleasure seemed blissfully ignorant of Reid's pain. "I'm 32. I hadn't won a major, and everybody all over the world is always asking me why," he said. "They did the same thing to Curtis and look what happened. He won back-to-back U.S. Opens." The contrast of Stewart's self-satisfaction and the unself-conscious tears of the mild-mannered Reid was so stark that what should have been the affirmation of the skill and ability Stewart always believed he possessed became, instead, the coast-to-coast confirmation of his most unpleasant character traits. It would not be the only time.

Very soon after Dr. Coop began working with Stewart, he suspected his new client had attention deficit disorder (ADD) and sent him to a clinician for a proper diagnosis. "I've got to give him tremendous credit," said Coop. "When he found out what he had, he talked to people about it. He didn't hide it. God gave him tremendous rhythm and tempo and neuromuscular skills but God didn't give him concentration." The knowledge of the condition led Coop and Cook to devise practice sessions tailored for someone whose ability to concentrate was, at times, tenuous. It wasn't always, though. "With the ADD, the U.S. Open was always set up so hard that he was able to focus during the tournament," said Cook. "The rough was so tough and greens were so fast and hard, it created a lot of focus for him that he didn't have in a run of the mill tournament."

In March '91 Stewart was wearing a brace to stabilize a herniated disk in his neck that had caused him to lose strength in his left arm. Reduced to nothing more than a spectator in his own backyard at Bay Hill during Arnold Palmer's tournament, he was out for ten weeks and unable to play in the Masters. An exercise regime helped rehabilitate the neck, but Stewart would struggle the rest of his career with three degenerative disks in his lower back. He played at Harbour Town the week after Augusta, tied for fourth, and took aim on his most prized goal, the U.S. Open at Hazeltine CC, outside Minneapolis.

The U.S. Open had been at Hazeltine on one previous occasion, when the Englishman Tony Jacklin won in 1970, and the layout of architect Robert Trent Jones was mocked as if it had been drawn up by a four-year-old with finger paints. It was characterized as a waste of perfectly good Minnesota farmland, most notably by Dave Hill, who developed an insult-comedy routine worthy of Don Rickles. As a young man Jones had apprenticed with the great Canadian golf course architect Stanley Thompson, working on the magnificent Canadian Rockies course in Banff National Park. He'd designed his own program at Cornell University because no existing major suited his ambition to become a builder of golf courses. He reworked Oakland Hills CC in Detroit for the 1951 U.S. Open, creating what Ben Hogan famously referred to as the Monster. By crushing lava to use as soil, he was able to build a course, Mauna Kea GC, on a barren landscape on Hawaii's Big Island where no one believed such a thing could even exist. Hazeltine, however, was not one of his triumphs. It had more doglegs than a pack of coyotes. After the '70 Open Jones made some changes, augmented later by his youngest son, Rees, a second-generation golf course architect like his older brother, Bobby. Years later the pair would take legal action against one another in a fight over the legacy of their father.

By the time the U.S. Open returned to Hazeltine, it had a trio of finishing holes as tough as any in golf, holes that would cost Scott Simpson a second national championship. Simpson, who would later become almost as well known for being actor Bill Murray's patient partner in the annual Pebble Beach pro-am started by Bing Crosby, birdied the fourteenth, fifteenth, and sixteenth holes in the '87 U.S. Open at Olympic Club outside San Francisco to beat eight-time major champion and local favorite Tom Watson, who'd attended Stanford University, just down the 101 Freeway. Simpson, a University of Southern California product himself, finished in the top ten in the next two U.S. Opens, too, the ones won by Curtis Strange, to earn a reputation as a dependable Open player. He had an unusual action. At address he'd slowly lower his upper body toward the ball and then rise up as he took the club back to the top. Though their swings were as similar as a Van Gogh and a mechanical drawing, Stewart and Simpson had at least one trait in common—neither was given to making the big mistake. In a U.S. Open brilliance has far less to do with swashbuckling shot making than it does the ability to avoid calamity, shot by shot, hole by hole, until you've simply outlasted your peers. It's about as glamorous as being stuck with the check.

Just like Kemper Lakes two years before, a violent summer thunderstorm hit Hazeltine, but this was far worse than just an interruption in play. A darkening sky filled with electricity halted the first round just after one o'clock, and six men took shelter underneath the branches of a small willow tree thirty yards or so from the eleventh tee. Two flashes of lightning knocked all six to the ground. William Faddell, who was not even a golf fan but who had been given the tickets by his father, died of cardiac arrest. Two months later, at the PGA Championship at Crooked Stick outside Indianapolis, another spectator, Thomas Weaver, would be killed by lightning in the parking lot. The confluence of tragic events led to golf's organizers forever changing the way they treated hazardous weather.

When play resumed, the rain-softened course gave up some good scores, including Stewart's opening 67 that tied him with Nolan Henke, a Battle Creek, Michigan, native who would just as soon have been fishing as leading the U.S. Open. By the end of three rounds Stewart and Simpson had managed to separate themselves from the field by three shots. For almost all of Sunday Simpson was in firm control. *Almost* is the operative word. He reached the final three holes with a two-shot lead over Stewart but bogeyed the sixteenth and eighteenth, while Stewart made a brave five-footer at the last to force the Monday playoff. By the next day Hazeltine's greens had baked out, turning crusty and unforgiving.

Again, Simpson came to the last three holes with a two-shot lead, and again, it wouldn't hold up. Stewart made a twenty-footer for birdie on the sixteenth, while Simpson missed from inside three feet for bogey. Rattled, Simpson pulled his four-iron on the seventeenth into the pond and scrambled for another bogey. Now, he was down a shot. Simpson's approach at the eighteenth ran through the green, and with Stewart five feet away for par, he tried to chip in but couldn't. Stewart won, 75–77.

"It's disappointing to lose the U.S. Open two days in a row," said Simpson, who had played those last three holes eight over par for the week to Stewart's one under. When it was over Stewart bought champagne for the media, a grandiose gesture he now shared with Tony Lema, who died in a plane crash thirty-three years before Stewart did. "I come off as arrogant sometimes," Stewart explained to the press. "Maybe you guys caught me at the wrong time a couple of times. If you got to know me, I'm a pretty nice guy, and by God, I'll buy champagne anytime you want it."

In some ways the next few years were not kind to Stewart. In others they were the kindest of all. With two major championships he could command lucrative, for those days, endorsements, and he landed an equipment deal that paid him handsomely but poisoned his game. If Scott Simpson had had a reputation as a man who showed up in the U.S. Open, Stewart did, too, finishing a gut-wrenching second to Lee Janzen, not once but twice. In 1993 at Baltusrol GC in New Jersey, Janzen hit it through trees on the tenth, chipped in on the sixteenth, and caromed a shot off another tree and into the fairway on the seventeenth. He hit just six fairways and eleven greens on Sunday and beat Stewart by two.

Stewart's back had become a never-ending source of discomfort. And, by 1994, he had the kind of midlife career malaise many top players experience. He began to wonder if it was all worth it. There is little doubt Stewart became a different person the last years of his life. He found a peace of mind that had eluded him from the time he was a boy in the balcony of Springfield's Grace Methodist Church where he couldn't sit still and his father sang too loudly. "The last two years of his life, he was a really good person," said Hicks. "He just walked a different walk."

Everyone who knew him saw it. "He was so much more thoughtful. He was so much more concerned about other people," said Coop. "He was more at peace with himself, too. It wasn't a logical peace. He fought to find that peace by playing harder or playing better or being more popular and that's just not where it comes from. The religion really gave him a sense of what was important. I think he didn't try as hard to be liked, and he was liked more. He was accepted more by not trying so hard to be accepted."

Stewart, who had won only once following Hazeltine, finished second to Janzen again in the U.S. Open, this time at the Olympic Club in '98. On Friday the USGA used a lamentable back-pin position on the steeply sloped eighteenth green, and with the possible exception of Tom Lehman, who four-putted it, few were bitten harder than Stewart. After missing a short, curling birdie putt, Stewart could only fold his arms, furiously chew his gum, and watch stone-faced as his ball rolled and rolled twenty-five feet back down the slope. Though he'd held a four-shot lead going into Sunday, Stewart played poorly in the final round. While luck shined on Janzen once again, this time on the fifth when his tee shot into the tops of the cypress trees dropped to the ground even as he was walking back to retee, Stewart wasn't as fortunate. After struggling to find a fairway, he finally did with a three-wood on the twelfth, but the ball settled into a sand-filled divot. The bad break led to two more bogeys, the most critical at the sixteenth, and he eventually lost to Janzen by a shot. But this was a far different Stewart than the one who had seemed so callous in victory over Mike Reid at Kemper Lakes. "He was about as gracious a loser as you could possibly have," said Cook. "He congratulated Lee. Talked about how well Lee played, about how he just didn't have it that day."

The following May at Jack Nicklaus's Memorial Tournament in Dublin, Ohio, Janzen and Stewart were paired together the first two rounds. A few weeks later Stewart would win his second U.S. Open on the No. 2 Course at Pinehurst, North Carolina. "I always enjoyed playing with him," said Janzen of Stewart.

We liked to needle each other. We both layed up on the fifth hole, I can't remember who we were playing with, but we walked off to the side to wait for him to go for the green. Payne took his hat off and ran his fingers through his hair and it was basically orange. I asked him what color he was shooting for. At first he wanted to get mad, then he realized, there's no hiding it. He told me he tried to lighten it up and it didn't work out and so he had to get somebody to fix it and orange was the best they could do. We had a good laugh then.

Stewart's showing in San Francisco had reinforced his self-belief for the following year in Pinehurst. Generally considered Donald Ross's finest work among the four hundred or so courses he created, the heart and soul of the No. 2 Course are its domed greens. The Pinehurst Resort suffered through some tough financial times in the '70s and '80s, and the No. 2 Course's reputation had taken a hit as well. With rough grown up right to the collars of the putting surfaces, it was thought to be too easy a mark for the modern player. It wasn't until PGA Tour commissioner Deane Beman brought the Tour Championship there in 1991, shaving the green embankments to restore the character of the course, that No 2's challenge emerged from its own shadow. The only course in America easily identified simply by an integer, only the best-struck shot would hold No. 2's greens. If a player's ball rolled off into a collection area, his next shot offered a dicey set of choices—lob it up on top, pitch it into the bank, putt it up the hill. That's all well and good if you're smoking cheap cigars and playing a five-dollar Nassau with a group of high handicaps, but when there's a national championship at stake, those decisions become a hall of mirrors.

Stewart traveled to North Carolina after missing the cut in Memphis. He put the weekend to good use, playing a practice round with Cook and carrying just his chipping clubs and a putter. They mapped the greens, marking them with red lights, green lights, and yellow lights for the places he could not, or should not, hit the ball. Pinehurst wasn't the first time he and Cook had plotted a course that way. They did the same thing for every Open Championship links, too. Pinehurst, however, was the only time Stewart ever carried his yardage book himself, usually preferring to leave that job to his caddie, Hicks.

For the second straight year Stewart went into Sunday's final round with a lead, just one stroke this time instead of the four shots he had in hand at the Olympic Club. And, for the second straight year, he was overtaken on the back nine, this time by the man he was playing beside, Phil Mickelson. And, for the second straight year, he had a tee shot land in a sand-filled divot, this time on the fourth hole. But after his experience at Olympic, he'd spent time practicing the shot and saved his par. Vijay Singh and Tiger Woods took runs at the lead, but in the end, the championship came down to Stewart and Mickelson and the final three holes.

Only once during the week did Stewart make a red-light mistake, missing the green in the worst possible spot on the par-three fifteenth on Sunday. The designation earned its distinction when he had to make a long putt just to salvage the bogey that dropped him a shot behind Mickelson. Sunday of the U.S. Open always falls on Father's Day, and Mickelson, who had just turned twenty-nine and had yet to win his first major, was carrying a buzzer in his golf bag waiting for a call from his wife, Amy, who was expecting the couple's first child.

On the sixteenth, normally a par five played as a par four during the Open, Mickelson gave Stewart's shot back with a bogey of his own. Both players missed the green, and Stewart hit one of his weakest chips of the week, leaving himself a downhill, double-breaking twenty-footer. When he curled it in the center, he barely reacted. For Coop, this was one of the most telling moments of their eleven years together. "That putt on 16, you couldn't make with a bushel of balls," said Coop. "All he did was raise his right index finger to acknowledge the crowd and went right back into concentration. We worked so hard on that, so hard, not to get too high, not to get too low. He worked on his deficiencies." With Stewart in the hole with par, Mickelson's eight-footer missed, and now they were tied again with two to play and no one else really in the game after Woods's bogey at the par-three seventeenth.

Stewart hit his six-iron four feet from the hole on the seventeenth, and Mickelson followed with a seven-iron eight feet away. Mickelson missed on the right, and Stewart holed to retake the lead going to the last, an uphill par four of 446 yards. Mickelson found the fairway, but Stewart's drive landed in the right rough. All day it had been wet and uncharacteristically cool for North Carolina in June, when it's more likely to be in the nineties than the sixties. On the practice ground, a place called Maniac Hill, Stewart had taken out his navy-blue rain jacket during his warm-up but didn't like the way it restricted his swing, so he cut the sleeves off with a pair of scissors. As Hicks and Stewart walked up the hill against the cold drizzle, the carillon from the Village Chapel, just a couple blocks away, chimed "Amazing Grace."

The moment Stewart saw his lie in the thick Bermuda rough, he never thought of anything but laying up short of the cross bunker. From there he'd have a seventy-five-yard wedge shot into the back-left pin. Mickelson hit his second on the green but left himself a twenty-five-footer with a huge right-to-left swing in it, hardly a putt he could expect to make. Trying to cobble together a classic, scrambling U.S. Open par, Stewart wedged his third twenty feet below the hole. Mickelson missed, and Stewart made his right in the middle again. This time he rose up on one leg and punched the air. Hicks tossed the flagstick away and flew into his player's arms, wrapping his legs around him. After picking up his golf ball Stewart took Mickelson's face in both his hands and told him, "You're going to be a father. You're going to be a father." That night the Open champion and his caddie drove to Mebane, North Carolina, Hicks's hometown, for a fund-raiser the following day. Stewart never entertained the notion of not showing up. Instead, the two of them sat up most of the night in Hicks's kitchen taking turns drinking champagne from the U.S. Open trophy until the caddie could sneak away to bed unnoticed.

In September as the days shorten, the Ryder Cup Matches have early starts, particularly the morning sessions of either four-ball or foursomes. Warm-ups can begin before sunrise, and often the matches don't end until dark. Stewart loved his music. He played in Peter Jacobsen's band Jake Trout and the Flounders, and he was a devoted Jimmy Buffett parrothead. He traveled with a case of harmonicas in a range of keys, all of which he could violate without the slightest hint of remorse. But he was never more purposefully musical than he was at a Ryder Cup. Whenever Stewart was on the U.S. side, which he was five times, wake-up calls were completely unnecessary. Up before any of his teammates, Stewart would blast Bruce Springsteen's "Born in the USA" at full throttle for everyone in the hotel, American and European alike, to hear. If Seve Ballesteros liked nothing better than beating Americans, Payne Stewart liked nothing better than playing for his country.

At The Country Club in Brookline, the course where Francis Ouimet won the 1913 U.S. Open in a playoff against British legends Harry Vardon and Ted Ray, the U.S. team fell woefully behind after the first two days. The Americans were four points behind, 10–6. No lead that large had ever been overcome in the history of the matches. U.S. captain Ben Crenshaw front-loaded his lineup, and the Americans won the first six singles. When Justin Leonard rolled in an improbable monster putt on the seventeenth, the green near Ouimet's house where he made the crucial stroke against Vardon and Ray, the Americans stormed thoughtlessly onto the green while José Maria Olazábal stood in stoic dignity, still with a chance to tie. He didn't, though. Crenshaw kissed the green where Ouimet had beaten the Brits. The stunning U.S. comeback was complete but for one thing.

The match directly behind Leonard and Olazábal was Payne Stewart and Colin Montgomerie. The Boston crowd had been enormously unkind to Montgomerie, hurling insults about his game, his team, his body, anything they could think of. Some particularly well-lubricated and obnoxious fans were ejected from the grounds at Stewart's insistence. When Stewart picked up Montgomerie's ball on the eighteenth green at The Country Club, giving him the match, Hicks thought it was his player's finest moment, greater even than the eighteenth green at Pinehurst just months before.

"What he did with Monty was the proudest moment I ever had," said Hicks. "The old Payne Stewart wouldn't have done that. He wouldn't have been thinking about the big picture. I was proud of the way he handled himself the whole day. Those people were ruthless." The first person Stewart saw on the green was Montgomerie's wife at the time, Eimeer. He hugged her and apologized for the fans' behavior. At forty-two Stewart had become a man in full.

It was a cool morning in Orlando, Florida, on October 25 with a few puffy white clouds in the sky. By afternoon it would be in the seventies, a perfect day for golf, and flying. Michael Kling, a captain for Sunjet Aviation, came to work at 6:30 in the morning. His first officer, Stephanie Bellegarrigue, arrived fifteen minutes later. They inspected and fueled Learjet N47BA, loaded a cooler with ice and soft drinks on board, and left Sanford, Florida, for Orlando International Airport at 7:54 a.m. to pick up passengers, Payne Stewart; his agents, Van Arden and Robert Fraley; and Bruce Borland, a last-minute addition from Jack Nicklaus's architectural team who was anxious to work with Stewart on a golf course project near Dallas.

Stewart and his wife, Tracey, were up early that morning, too. She had an appointment with a chiropractor, and Payne made pancakes for the children, Chelsea and Aaron, before the three of them left for school around 7:30 a.m. Stewart had angered some of his professional friends because he'd backed out of a commitment to play in a fund-raising event that day hosted by Arnold Palmer at Bay Hill. Instead, he would stop in Dallas on his way to Houston for the Tour Championship.

The Learjet took off from Orlando International Airport at 9:19 a.m. After a series of altitude clearances, at 9:26 a.m. the pilot was instructed to change radio frequency and contact a Jacksonville controller, who cleared them to climb to, and maintain, flight level 390 to Dallas. The response, "Three nine zero bravo alpha," are the last known words to have been spoken on the airplane.

From that moment until 12:12 p.m. central daylight time, N47BA was first intercepted by an F-16 from the Fortieth Flight Test Squadron at Eglin Air Force Base, then followed by two Oklahoma Air National Guard F-16s, joined by a pair of North Dakota Air National Guard F-16s. All reported the windows fogged or frozen and no signs of life. A cataclysmic loss of cabin pressure had turned it into a ghost ship. For nearly four hours, first in great confusion and then heartbreaking resignation, the saga played out on cable news as the Learjet flew like a porpoise through the air. Stuck in a climb, it bumped up against its maximum altitude of 48,900 feet, descended to a level where its engines functioned more efficiently, and then climbed back to its apex over and over again until its fuel tanks ran dry.

It came down like a javelin in a field outside of Mina, South Dakota, down a dirt road, behind bales of hay, where Jon Hoffman's cows grazed. The entry wound in the earth was shockingly compact, as much a grave as a crash site. "That's where they are," Hoffman said. Stewart's last flight ended on land owned by a working man who built his own driving range just off his back porch so he could hit balls on summer evenings.

A polished stone unearthed by the force of the crash serves as its memorial. In part the engraving on it says:

He brought me up out of the pit of destruction,
Out of the miry clay;
And he set my foot upon a rock
And he gave me a firm place to stand.

# 5

## Phil the Thrill

Golf became more interesting the day Phil Mickelson, nothing more than a toddler at the time, mirrored his father's right-handed swing and then stubbornly refused to switch. Phil was doing things his own way before he was out of Pampers, which maybe explains why he's been flying by the seat of his pants his whole life. There were better players, one in particular, but no player made golf a more deliciously, impishly curious place than the naturally right-handed, thus inappropriately nicknamed, Lefty.

Who else gets a dinosaur head for his birthday? Which just happens to be June 16, which just happens to be more or less during the U.S. Open, which just happens to be the major championship he's been second in a record six times. Who's your fossil?

Growing up in a middle-class neighborhood in San Diego, Phil was the middle child of Phil Sr., who flew F-8s for the navy until he left the service in 1965, just before Vietnam heated up big time, to become a commercial pilot beginning with Hughes Airwest for fifteen years before being forced to retire because he was diabetic, and Mary, a nurse who would later play on the U.S. Senior Women's Olympic basketball team. The backyard had a basketball goal with enough space around it for a decent game of H-O-R-S-E and a mini-practice facility for golf with a bunker and a green Phil Sr. constructed to USGA specifications, being the kind of man who paid attention to detail. Beyond the green the yard fell off into an arroyo. There were lost balls in one direction and broken windows in the other. In between was the parade ground of an athletic genius. Or knucklehead. Over the sweep of his career, Phil the Younger would give you plenty of reasons to believe he was both, which is why there hasn't been a player in the past fifty years who could break your heart as often as he stomped on his own while still enjoying every moment of it and delighting us as well. He was the full package.

At Arizona State University (ASU) Mickelson won three NCAA individual titles, one NCAA team title, and the 1990 U.S. Amateur and was a four-time All-American. He became one of just four players to win a PGA Tour tournament as an amateur when he won the Northern Telecom Open in Tucson in 1991. Pictured on the cover of *Golf World* with the trophy, a shiny silver conquistador helmet on his head, he had the hand-in-the-cookie-jar look of an adolescent who'd just been caught passing notes to his girlfriend in Ben Stein's economics class. It was a fashion statement the gregarious (in public, anyway) Lee Trevino could pull off. Not so much the sheepishly beaming Mickelson. That was the last time he would ever let his image gallop free in front of him.

Mickelson's coach at Arizona State was Steve Loy, who'd taken over at ASU after being at the University of Arkansas, where John Daly was one of his players. Let's just say the disciplined Loy and the wild man Daly didn't see eye to eye on much of anything. After Mickelson, far and away the best player Loy ever coached, graduated, the coach would leave college to become Mickelson's most trusted agent. No one knew Mickelson, the golfer, better. During one collegiate tournament at McCormick Ranch in Scottsdale, ASU was leading by a couple of shots in the team competition, and Mickelson was ahead in the individual. Designed by Desmond Muirhead, the eighteenth hole then was a par four with a large lake in front of the green. Mickelson's drive had finished underneath a small bush meant to mark the distance to the center of the green as 150 yards. Mickelson thought he might be able to get a club on the ball, if he took his stance on his knees. To do it, though, he'd have to play the shot right-handed. He took his eight-iron and turned it upside down, got on his knees, and was preparing to hit the ball from the right side when Loy came charging up. "What are you doing?" he demanded, mindful of the team's narrow lead and the water hazard right in front of them. "Coach," Mickelson protested, "I'm pretty sure I can skip it across." And that is everything you need to know about Phil Mickelson, the golfer.

"I'll tell you the first time I dealt with Phil," says Gary McCord, a PGA Tour veteran who is known as one of the architects of the all-exempt tour but even better known as the handlebar-mustachioed veteran golf commentator for CBS.

We were playing in Tucson, a practice round. I don't know if it was the year he won or not, but he was an amateur. We ended up playing late, nine holes. We come to the seventh hole, it's pitch dark. On a bet, he was playing my clubs right handed and I was playing his clubs left handed, in the dark. He absolutely killed me. Another time we're playing a practice round at the TPC [Tournament Players Club] with [Tom] Weiskopf. I obviously knew Phil and Tom wanted to play with him. On the tenth hole, the flag is right there, going downhill. "Phil," I said, "show Tom your spinner." So, he put the ball in the fringe and he hit it, whooooom. It went past the hole and sucked back, uphill. Weiskopf walked in. Just walked in. "I've seen enough," he said. I've been hustled by every shot Phil's got, and he's got a lot of them.

What he didn't have was the beginning to his professional career that he'd imagined all along would just happen as everything else had just happened for him. Mickelson's talent level was so off the charts, the right outcome had always come through naturally. Why should it be any different on the PGA Tour or in major championships? On another continent and another hemisphere, Ernie Els was born in Johannesburg, South Africa, eight months earlier than Mickelson. They seemed destined to go through their golfing lives joined at the trophy case. Except a funny thing happened on the way to ruling the upper and lower halves of planet Earth: Tiger Woods. Els managed to snatch a couple of U.S. Opens, in 1994 and 1997, before Woods really got up to ramming speed, even though he'd won the '97 Masters by a ridiculous twelve strokes. Phil, on the other hand, spent those early years, and quite a few thereafter, treading water and watching Tiger Woods snuff out the competition.

Mickelson had won ten PGA Tour tournaments by the time Woods won his first Masters. Through the remainder of '97, all of '98, and some of '99, Woods's work with Butch Harmon to alter his swing had yet to bear fruit. When those changes kicked in, he would begin winning major championships in great clumps, leaving little more than table scraps for everyone else. Prior to Tiger's dominance, the best Mickelson was able to muster was his first runner-up in the U.S. Open, finishing behind Payne Stewart on Pinehurst's No. 2 course in '99. A resurgent Woods was on their heels, finishing tied for third. Mickelson, it would seem, was capable of extraordinary golf, just not when it mattered the most.

The critics were merciless. Mickelson was too soft, inside and out. He was too rich. He was too stage-managed. He was too foolish. He gambled too much, on the golf course and at the gaming tables. He knew way too much about setting and beating point spreads in professional football games. By April of his thirty-third year he was zero for forty-six in major championships (forty-two as a professional), and that doesn't count missing the 1994 Masters after breaking his leg skiing in Flagstaff, Arizona—just another run-in with reckless behavior, it was supposed, even though he'd skied his whole life. He'd played on four Ryder Cup teams and five Presidents Cup teams and won twenty-two times on the PGA Tour. He was vilified for taking chances when it seemed like there wasn't one. Exhibit A was a shot he played on the sixteenth hole at Bay Hill from under a tree, trying to reach a par five in two with water in front when a simple punch-out would have certainly yielded at least a chance at birdie. Later, at the Players Championship, he was defensive about his approach to the game. "The fact is, if I change the way I play golf," he said, "one, I won't enjoy the game as much and, two, I won't play to the level I have been playing. So, I won't ever change. Not tomorrow, Sunday, or at Augusta or the U.S. Open, or any tournament." So there. Take that.

When he was asked prior to the 2004 Masters if that first major victory would be the hardest one to get, Mickelson deadpanned, "For me it's been." But he didn't stop at the punch line. "I've really enjoyed the challenge of trying to win a major, although I haven't broken through and won. I enjoy all the challenges in my life. I know I haven't done it yet but I've been close a number of times and I think that, when I finally do break through, it will be that much more rewarding for going through the difficulties of the last ten years of trying and not doing it." The posturing was gone. The defensiveness had vanished.

Frivolous Phil, the gambler, the skier, the oddsmaker, the pilot, the diagnostician of subcutaneous fat, seemed, well, different that April. The year before Amy had given birth to their third child, Evan, in March. She nearly died in childbirth, and so did Evan. Amy suffered a tear in a major artery, and their son didn't breathe on his own for almost seven minutes. Mickelson did play a few weeks later at Augusta, and while his ability to compartmentalize allowed him to play well, the rest of '03 was substandard, lacking a victory or even a runner-up finish. The realization that he could very easily have lost two of the people dearest to him had changed him in a fundamental way. When a major championship no longer mattered as much, he began to win them.

The opening round of the '04 Masters was the day Tom Watson, sitting in the champion's locker room, learned his longtime caddie, Bruce Edwards, had succumbed to ALS, Lou Gehrig's disease. Because players had to use Augusta National caddies prior to 1983, Edwards hadn't been at his player's side for either of Watson's Masters victories. It was Watson, in fact, who lobbied persuasively, and successfully, for players to be able to use their own caddies. Outside of the clubhouse, the food for the Masters is a high-fat cornucopia of sandwiches wrapped in what the green coats (the suit of armor sported by the members) consider to be inoffensive green plastic bags. Among the options are pimiento cheese, southern-style barbecue, and, of course, egg salad, no extra charge for the pieces of shell. Nothing is cooked on the grounds. The smoke and smell of, say, charred meat on a grill are anathema, unless of course they could figure out a way to make the beef green. After Edwards started coming to Augusta to caddie for Watson, he would eat an egg salad sandwich every time they got to the thirteenth tee, the last shot on Amen Corner. After Edwards's death Watson took to leaving a sandwich on the tee box as a remembrance.

That spring Tiger Woods had begun undertaking yet another swing change, this time with the help of Hank Haney, the teacher of his close friend Mark O'Meara. Following on the heels of Woods's personal troubles, Haney would write a book in 2012 about his six years with the world's best player, justifying it by saying they were his memories, too. The pause in Woods's dominance in '04 would be brief, but the opening was nonetheless real. By Saturday night Mickelson was tied for the lead with Chris DiMarco, a short-hitting, proud University of Florida alumnus with a somewhat stiff-armed move through the ball who possessed as much fight as any real-life gator. Ernie Els was just three back, tied with Bernhard Langer and K. J. Choi. They were a shot behind a young Englishman, Paul Casey. While the final round evolved into a contest between Mickelson and Els, DiMarco would play a key role, despite falling out of contention by playing the third through the seventh holes five over par.

After Els eagled the eighth hole, he was a shot ahead of Mickelson. As Els was going down the thirteenth Mickelson birdied the treacherous par-three twelfth to briefly join the South African. Els would make his second eagle of the day at the thirteenth to skip two ahead, but Mickelson answered with a birdie at the same hole to cut the advantage to one. He put his wedge on the fourteenth inches from the cup to tie the South African. Els birdied the par-five fifteenth, but Mickelson answered with a fifteen-footer for birdie at the sixteenth. Both parred the seventeenth. Els drove into the fairway bunker at the eighteenth and still had a fourteen-footer for birdie but missed. Mickelson took three-wood off the eighteenth tee to stay short of the bunkers, then hit an eight-iron eighteen feet above the hole. DiMarco had bunkered his approach, and when he blasted out his ball went just outside Mickelson's but on the same line.

School was in session. Mickelson saw the break from DiMarco's putt, and as Jim Nantz, the voice of CBS, observed from his tower, his time had come. Els was on the putting green, hoping to go down the tenth in a playoff. When Mickelson's birdie putt went in, the roar of the gallery surrounding the eighteenth told him extra holes wouldn't be necessary. He scooped up his golf balls with the back of his putter and walked into the clubhouse. Mickelson's celebratory jump would become fodder for endless one-liners. Eventually, even Phil would crack wise about his three-inch vertical leap, but that night, he slept in his green jacket. Lefty had achieved liftoff.

By the next year Tiger Woods had returned to form, winning both the Masters and the Open Championship, the latter for a second time on the Old Course at St. Andrews. The PGA Championship was returning to the New York Metropolitan area at Baltusrol GC in New Jersey. Woods had won a U.S. Open on Long Island in 2002 at Bethpage Black, but it was Mickelson who won the New York fans, both there and again at Shinnecock Hills GC just a few months after Phil's first major victory. The '05 PGA was supposed to be at The Country Club, the site of the '99 Ryder Cup where the U.S. team staged what was at the time the largest comeback in the history of the matches, but financial wrangling between the club and the PGA of America forced the relocation of the championship to Springfield Township, where, once again, Mickelson was hailed as New York's favorite son.

After every round Mickelson either led the championship outright or shared the lead. Playing a baby cut to keep the ball in the fairway, Mickelson went out on a brutally hot final day tied with Davis Love III, who had won his only major championship in the PGA at Winged Foot GC, another metropolitan area course in Mamaroneck, New York. Love was the son of a PGA professional, the renowned instructor Davis Love Jr., who died in the fog-induced crash of a small private plane flying from Sea Island, Georgia, to Jacksonville, Florida, in 1988. As Love III made his winning putt on the eighteenth green at Winged Foot in '97, a rainbow arched across the sky behind him. Play was halted by lightning on Sunday at Baltusrol with twelve players still on the golf course and Mickelson, at four under par, still to putt on the fourteenth green but holding a one-shot lead over the Dane Thomas Bjorn and Australian Steve Elkington, who had won the PGA at Riviera CC in Los Angeles two years before Love's rainbow PGA. Trying to win his third major championship of the year, Tiger Woods had an opening round of five-over-par 75 but shot 66-68 on the weekend to post a two-under-par total and led in the clubhouse when play was halted. Even though Mickelson, who would have to return Monday morning with the eleven other players to finish, was only two shots ahead of him, Woods boarded his private jet and flew home to Florida. Adios, New York.

Mickelson finished up his three-footer on the fourteenth and on the par-three sixteenth, his four-iron buried in the bunker, a position where he couldn't recover. Now he was tied at three under with Elkington and Bjorn, who had bogeyed the fifteenth but birdied the seventeenth. Baltusrol's Lower Course finishes with back-to-back par fives, the first virtually unreachable in two shots at 650 yards and the second a 554-yard scoring opportunity. Neither Bjorn nor Elkington birdied the eighteenth, giving Mickelson his opening.

His drive on the eighteenth finished just a few feet from a plaque in the fairway commemorating Jack Nicklaus's one-iron to the eighteenth green on his way to winning the 1967 U.S. Open there. Mickelson tapped the metal plaque with his three-wood for luck. His second came up just short of the putting surface in deep grass.

"If there's anybody you'll bank on to get it up and down from there in the world, it's Phil Mickelson," said Bjorn.

And he did. "It was a chip shot I'd hit tens of thousands of times in my back yard," said Mickelson. In sixteen months he'd gone from the best player not to have won a major to halfway to the career Slam.

A few weeks after Mickelson won his second major championship, Hurricane Katrina slammed into New Orleans. The levies broke. The city flooded. Entire neighborhoods were reduced to rubble. For blocks and blocks, sometimes as far as the eye could see, skeletons of houses were spray painted with the search-and-rescue X. In the months following the debacle of the initial response, multicolored placards grew out of telephone poles like flowers at Augusta National. Mildew Removal. Gutting. Quick Cash for Houses. Before Katrina the elevated i-10 was a parking lot at rush hour. After Katrina thousands of drowned vehicles were piled underneath the interstate as if they were trying to get out of the hot summer sun to rust away in their own aboveground graveyard. Much of the TPC of Louisiana, the Pete Dye course the tournament had moved to the year before the hurricane, was under water, and two thousand trees were destroyed. No way could it be ready to host a tournament in eight months. They would try to play the next April at English Turn Golf and CC, one of the tournament's previous sites, but the destruction everywhere was so massive, that too was far from a foregone conclusion. One of the first players to call the New Orleans tournament committee was PGA champion Mickelson. If they were able to have a tournament, he was committing to play in it then and there. He told them to use his name, his likeness, offered to do promos. Whatever they needed.

In April '06 Mickelson showed up at Augusta carrying two drivers. He'd experimented with the strategy the week before in the BellSouth Classic in Atlanta and blown the field right out of its ankle socks. The closest players to him were José Maria Olazábal and Zach Johnson. The first had won the Masters twice and the second would win it a year later, and they were thirteen shots behind Mickelson at TPC Sugarloaf. The concept behind the two drivers was one for a high fade to hit the fairway and the other for a low, screaming draw and extra distance.

If Mickelson arrived in Augusta with a heavy golf bag, Woods came in with a heavier heart. He knew his father, Earl, who had struggled with prostate cancer, was terminal. Far too ill to attend the tournament, the former Green Beret wouldn't last another month. Woods knew his father would be watching on television and that this would be the last time he'd have a chance to see his son win a Masters, or any other major, for that matter. There are few things more difficult in golf, in sport, than trying to win for someone else. Woods pressed all week and turned in one of his worst putting performances. In his final round of 70 he took thirty-three putts and finished three behind.

Thunderstorms on Saturday caused much of the third round to be pushed into Sunday morning. Many of the players faced what would amount to almost a double round. Mickelson was on the sixth hole, three shots behind the leader, Chad Campbell, who had played just four holes. By the time the round was completed Sunday morning, Mickelson had played his remaining thirteen holes in one under par and had the lead, a shot ahead of Campbell and Fred Couples. Playing with Couples in the afternoon, Mickelson took a two-shot lead over his playing partner with a par at the eleventh and, after a birdie at the fifteenth, led by four. This would not be the kind of white-knuckle landing he'd experienced two years previously. Mickelson eventually finished two shots clear of Tim Clark, a South African who played college golf at North Carolina State. Clark was one of the major proponents of the long putter, voicing his concerns about the USGA's intention to ban anchoring beginning in 2016. Though he adopted the long putter when he was in college because of poor results, it may have been necessary, too, since Clark has a congenital defect that prevents him from having a full range of motion turning his forearms and wrists.

Mickelson had no such problems slipping into another green jacket, his own. Now, he'd won two majors in a row, something only Tiger Woods had done in the past dozen years. The next week was New Orleans. The thought of skipping the tournament never entered Mickelson's mind. With the city still reeling from the hurricane, he showed up and did every interview they asked. He signed autographs until there weren't any more people standing around with anything that would hold ink from a Sharpie. He took his family on a tour of the destruction in the Lower Ninth Ward, some of the worst in the city. After he won his first Masters Mickelson took his victory lap on the New York City talk shows. This time he had something more important to do.

When Phil returned to Augusta the following year, he was asked about going head-to-head against Woods. "I think it's a fun challenge to beat him. He's most likely the best player the game has ever seen. It's between he and Jack, and to be able to play against him in his prime is a great challenge," said Mickelson. "If I have a great rest of my career, and I go out and win 20 more tournaments and seven more majors to get to 50 wins and ten majors, which would be an awesome career, I still won't get to where he's at today. So I don't try to compare myself against him." Just as he had discovered winning majors was easier once they were less important, when Mickelson admitted to himself his record would never be the equal of Woods's, beating the world number one got easier, too.

Mickelson wouldn't win his next major until his third Masters championship in 2010, the year Woods returned from his self-imposed, scandal-induced exile. When Woods announced his return to professional golf would be at Augusta National, the tournament went into full bimbo defcon 2. It seemed as though behind every tree lurked a security guard, some in uniform and some in plain clothes, all packing portraits of various potentially disruptive blondes.

But the blonde of the week, who was also returning to golf, was Amy Mickelson. If she was strong enough to actually come to the golf course, it would be her first appearance at a tournament since being diagnosed with breast cancer a year earlier, undergoing radical surgery and all the accompanying therapies. It was also the year that Nicklaus joined Palmer as the ceremonial opening-shot twosome, to be joined by the third member of the Big Three, Gary Player, two years later. Mickelson went into the last round paired with, and a shot behind, Lee Westwood, a thirty-six-year-old Brit and repeated challenger in the majors—but never a winner—who once plummeted from 4th in the world to 256th, only to claw his way back to 4th again.

In the previous two decades, only one Masters champion had come from anyplace but the final twosome on Sunday, so it was no surprise it came down to Mickelson and Westwood at the end. Mickelson made the turn in one under par, Westwood in one over. Each was struggling mightily with the driver. Mickelson made spectacular par saves from the woods after hooking his drives badly on the ninth and tenth and got a lucky break when his tee ball caromed off a patron to stay in play on the eleventh. Fred Couples, the champion of the Champions Tour, was the first to take a run at the final pair, going out in 33. A bit of karmic reckoning finished him off when his tee shot on the twelfth landed more or less in the same spot as 1992, the year he got his green coat, only this one didn't stay on the bank. It was as if the ball had taken eighteen years to finally slide back into Rae's Creek. K. J. Choi also went out in 33, and a birdie at the tenth tied him for the lead with Mickelson at twelve under until he made his worst swing of the day, found the back-left bunker on the thirteenth, and took a crushing bogey on the par five. Y. E. Yang had outdueled Woods in the PGA Championship the previous August, and when Choi dropped another shot at the fourteenth, the dreams of back-to-back Korean-born major champions was finished. Up ahead an American-born Korean, Anthony Kim, a rookie star of the victorious U.S. Ryder Cup team in 2008, looked like he might be able to put up a number, sit back, and watch the carnage play out behind him. Kim played the thirteenth through the sixteenth holes five under par and posted twelve under. It wouldn't be enough, however. If this was a Masters that marked returns, Kim, a player of great promise who was given to wearing flamboyant belt buckles, would do just the opposite, virtually disappearing from golf, sidelined by a series of injuries to his thumb, wrist, and Achilles' tendon. From then on he would be seen more at poker tables than golf courses.

A two on the twelfth put Mickelson back in firm control. On the majestic thirteenth, where the day before he'd made the first of his back-to-back eagles, he played the shot of the tournament. This time instead of attacking the pin from a perfect spot in the fairway, he'd driven it through the dogleg and into the pine trees. To Mickelson, perhaps, the opening looked to be four or five feet wide. His longtime caddie, Jim "Bones" Mackay, was measuring it more in inches. Mackay politely suggested to Phil that he entertain the notion of laying up. All week, though, Mickelson had had an air of destiny rather than recklessness. After back-to-back eagles on Saturday, hadn't he layed up on the fifteenth? He'd taken on the impossible back-left pin on the thirteenth the day before. He was going to challenge the hole again. It was a six-iron off pine straw, just the kind of gamble that finished so often in disaster in his past. In a spray of dirt and pine needles, he stiffed it to four feet. Though he missed the eagle putt, his birdie at the fifteenth put him three clear of Westwood and Kim, and it was then a matter of getting it to the house, and Amy, where he also joined Jimmy Demaret, Nick Faldo, Gary Player, and Sam Snead as three-time Masters champions, adding considerable elevation to a major record that began there with a leap of inches.

Mackay was the first one in the last group to see Amy standing near the scoring hut behind the eighteenth green. Neither he nor Phil was sure she'd be able to make it to the course. Still frail, she hadn't been there yet that week. Mackay walked to the front of the green with his head down, reduced to a puddle of emotion. Phil saw her before he made the birdie putt that gave him his sixteen-under-par winning total of 272 and his three-stroke victory over Westwood. The tearful hug the husband and wife shared as the three-time Masters champion came off the course was reminiscent of Woods and his father, Earl, and yet, oh, so different. One marked arrival, the other survival.

In 2013, now forty-three, Mickelson picked off the third, and in some respects the least likely, leg of the career Slam with a magnificent Sunday 66 at the Honourable Company of Edinburgh Golfers, adding an Open Championship to his three Masters and his one PGA. Over the final nine holes, he was as unstoppable as the honorable company of previous Muirfield champions, joining Vardon, Braid, Hagen and Cotton, Player, Nicklaus, Trevino, Watson, Faldo, Els, and more.

But poor Lee Westwood. For the second time in his career, he had the lead going into the last round of a major, and Mickelson pipped him in both, giving the Englishman a nightmare package deal of the world's most exclusive clubs, Augusta National 2010 and Muirfield 2013 among his eight top-three finishes in major championships.

As Westwood went backward on Sunday, the field closed in. The Swede Henrik Stenson, Ryder Cup hero Ian Poulter, and Zach Johnson were in the mix. Adam Scott, that year's Masters champion, even led briefly until four straight bogeys on the thirteenth through the sixteenth reprised his finish from the year before at Royal Lytham and St. Annes. Ultimately, it was Mickelson who seized the opportunity. "My only goal was to get it to even par in the championship at the turn," said Mickelson. He reached the par five with a four-iron and a six-iron and two-putted for birdie and a front nine of 34. "Now it's a nine hole competition and I'm right in the thick of it," he said.

He birdied the thirteenth and fourteenth, made a magnificent par save at the sixteenth, and birdied the last two for a back nine of 32. The par at the sixteenth might have been the most important of his life. "I hit a perfect shot, I thought," he said of his six-iron off the tee. "It was right in the middle of the green. I thought it was 25 feet from the hole. Well, it *was* 25 feet from the hole but it didn't end up 25 feet from the hole." More like twenty-five yards after it rolled back down the slope. Mickelson wedged it up and made a seven-footer.

At the seventeenth Mickelson launched two scalding-hot three-woods that reached the green into the wind and two-putted for a birdie to give him a two-shot lead. The eighteenth was pure theater. After striping a hybrid through the cold-hearted left-to-right wind, his six-iron approach teased the greenside bunker but finished fifteen feet behind the hole. "I was trying to start right on the left edge of the green and just let the wind kind of bring it back and it didn't move it much," he said. He rolled the putt in and raised his arms over his head. Mackay, his caddie, put the pin back in the cup and delivered a roundhouse, bent-at-the-waist, two-o'clock-to-eight-o'clock counterpunch through the air. They hugged. They cried. "I did it," said Phil.

There were family and friends and tears and a lot of time to kill as the rest of the field straggled in. No one could come close to Mickelson's mark. Mackay couldn't hold it together. "If you work for a guy for 21 years, it's pretty cool when you see him play the best round of golf he's ever played in the last round of the British Open," said Bones, his voice quavering. "He's gotten pretty good at this links stuff."

Only Mickelson was in red figures by the championship's end. Two years earlier Mickelson had consulted a sports psychologist, Julie Elion, before his second place at Royal St. George's. She helped him find a new mental compartment, where every links was his playground, a game within a game, inventing shots, taking it on with a sparkle in his eye. His Scottish Open victory at Castle Stuart the week before Muirfield marked the second time he'd won the week prior to a major, and it screamed the reality that links golf was no longer some inscrutable mystery to him.

No sooner had his birdie putt hit the bottom of the cup on the eighteenth in Gullane than the world was reminded of his six runner-up finishes in the U.S. Open—the one major title he lacked—and that the next year that championship would return to Pinehurst's No. 2 Course, where all the seconding began.

Mickelson's checkered history with his own National Open really began before he started finishing second in it with such appalling regularity. The ifs and buts first surfaced in 1995 at Shinnecock Hills GC on Long Island (where nine years later he would later finish second, of course, to South African Retief Goosen) when Mickelson played the 544-yard sixteenth hole six over par, including a double bogey on Sunday. He finished four shots behind Corey Pavin, the thirty-five-year-old LA product with a body as thick as a ramen noodle who was, at the time, decorating his five-foot-nine frame with a Groucho Marx mustache. A short-game and long-iron wizard, Pavin played a majestic four-wood on the seventy-second hole to nail down a one-shot victory over Scott Simpson. If (and here it begins) Mickelson had played that one par five less aggressively and made par every day, he would have won by two.

Of course, the official runner-upping began piling up in '99 at Pinehurst. With wife Amy at home holding off—as best she could—the birth of their first child, Amanda, and Phil toting Beeper in a Bag all week, Payne Stewart made a long and almost impossible par putt at the sixteenth to tie Mickelson after Phil had taken the lead the hole before. Going to the par-three seventeenth, both hit wonderful tee shots, but Stewart converted his birdie and Mickelson didn't. On the eighteenth Stewart drove in the rough, gouged it out short of the cross bunker, wedged on, and made a USGA world-class par four to win. Cameras captured Stewart, who would die in a plane crash just months later, taking Mickelson's head in his hands on the eighteenth green.

"I lost by a shot but what I remember is the next day I had the birth of my first child," said Mickelson. "It was an emotional experience, an emotional week, and things, you know, worked out the way they should have."

His least-worst second came three years later at Bethpage State Park on the infamous Black Course, mostly because it was 2002 and this was Tiger Woods in full flight. Woods went into the final round with a four-shot lead but stumbled out of the blocks with two bogeys. First-tee jitters would plague Woods his entire career. Mickelson, meanwhile, had been adopted by the New York fans just as much as they showed a vocal antipathy for the nervous gripping and regripping of Spaniard Sergio Garcia, and after Phil made birdie at the thirteenth, he was within a couple of shots of Woods who, at twenty-six, had already won seven major championships, including the Masters that April. Woods birdied the thirteenth right behind Mickelson, and Phil dropped four back with a bogey at the sixteenth to finish what was, in reality, a distant second to one of the best players who ever lived playing at the top of his game.

Goosen got the next Mickelskin to hang on the wall when the Open returned to Shinnecock. After Phil, who had won his first major championship that April in Augusta, made back-to-back birdies on the fifteenth and sixteenth holes, he was a shot ahead. He bunkered his six-iron tee shot on the par-three seventeenth, however, and double-bogeyed. Behind him Goosen also birdied the par five, the same hole Mickelson had butchered in '95. Mickelson finished two behind. "I was one of the persons that has taken one away from him," said Goosen, who was a demon on the greens Sunday, one-putting six of the last nine holes in the very year one green, the Redan par-three seventh, got baked so badly the USGA had to resort to periodically watering it on Sunday just to make it playable, if somewhat unfairly. After all, who got to play to the softer green and who didn't?

Sometimes second doesn't meet you face-to-face, like Stewart did at Pinehurst; sometimes it sneaks up from behind swinging a Winged Foot. This is the hardest of the runner-ups to forget and, in some ways, the easiest to forgive because Mickelson never should have been in a position to lose it in the first place. "It was a week where, literally, 63 of the 72 holes, he had virtually no idea where the ball was going," said Mackay. Mickelson was carrying a four- instead of a three-wood and using it like a utility club to rescue himself from deep lies in the rough. When he came to the eighteenth tee with a one-shot lead, and lacking the safer option of a three-wood when a four-wood wouldn't clear the dogleg, he blasted driver so far left it bounded like a trampoline off the roof of a giant hospitality tent. As errant as the tee shot may have been, what really cost him the tournament was an ill-advised second shot. Mickelson tried to cut a three-iron around a maple tree from a good lie in the rough, but the shot hit the tree and kicked back at him, stopping some thirty feet from where he had played his second. Forced now to gamble, his third ended up buried in the left bunker, and his double-bogey finish (along with the collapse of several others, including Colin Montgomerie) gave the championship to Geoff Ogilvy, a lanky Australian with a lazy gait and a first-class mind. Knowing that a bogey at the last would have forced a playoff the next day, Mickelson crouched on the eighteenth green with his head in his hands. Afterward he said, simply, "I just can't believe that I did that. I am such an idiot."

In 2009, back at Bethpage Black, with his wife, Amy, and his mother, Mary, having both been diagnosed with breast cancer, Mickelson went into the final round, delayed a day because of repeated spells of abysmal weather, five shots off the pace set by an athletic Californian, Ricky Barnes, whose father, Bruce, had been a punter for two seasons for the New England Patriots. Barnes, the son, would marry professional beach-volleyball star Suzanne Stonebarger a year later. He couldn't hold serve on Bethpage's waterlogged course, however, and when Mickelson birdied the twelfth and eagled the thirteenth, he was at four under par, the eventual winning score, but let it slip away again. "I thought Bethpage was crazy," said Hunter Mahan, who played with Mickelson that day. "I just remember the energy was through the roof. The will and desire for him to win was just incredible. And he was in it all the way until, I think, 15. It was a fight to the end for him, for sure." After another bogey at the seventeenth, Mickelson finished in a three-way tie for second, two shots behind Lucas Glover, an ambling lowball hitter from Greenville, South Carolina, who played at Clemson University and whose estranged biological father, Ron Musselman, pitched in forty-eight games in the Major Leagues with stints with the Seattle Mariners and the Toronto Blue Jays. At the trophy presentation a silver medal is given to the runner-up but, of course, they only had one. Mickelson looked at fellow second-place finishers Barnes and David Duval and demurred. "I've got four of those. I'm good," he said. Later he added, "I've been second five times. But I don't know where to go with this because, you know, this time I feel different. I've got more important things going on. And, oh, well."

The sixth, and final, second was nearly as painful as Winged Foot. The U.S. Open had returned to nearly inaccessible Merion GC, the site of Ben Hogan's 1950 comeback from his horrific car crash and the place where Bobby Jones completed the Grand Slam in 1930. The week began with Mickelson jetting home to San Diego on Wednesday to watch the eighth grade graduation of Amanda, then returning to Philadelphia in the wee hours Thursday morning. By Saturday night he was the only player still under par and had a one-shot lead over the threesome of Charl Schwartzel, the South African who finished with four consecutive birdies to win the 2011 Masters; Wisconsin native Steve Stricker, who twice had won the PGA Tour's Comeback Player of the Year Award; and Mahan, who once again would play with Mickelson during a final round, all at even par. Mickelson had either shared or led outright at the end of each of the first three days. He got off to a poor start Sunday, however, going three over par after five holes with double bogeys at both the third and the fifth holes, three-putting each. "Those are tough holes. And those were costly doubles," he said.

After taking a long iron off the tee on the short, tempting tenth, Mickelson holed a wedge for eagle. The shot was seventy-six yards from the pin and fifty-four yards from the plaque commemorating Jones's completion of his Slam on the next hole, 8 and 7 over Eugene Homans. The roar went up just after Justin Rose, the Englishman who burst on the golfing scene as an eighteen-year-old amateur in the '98 Open Championship at Royal Birkdale, had three-putted the eleventh, dropping him instantly a shot behind

Mickelson. Rose responded by going birdie-birdie, while Mickelson began making mistakes. The first was taking on a sucker pin and hitting his wedge over the tiny par-three thirteenth and making bogey. He added two more bogeys at the fifteenth and the long eighteenth. Rose closed with impressive pars on the last two murderous holes, including driving it nearly on top of the plaque in the eighteenth fairway commemorating Hogan's one-iron approach there—which, according to Charles Price, who was directly behind Hogan, and Dan Jenkins, who got the information directly from Hogan, was a two-iron—for a two-shot victory over Mickelson and Australian Jason Day. "This one's probably the toughest for me, because at 43 (it was Mickelson's birthday, too) and coming so close five times, it would have changed the way I look at this tournament altogether and the way I would have looked at my record," he said. "Except I just keep feeling heartbreak."

Amazingly, Mickelson would turn around in just a few weeks and win the Open Championship at Muirfield. "I thought it could go either way. You have to be resilient in this game because losing is such a big part of it," he said after winning his fifth major. "And after losing the U.S. Open, it could have easily gone south, where I was so deflated and I had a hard time coming back. But I looked at it and thought I was playing really good golf, some of the best of my career, and I didn't want it to stop me."

If his six seconds in the U.S. Open are a mark of futility unmatched in major championships by any other player in history, his record of disappointment in the Ryder Cup was almost as striking. Mickelson had played on ten Ryder Cup teams beginning in 1995 (Nick Faldo played in one more) and had been on just two winning teams. Only Jim Furyk, in nine cups, lost more matches than Mickelson. In addition to his Ryder Cup appearances, Mickelson played on each of the first eleven Presidents Cup teams where the U.S. advantage was as pronounced as it was poor against the Europeans. As you might expect, Mickelson's own record was more successful, too. Though his results were spotty, his love for both events was anything but. No one, particularly as he grew into a veteran presence, spent more time playing practice rounds, sometimes insisting on high-stakes games, to prepare the younger American players like Dustin Johnson, Rickie Fowler, or Jordan Spieth for cup play than did Mickelson.

So upset was Mickelson after the U.S. team lost to Europe at Gleneagles in 2014, he took the U.S. captain, sixty-five-year-old Tom Watson, to task at the closing press conference, extolling the virtues of a previous captain, Paul Azinger, by comparison. "He got everybody invested in who they were going to play with, who the picks were going to be, who was going to be in their pod, when they would play. So, we were invested in the process. Nobody here was in any decision," Mickelson said of the twelve players at Gleneagles.

If going public was considered unseemly, it was not unusual. Mickelson had done the same thing concerning the rough he considered too deep and too dangerous when, with an injured wrist, he missed the cut at Oakmont CC in the 2007 U.S. Open; he played with a "grandfathered" wedge at Torrey Pines to highlight a change in the groove rule he didn't like in 2010; in multiple interviews he staged a running feud with Rees Jones, criticizing his work as a golf course architect; he withdrew from the 2012 Memorial after shooting 79, complaining of the use of cell phones to take pictures on the course, even texting PGA Tour commissioner Tim Finchem during the round; he lamented what he believed to be an excessive rate of taxation in the state of California at the Humana Challenge in Palm Springs in 2013 and apologized for the problems of the 1 percent later at Torrey Pines; after winning the Deutsche Bank Championship in 2007, he expressed his disappointment that Finchem had ignored his input on the format of the new FedEx Cup Playoffs and then skipped the next event. And so it goes.

If Mickelson's life took a turn for the serious in 2003 when Amy had such a dangerous experience in childbirth, there were more challenges to come. Besides the breast cancer of his wife and mother, his own physical ailment arrived in 2011. At the U.S. Open at Pebble Beach, Mickelson could barely walk and couldn't grip the club normally. "My index finger, which was the first sign for me that I had arthritis, I couldn't bend," he said. "If you noticed, it was straight. But it was my bottom finger and I just let it hang off the shaft." By then Mickelson had been working with swing instructor Butch Harmon, who had also done stints with Greg Norman and Tiger Woods, for three years. "On Thursday Amy calls and says Phil is going to be late getting there, that he's in a lot of pain and is having difficulty walking. He can barely get out of the car," Harmon told *Golf Digest.* "He has terrible pain running down his legs to his ankles, then back up all the way to his hands. Phil says, 'Can you walk with me?' We surround him and hide his limping. He gets to the range, and every swing is agony." He finished fourth. A week later, on vacation in Hawaii, Mickelson couldn't get out of bed. He tried to play golf but couldn't even get the club back. The diagnosis was the chronic inflammatory disease psoriatic arthritis.

Other challenges Mickelson brought on himself. Just as he was heading to Pinehurst in 2014 to try to complete the career Slam at the U.S. Open back on the No. 2 Course, a goal the importance of which he made no effort to disguise, he was being dogged by Federal Bureau of Investigation (FBI) agents concerning accusations of insider trading. "I just think it's easier to be honest and up front about what I'm feeling and going through than it is to try and deny it," he said. "There's such a difference in the way I view the few major champions that have won all four. The guys that have won all four, I view in a different regard." But it's not easy chasing a goal when the FBI is chasing you. They confronted him in 2013 at Teterboro Airport in New Jersey and in 2014 at the Memorial Tournament after the second round. He was being linked to billionaire Carl Icahn but also, more insidiously, to William "Billy" Walters, one of the most notorious sports gamblers in Las Vegas. "As a player you have to be able to block out whatever is going on off the golf course and be able to focus on the golf course," he said at the Memorial. "It's not gong to change the way I carry myself. Honestly, I've done nothing wrong. I'm not going to walk around any other way." But with the exception of the run he made at Rory McIlroy at the PGA Championship in August at Valhalla GC, the thrill was gone.

But not forgotten. Not with Phil. "The game, to him, is so much serendipity," said McCord. "To keep it as simple as possible, Phil has short term memory playing golf. All these guys lather up and deal with their past problems on the golf course. Phil just gets rid of it and goes to the next hole and tries something that is other-worldly all the time. That's what keeps his ego going, that's what keeps him as a person going. Really, he forgets it and there's not many guys that have that ability, to forget. He's always been that way, kind of whimsical playing the game, trying stuff nobody ever tried."

Over the span of his entire career, Mickelson was never able to become the number-one-ranked player in the world. He settled for being the most riveting.

# 6

## Long, Gone John

If the question is, how far can you get on talent alone, the answer is John Daly.

In 1991 he wasn't just a story, he was the Daly Planet. A rookie, he gets into the PGA Championship as the ninth alternate, replacing Nick Price, the genial Zimbabwean who would win the same championship the following year. Using Price's caddie, Jeff "Squeaky" Medlin, who would die of leukemia in 1997, he's playing a golf course, Crooked Stick, north of Indianapolis, that was stretched to what seemed like absurd distances, but he hit the ball so far, with a swing that seemed so freakishly Gumbyesque, that he cut the course off at the doglegs and flew its hazards as if they weren't even there. He took the club so far past parallel, he looked like a tweedless, cleekless, mullet-haired caricature out of a Scottish painting from the 1800s. The players in front of him walked faster than usual just to escape what they knew would be his landing area. Once they got down range, they turned to watch the ball and shake their heads.

No one had ever seen anything quite like Daly. He led the championship from the second round on and was the darling of the gallery with his long blond hair, his chain-smoking, his whoop-whoop circular gesture with his right fist over his head, adapted from the popular Arsenio Hall television talk show. When it was all said and done, and he'd won by three shots over Kenny Knox, he donated thirty thousand dollars to the family of a man who had been killed by lightning in a parking lot near the fifteenth fairway on Thursday. On the Sunday night when he left Crooked Stick in a limo with the woman who would become his second wife, Bettye Fulford, and the Wannamaker Trophy, they went to a McDonald's drive-through. At the window John paid for their hamburgers and got the food standing up through the sunroof.

But we were just beginning to get to know John Daly. There was the Jack Daniels and Coke (the favorite drink of his father, too, who would years later pull a gun on him), at least one binge bad enough to land him in a hospital. There was the gambling. Millions of dollars lost. There was the assault charge involving Bettye. There was rehab. There was a domestic violence program. There were disqualifications. There were the marriages. Though the PGA Tour has a bizarre policy of not publicly announcing suspensions, there were the suspensions. By the time Daly won the Open Championship at St. Andrews in 1995, he was, for the moment, sober and, for the moment, married to his third wife, Paulette.

And he was magnificent. While this Open Championship is remembered more for Constantino Rocca's chili-dip pitch into the Valley of Sin and the fifty-footer he made to force the four-hole aggregate playoff Daly won by four shots, what can't be glossed over was Daly's sheer genius around the greens. He lag-putted brilliantly. He chipped superbly. He ran the ball along the ground as if he'd grown up in Gullane and not Dardenelle, Arkansas, and Locast Grove, Virginia, and Jefferson City, Missouri. That a man not far removed from the delirium tremors could have the touch and feel Daly possessed around the Old Course's immense double greens was nothing short of astonishing. Here was a fellow blessed with the long game of Paul Bunyan and the idyllic touch of Paul Gauguin.

Plus all the weaknesses human frailty can muster and then some. To Daly's credit, if that's what it is, he has never tried to disguise a single one of his proclivities, of which there were many. He chain-smoked cigarettes, chain-drank Diet Cokes, and was as kind-hearted a person as you'd ever want to meet, most of the time. After St. Andrews there was more drinking. Another divorce. Suicidal thoughts. Another marriage. More gambling. More drinking. He was shaking and sweating on the golf course in Vancouver. He was shuttled off the golf course when he was shaking and sweating and couldn't finish a round in Pennsylvania. He played hockey on greens in Mississippi. He hit six shots in one water hazard in Orlando. His giveupmanship reached staggering, literally, heights. His fourth wife—there was another doomed relationship in between—Sherrie, was arrested along with her parents on drug and money-laundering charges. He showed up at the tournament in Memphis with what looked to be fingernail scratches on both cheeks and insisted Sherrie had attacked him with a steak knife. She and her parents pleaded guilty to money laundering. All followed by more of everything, including a rolling John Daly megastore for selling his personalized logo merchandise in Hooters parking lots.

And so it went, until it finished in lap-band surgery; blond hair dye; yet another woman, Anna; and slacks that could outfit every clown car under the big top.

Raymond Floyd, the four-time major champion, had a reputation as a partyer early in his career. "I was a young guy. I was enjoying the environment, if you would," says Floyd. That ended when he met and married, Maria, his wife of nearly forty years who passed away in 2012. The story Floyd often tells is when he and Maria were in a hotel room in Jacksonville, Florida, after he'd withdrawn from a tournament, hell-bent for a racetrack in Miami. Throwing his clothes in a suitcase, he told Maria to pack. She refused. She told him he was still young, just thirty-one, and if there was something else he wanted to do in life, well, he should make up his mind and do it. Otherwise, grow up. "That was like hitting me beside the head with a bat," says Floyd. "From that day forward, I never gave it less than 100 percent. I've known players through my years that had the ability but they didn't have the support behind them. It's a very, very difficult career path. Nothing says that all of a sudden something happens, your abilities lesson, injury, many things that can all of a sudden wake you up and now it's too late. You didn't give it your best. I was blessed. I played from 20 to 30 just rambling around. Then from 30 forward, I got my act together."

Daly wasn't so lucky. Poet W. H. Auden once wrote, "All we are not stares back at what we are." In Daly's case it's a long look.

# 7

## Lady Inkster

The lady was a jock. She was a jock with a Hall of Fame career that left footprints in four decades. She began by beating Kathy Whitworth and finished competing against Lydia Ko, who were born fifty-eight years apart. In between she crossed five-irons with all the great ones just because she loved doing it.

Juli Inkster, née Juli Roy Simpson, was born in Santa Cruz, California, and after the age of three grew up in a home on the fourteenth hole of Pasatiempo Golf Club, the Alistair Mackenzie–designed course built by Marion Hollins, a daughter of wealth and privilege from Long Island, New York, and one of the finest woman golfers of the Jazz Age. Hollins began her association with Mackenzie, who would eventually live on the sixth hole of Pasatiempo himself, when they partnered in building the Cypress Point Club on the Monterey Peninsula. At the request of Hollins and Samuel F. B. Morse, the developer of Pebble Beach, Mackenzie took over the Cypress Point project after Seth Raynor died suddenly of pneumonia in West Palm Beach, Florida, in 1926 at the age of fifty-one. In 1929, still a year away from both the Grand Slam and retirement, Bobby Jones came west to play in the U.S. Amateur at Pebble Beach. Mackenzie was, of course, aware of Jones. Who wasn't? They'd probably met. He'd seen Jones play at St. Andrews in the Walker Cup and in Jones's Open Championship victories both at Royal Lytham and St. Annes and his successful defense at St. Andrews after which Jones got the first of his two ticker-tape parades in New York City. But it wasn't until Jones lost to Johnny Goodman, a Nebraska boy who traveled to California by cattle train, in the opening round of match play at Pebble Beach in 1929 that the greatest golfer of the Gatsby era (already smitten with Cypress) would have engaged in his first serious conversation leading to Mackenzie designing his Augusta National Golf Club. After the U.S. Amateur Jones played an exhibition alongside Hollins at the opening of Pasatiempo, losing to Cyril Tolley and Glenna Collett. The match would have been arranged months in advance, but it wouldn't have been the least bit surprising to have Emperor Jones, one of the sporting gods of the day, there. Swimming in a vat full of Vanderbilts and Rothschilds, with the occasional Will Rogers or Mary Pickford floating by, was standard operating procedure for the affluent and well-connected Hollins.

Inkster was neither wealthy nor well connected. Her father, Jack, drafted as a shortstop by the Cincinnati Reds organization, played two years in the Carolina League before moving back to California, where he worked for the Santa Cruz Fire Department for three decades. Her mother, Carole, was a housewife. She had two older brothers, Danny and Mike, and if Juli wasn't one of the boys, she was at least one of the guys. She played basketball and golf and worked at Pasatiempo in the cart barn, picking up range balls and selling sandwiches and drinks at the turn in Hattie's Snack Shack. She took golf lessons from one of Pasatiempo's assistant pros, Brian Inkster. They were married just weeks before she won the first of her three straight U.S. Amateur Championships in 1980.

One of Inkster's charms, and one of the reasons she became the player she did, is that she never really knew how good she was. Margaret Leonard, a neighbor and later a lawyer, is the person who pushed Inkster into qualifying for the 1978 U.S. Women's Open in Indianapolis. "I didn't expect to make it in the qualifying round," she said. "I ended up being medalist and my parents looked at each other and said, 'Now what do we do?' What they did was send me to Indianapolis for the Open and I shot 80-72-72-75." That was ten shots behind the winner, Hollis Stacy.

Inkster was a three-time All-American at San Jose State. One of her teammates, for a year, was Patty Sheehan, another all-around athlete who would become a friend, mentor, and the person who dealt Inkster the most devastating defeat of her career in the 1992 U.S. Open at Oakmont. In 1980 Inkster won the first of her U.S. Amateur titles at Prairie Dunes in Hutchinson, Kansas, a relatively short golf course designed by Perry Maxwell and built with equipment drawn by horse and mule. It was fashioned out of a gnarly landscape of sand hills, a rolling remnant of North America's inland sea that existed along with the dinosaurs in the Cretaceous period. If that amateur was her first major victory, her last came at the same place twenty-two years later, a U.S. Open bookend she was able to snatch away from Annika Sorenstam on as dramatic a final day as that championship has ever seen. "I've been there three times in my life," Inkster says of Prairie Dunes. "I'm sure I wasn't the best golfer for the U.S. Amateur but I got a little better each day and I'm sure I wasn't the best golfer with the U.S. Open but I made the shots when I had to make them. Then, a couple of years ago I was in Wichita with a friend of mine and he goes, 'Let's go play Prairie Dunes,' and that's the other time I've been there. I've only been there three times in my life and I've won two majors so, yeah, it's an amazing place."

Inkster won the second of her U.S. Amateurs at Waverley CC in Portland, Oregon, on a golf course built on the site of an orchard once owned by Seth Lewelling, a horticulturist who along with his Manchurian laborer Ah Bing crossbred the cherry that would forever bear the name of the Chinese foreman. Inkster trailed Australian Lindy Goggin, one down with two to play in the final, and birdied the last two holes along the Willamette River for a one-up victory, becoming the first back-to-back winner of the championship in forty-one years. The next year on what was then called the South Course at the plush Broadmoor resort in Colorado Springs, Colorado, Inkster won a third consecutive amateur title when she beat Cathy Hanlon 4 and 3 in the finals. It was Inkster's eighteenth straight match victory in the championship and the first time any woman had won three in a row since Virginia Van Wie's hat trick from 1932 through 1934. In the championship match in '32, Van Wie beat Glenna Collett, the woman who would help Marion Hollins christen Pasatiempo. After Van Wie's third straight crown she was named the Associated Press's female athlete of the year. While the reputation of amateur golf wasn't nearly as robust in the early '80s as it was in the '30s, there was no disputing Juli Inkster was a phenom.

In her rookie season on the Ladies Professional Golf Association (LPGA) (in those days it was calculated based on the anniversary of joining the tour rather than a simple calendar year), she won once and nine months into her professional career tacked on her first major championship, the Nabisco Dinah Shore in Palm Springs, the first of seven career majors. Inkster won on the first hole of a sudden-death playoff, beating Pat Bradley. Inkster shot a hard-charging 68, including a birdie on the eighteenth when she wedged the ball to three feet on the par five, to go with birdies on the thirteenth and fifteenth—a hole that would prove pivotal for several reasons. Playing a group behind, Bradley was iced on the fifteenth tee for somewhere between five and ten minutes by NBC-TV because the producers thought they were playing too fast and the tournament would end before the telecast. Bradley never hit another good tee shot. She managed to save par at the fifteenth, bogeyed the sixteenth after driving into a stand of trees, and had to salvage another par on the eighteenth after hitting a screaming hook off the tee. When the twosome of Bradley and Inkster returned to the scene of the slowdown, the fifteenth, for the playoff, Bradley nearly drove it out-of-bounds and took four just to get to the green. Inkster's par from the fringe was an easy winner. After it was all over Bradley exchanged a few choice words with NBC producers Don Ohlmeyer and Larry Cirillo. Whether the yellow flag television pulled out for Bradley's group was a contributing factor or not, Inkster's final-round 68 had been a thing of beauty, if something of a shock to her playing partners, Sally Little and Beth Daniel. "Man, those two were tough," Inkster says now with her customary laugh. "It was my rookie year and I was making putts from everywhere and it was just pissing them off. I ended up winning the tournament and they were not happy. Beth and I are great friends now and she says, 'No, I didn't do that,' and I go, 'Oh, yeah, you did.'"

In July '84 Inkster added her second major title, the du Maurier Classic in Toronto. Over the years the women's professional game has struggled off and on with figuring out which tournaments would serve as the barometer for career success the way the Masters, U.S. Open, Open Championship, and PGA Championship do for the men. In fairness it wasn't always exactly cut-and-dried among the men, either. The Western Open was held in the highest esteem in the early years of its existence but was gradually supplanted by the now standard four, though from time to time it seems like the PGA is hanging on to its status like Indiana Jones walking on a rope bridge. With the notable exception of the U.S. Women's Open, which has always been the queen jewel, the shuttling in and out of majorhood among the women has most often relied on the appearance of deep-pocketed strangers. Money talked and majors walked. The du Maurier got its title from the cigarette brand named for a British actor who died in 1934 and whose most prominent theater role was his original portrayal of Captain Hook in *Peter Pan*. In fact, Gerald du Maurier's nephews were the inspiration for Peter and others among the lost boys in J. M. Barrie's story. The tournament had a prestigious run until tobacco became socially unacceptable, and it was stubbed out in 2000. On the flight to her second major, Inkster built a four-shot lead after opening rounds of 69-68 but surrendered it in the third round, largely over a three-hole stretch with bogeys at the fourteenth and fifteenth and a double bogey at the sixteenth after shanking a four-iron. Her 75 put her a shot behind Betsy King, who turned out not to be the ticking crocodile in this particular interpretation. Inkster gave yet another virtuoso Sunday performance with a bogey-free 67 to finish one shot better than the Japanese star Ayako Okamoto. The victory, still within her allotted first twelve months on tour, swamped all competition for rookie-of-the-year honors.

Inkster didn't exactly disappear after her rookie season, but she wasn't the force her explosive beginning advertised. She won eight more times before her next major victory, a second Dinah Shore title in 1989. Not even TV could slow her down. Prior to arriving in Palm Springs, she hadn't played well, but you couldn't tell it from her opening round of 66, and Inkster never looked back. "One week out there you are God, next time you're the devil," she said. Inkster took a five-shot lead into the final day, the eventual winning margin, and the closest anyone got to her was three. Presaging something very similar to what would happen to Inkster herself at the U.S. Open at Pinehurst in 2014 at the age of fifty-three, the closest pursuer in the Dinah Shore was JoAnne Carner, two weeks removed from her fiftieth birthday. After it was over Inkster joked, "JoAnne played very well, for an older lady."

The next years were among the best and worst of Inkster's career. On the plus side she gave birth to her two daughters, Hayley in 1990 and Cori in 1994. In between she suffered a tearful defeat at the hands of her former college teammate Patty Sheehan in the U.S. Women's Open at Oakmont CC in 1992. With just two holes to play, rain and lightning forced a two-hour delay with Inkster two shots ahead after Sheehan's three-putt on the sixteenth. When play resumed Sheehan birdied the short seventeenth, the tiny uphill par four, after Inkster had lipped out her try to close to within a shot. It's the eighteenth, however, that still bothers Inkster. Sheehan drove into the right rough, drawing a thick downhill, side-hill lie from which she never would have been able to reach the green. Taking her stance in a wet area, Sheehan was given relief from casual water. The nearest drop was back in the fairway. Playing from a pristine lie, Sheehan's five-iron settled inside twenty feet below the hole, and she made the putt to force an eighteen-hole playoff that she won the following day by three shots. Inkster had hit seventeen greens and missed just one fairway the last day, and it hadn't been good enough. Sheehan and Inkster were friends, sure, but friendship ceases at the edge of a U.S. Open. Sheehan's victory soothed a gaping wound she carried after losing a seven-shot lead in the Open two years previously. Inkster, to this day, refers to the relief Sheehan got on the seventy-second hole as the worst ruling in the history of golf. It probably isn't even the worst ruling in the history of Oakmont. That distinction likely belongs to the line-of-sight relief granted Ernie Els on the first hole of the final round in 1994 when the television camera that was blocking his shot could easily have been moved. He also went on to win in a playoff. Either way, it was a devastating defeat for the übercompetitive Inkster, and she took it hard. "You never really know if you're going to get back there again," she said.

With her time divided between children and golf, it was unclear whether she ever would. When she did, at Old Waverly in Mississippi in 1999, she won her first U.S. Open in a satisfying walk. Her career broke into halves, before the birth of her daughters and after she realized she could, as she once put it, "have a professional golf career and raise two normal kids." That was sometime around 1997. "I was kind of straddling the fence," Inkster said of her duel roles as basketball coach to her young starlets and three-time major champion. "Do I quit? Do I play? Do I quit? And, if I'm going to do this, I've got to start working on my game," she has said. Her husband, Brian, the professional at their club in Los Altos, had been her coach since her teenage days. She began working with Mike McGetrick instead. "Pre-children she was a wonderful golfer," her husband said, "but I think she's a better player today."

Old Waverly was there for the taking. A cool spring held back the growth of the Bermuda rough, rains softened the course, and Inkster took full advantage of it. She won by five, set the record for the lowest fifty-four-hole score, and broke the U.S. Open seventy-two-hole scoring record, against par, by six. She shot 65-69-67 to open a four-shot lead on her way to claiming the title that brought tears to her eyes after the muck and mire of Oakmont. Then, just a few weeks later, she added her fifth major championship, the McDonald's LPGA Championship, winning at the DuPont CC by four with another textbook final round, this time a 65. Inkster took the lead with birdies on the eighth and ninth holes Sunday, but it was her finishing kick that blew everyone away. She was paired with her close friend Meg Mallon. "It was her destiny to win," Mallon said. "I mean, who else plays the last three holes four under to win a major championship? After she made the eagle putt on

16, I had chills." The victory meant that Inkster had collected all of the major championships the LPGA currently had on offer. The only players to have done it before her were Mickey Wright, Louise Suggs, and Pat Bradley. When she saw Brian, Hayley, and Cori in the gallery at the last hole, she hugged the girls and said, "Can you believe this?" At the presentation she pointed to them and said, "These guys are my Hall of Fame." The once and future phenom had turned thirty-nine the day of the first round, and it looked like she was just getting started.

A year later, on her fortieth birthday, Inkster shot a six-under-par 65 on a remarkably different DuPont CC on the way to back-to-back LPGA Championships. That night she had a party. Hayley gave her a handmade piece of pottery with clouds and the sun painted on it, and Cori made her a multicolored stuffed bear. The next day DuPont CC was less festive. Unlike the previous year the rough was up and the greens hard. "It's two different courses," she said after beating Italy's Stefania Croce on the second hole of sudden death. "It was like an Open out there. I never thought I could shoot four over and win this tournament." Inkster's final-round 75 was just one of twenty-nine rounds of 75 or worse. She came to the last hole with a one-shot lead but, after gouging a five-iron out of the rough into the greenside bunker, missed a six-foot par putt that would have won it outright. On the second playoff hole, the tenth, Croce's approach carried over the green, "which is jail," Inkster said, and her two-putt par proved good for a sixth major championship.

It's a lot more stressful having a one-shot lead and bogeying the last hole. That's the stuff you have nightmares about. I told Hayley, "I'm getting too old to do this stuff." It means a lot to me, personally, just to prove to myself I can still play with these girls and I'm still one of the top players. I work hard at my game and I love the game of golf. I love competing and sometimes it's not easy. You know, you bogey the last couple holes and you lose a tournament and you fret the whole week. Why am I doing this? I don't need to do this. But, you know, next week you tee it up and you're right back at 'em. It's in my blood. I love to compete.

The exclamation point came two years later, back where it all started, at Prairie Dunes. For three days Inkster spent most of her time in the yucca plants, plum thickets, and soap weeds. Her game was a shambles. "I was hanging on by my fingertips," she said. She was making five-, six-, eight-footers for par, getting up and down from parts of the golf course other players didn't know existed. It left her two shots behind the best player in the world, Annika Sorenstam, who had won six of her last thirteen events and fourteen of her last thirty-six on the LPGA. Sorenstam hadn't won a U.S. Open since her back-to-back victories in '95 and '96, but to say she was anything less than the prohibitive favorite would have been like betting against Tiger Woods in 2000. Forget about it.

After her third round Inkster looked utterly dispirited. She knew she had to find an answer for her undependable ball striking or she'd have no chance whatsoever. Annika wasn't going to make mistakes. Mike McGetrick recorded the third round and studied his pupil's swing from the TV angles. He told her to get her weight a little bit more on her heels and make a better turn away from the ball. "I didn't sleep all that night trying to figure out what the hell I was doing out there," Inkster said. Never has anyone looked so lost one day and so found the next.

"It's like 15 minutes before I had to go, Brian just said, 'You need to make a better turn.' We have a drill that we do to help me turn back to the ball and I did a few of those and finally started to feel like I was behind the ball and could drop my arms down," she said. She hit a half dozen solid shots and was ready to go.

Inkster birdied the second, chipped in from sixty-five feet on the sixth, and birdied the seventh from the fringe to take a two-shot lead by the turn. The decisive swing happened at the fifteenth and sixteenth holes. Sorenstam, playing the group behind Inkster, had birdied the fourteenth to pull within a shot. Inkster missed the par-three fifteenth green to the left and chipped fifteen feet past the hole. As Sorenstam ate a banana on the tee and watched, Inkster drained the putt for par. Sorenstam missed the green short and right, nearly chipped in, but then missed the five-footer coming back. The lead was back at two. When Inkster rolled in her birdie putt on the sixteenth and punched the air, the pro-Juli, pro-USA

Fourth of July crowd erupted. Sorenstam bogeyed right behind her, and it was, effectively, over.

"Every time I win a tournament I surprise myself," said Inkster afterward. "You know, everybody asks me why I play. I play because I love to play and how can you not love to do what I did today? I mean, the crowds were great. When I made that putt on 16, my heart was pumping so hard. It was fantastic." Was it the best round of her career, given the pressure, the opponent, the size of the prize? "It is right now," she said. As Walter Hagen once said, "Anyone can win one Open. It takes a hell of a player to win two." In the television booth NBC's Johnny Miller called it the best putting round in a major championship, man or woman, he'd ever seen.

After reaching the grand age of fifty-three, Inkster decided she'd had enough of the nerve-fraying grind of U.S. Opens. She announced that Pinehurst in 2014 would be her last. It would be her thirty-fifth, contested in twenty-two different states. At that point she had played in more than half of the U.S. Women's Opens ever held. "It's still the coveted trophy that everybody tries to win," she says. "Two for 35? I would be sitting on the bench if I was a baseball player."

Then, on the No. 2 Course on Saturday in North Carolina's summer swelter, a mere seventy-two hours shy of her fifty-fourth birthday, she shot a remarkable 66, the lowest round of the tournament so far. She was tied for third, four off the lead. Hogan had done the same thing at the age of fifty-four at Augusta National in 1967. Both plummeted back to reality with final rounds of five over par. On the way to her 66 Inkster missed one fairway and one green. On Sunday she hit more bunkers than greens. There is no burden quite like the end of time. She felt it before she even got to the tee Sunday. "You can think and you can dream all you want but, the bottom line is, you've got to come out and make the shots," she said. It was a curtain call full of sweat and grit and sandy bogeys.

"I was disappointed in the way I played today, as a golfer," said Inkster. "But, as a person, I just felt a lot of pride that people root for me like that. Especially the reception on No. 1 tee and the reception on 18 and all around the golf course. It was great. Very, very, very honored."

In September 2015 Captain Inkster took her Solheim Cup team to Germany to play the Europeans. The same woman who sang "You've Lost That Lovin' Feeling" over the bus public address system when she was a player was now in charge. The American team fell behind by a staggering four points after the foursomes and four-ball matches. Early in the week Inkster had given her twelve players gifts—a red, white, and blue lunch pail. They showed up for the opening ceremony wearing Chuck Taylor sneakers. Having lost two cups in a row, it was time to go to work. Aided by a controversy over the nonconcession of a putt, Inkster rallied her team to the biggest comeback in the history of the Solheim Cup, equaling what the U.S. men had done at The Country Club in '99 and what the Europeans pulled off at Medinah in 2012.

One of Inkster's memories from her very first U.S. Open in 1978 at The Country Club of Indianapolis was being impressed by the quality of the new Titleist range balls. The fifteen-year-old stuffed her golf bag full of them for the trip home. By the age of fifty-three, she'd given it all back, with interest. Few players ever squeezed as much out of a golf game, and fewer still ever made the game of golf so much better for it.

After four decades of championship golf, what follows are just a few of Inkster's reflections on some of the players she competed against. For the sake of simplicity, the Dinah is referred to throughout as the Dinah, rather than Nabisco or its current ANA Inspiration, and of course, career highlights run through 2015. Some have a lot of golf left to play:

JoAnne Carner, born 1939; the Great Gundy; five U.S. Women's Amateur Championships; two U.S. Women's Open Championships; three times LPGA Player of the Year; five-time winner of the Vare Trophy for low stroke average.

She's probably one of the people I loved playing with the most. It didn't matter where she was, you knew the ball was going to get somewhere on the green. She just had the greatest shot imagination and hands to play the game. She's gruff but what a nice lady. She got up there and let it fly. She didn't care where it went; she would just go get it. She's still that way. She's still playing. She's a lot like me. She just loves the game of golf. She loves playing. Her sand game and her game around green was just amazing. You might be thinking there's no way she's going to get this up and down, then she gets it up and down and she gives you that little smirk, you know? I remember her giving me a sand lesson, "You gotta get low in there. You gotta get really low." Just stuff like that. What a great lady. And great for the game.

Kathy Whitworth, born 1939; pupil of Harvey Penick; two Title-holders Championships; three LPGA Championships; one Women's Western; eighty-eight career victories, most of any man or woman; seven times LPGA Player of the Year; seven-time winner of the Vare Trophy.

Whit was a little more standoffish. She was always kind of Negative Nellie. Always kind of, "I can't believe I hit that shot. I can't believe they let me have my card out here. I suck. I'm not that good." She won eighty-eight times! She was old school. She just kind of went about her business. The first tournament I ever won I beat her. It was in Kent, Washington and it was a horrible day. I think I was five or six shots back, and I think I shot 70 and ended up winning. She just made me laugh. She'd hit a shot and she'd be like, "Gawd," and you'd get up there it was like, this far [Inkster puts her hands two feet apart].

Donna Caponi, born 1945; two LPGA Championship; two U.S. Women's Open Championships, back to back.

They called her the General. She took charge of the group out there. Went by the book. I was chipping one day with range balls or something and she goes, "Juli, always chip with your golf balls; never chip with range balls." I still do that. She was always very helpful. One time I was struggling with my putting, and she'd come up and help me out a little bit. I've gotten to know her pretty well. She had kind of a different swing, real slow backswing and through the ball.

Judy Rankin, born 1945; twice LPGA Player of the Year; three-time winner of the Vare Trophy.

She's the best. I love Judy Rankin, but I didn't really know Judy Rankin. I never really played against her. It took me a long time to get to know Judy. Judy's really quiet, reserved. I kind of got to know her in 1992–93–94 and really in 1998 when she was my captain for Solheim Cup. I really got to know her then. We've been great friends ever since. I talk to her a lot. She's kind of my go-to person. She's the one that kind of pushed me to try television. She knew I was kind of cutting back, and she wanted to kind of cut back. And she decided I'd be good at it. I did five Golf Channel telecasts with her. She is the nicest lady. She was a phenomenal golfer, but she's been a phenomenal broadcaster, too. Afraid of heights. Yeah. She's just a good-hearted Texan lady. I really admire her.

Pat Bradley, born 1951; three du Maurier Championships; one U.S. Open; one LPGA Championship; one Dinah Shore; twice LPGA Player of the Year; twice the Vare Trophy winner.

Pro? Pat Bradley, she was tough. She was the epitome of a pit bull. She never knew anybody's name. You ask her—she didn't want to get close to anybody. Her job was to beat you. She didn't want to have any of that connection of friendship or anything like that. I think she regrets that today. Now, she's just the opposite. She's the best. She even told Keegan [Bradley, her nephew], "Don't do what I did." Pat Bradley, she probably was the best course-management person I ever played against and probably the best putter from 20 feet I've ever played against. She was a phenomenal lag putter. She would just go for the middle of the greens, take her par or whatever. If she made it, fine. And she'd attack the holes that set up perfect for her. But, Pat, she was tough.

Ayako Okamoto, born 1951; forty-four victories on the Japan LPGA Tour; seventeen U.S. victories; one LPGA Player of the Year.

Ayako probably could play a golf course without a yardage book. She totally felt everything. She had the best wedge play I've ever seen. Her demeanor out there, she was probably my favorite person to play with. She was just kind of carefree, she would just kind of get up there and hit it, but from 150 yards in, she was money.

Hollis Stacy, born 1954; one du Maurier Championship; three U.S. Women's Open Championships.

Hollis was tough. I always felt there was an agenda with Hollis. There was some gamesmanship out there, but I never had a problem with her. I remember my first Open as the amateur champ, I got paired with Hollis and Pat Bradley at Del Paso, the year Janet Anderson won. I was really looking forward to it. Those two hated each other. Maybe not "hated" each other, but they just didn't get along. Two days of just them [bitching] . . . I'm like, "Oh, my God, is this what I want to do?" Some people just cannot talk on the golf course. They have to focus. Hollis couldn't shut up. The better she played, the more she was in your ear. You couldn't get anything out of Pat Bradley. Back then, it was just a little more . . . not competitive, but I think there was just a smaller group that could really win out there, and they were really competitive with each other. Everybody had to have the upper hand—at least everybody had to feel like they had the upper hand. It's so different out here now. There's so many people that can win and so many diverse nationalities. Then it was just more intense in that small group. Hollis could work the ball. Shape the ball. Amy the same way. They enjoyed that part of the golf, working the ball, shaping the ball. Patty Sheehan, too.

Betsy King, born 1955; one LPGA Championship; three Dinah Shore Championships; two U.S. Women's Open Championships; three-time LPGA Player of the Year; twice the Vare Trophy winner.

There's someone that struggled at the start, didn't really have much success at all but was a hard worker, a grinder, and just ended up having a phenomenal career. She went to Furman—smart. She did everything good but was kind of unorthodox. She used to put the putter behind it and take her practice swings. Stuff that you never see today. She just plodded. That's another one you couldn't tell if she was shooting 66 or 76. I thought she was a good ball striker. She probably didn't do anything great, but she did everything really, really good. Consistent and very kind of straitlaced.

Amy Alcott, born 1956; three Dinah Shore titles; one U.S. Women's Open Championship; one du Maurier Championship; one Vare Trophy.

Amy Alcott, just out there. I didn't play a lot with her. Amy's iron play was probably one of the best. She just hit it straight, on a line. Not real high, just a bullet. I don't think she went to college. I think she just came right out when she was eighteen. She was kind of from the school of hard knocks, man. A little airy. Some of the things that came out of her mouth were like, okay, are you messing with me or is it just you? I never knew where she was coming from. Total LA. Loves the Hollywood scene. Loves name-dropping. She's Amy. You never know what's going to come out of her mouth, but golf-wise, she could hit it.

Beth Daniel, born 1956; one LPGA Championship; three-time LPGA Player of the Year; three-time Vare Trophy winner.

Oh, my gosh. One of the all-time-best golf swings. Great ball striker. There wasn't anybody who was harder on herself than Beth Daniel. She was a perfectionist. Not the easiest person to play with. She would kind of give everybody the wrath out there. Off the golf course, she's great. On the golf course, it's just like another person. She has to hit every shot perfect. If she doesn't, she's pissed. That's what made her tick. As far as pure ball striking, she's probably one of the best I've ever seen. Now, I never played with Mickey Wright. Beth was . . . I hated playing with her. You knew it was just going be a grind. You didn't know what to say. You didn't know when to say it. And Beth's a good friend of mine. We're great friends now, but she was tough when I was coming out.

Patty Sheehan, born 1956; one Dinah Shore; three LPGA Championships; two U.S. Women's Open Championship; one LPGA Player of the Year; one Vare Trophy.

Inch for inch, one of the best. Grew up with three older brothers. I had two older brothers. She could do everything. She was just athletic. She was a great skier. She had great hands. Good ball striker, great putter. Huge heart. If you wanted somebody to make a five- or ten-footer to win, she was the one you wanted to do it. A good friend. I played a year with her in college, and I learned a lot from her. I really picked her brain when I first came out—what tournaments to play, how to go about it. She was a good mentor for me. She was a great golfer, and she had a lot of outside stuff that she liked to do. Golf wasn't her number-one thing. She loved to ski. She loved to hang out with her family. She was kind of an outdoorsy woman. Patty always told me, "You gotta learn to cut the ball on the LPGA Tour," because Patty Berg always told her that. So, that was kind of our big thing.

Nancy Lopez, born 1957; three LPGA Championships; four-time LPGA Player of the Year; three-time Vare Trophy winner; heartbreakingly four-time U.S. Women's Open runner-up; won five straight tournaments as a rookie.

There are a few people who have "it." Nancy has "it." [Arnold] Palmer has "it." They have a charisma. They're just kind to people whether they're in the gallery or in the locker room. Nancy's just a great lady, very motherly, very warm and fuzzy, great with hugs, would do anything to help you. I didn't really play with Nancy in her prime, but I know she was just a phenomenal putter. I played with her kind of at the end of her career. She would just stop and say hi to the most random people. I learned a lot from her. How to treat people. How to balance the golf and do the other side of it. When you shoot 76, you don't really feel like signing autographs. She always did. No matter if she shot 76 or 66, she would sit there and smile that amazing smile.

Dame Laura Davies, born 1963; two LPGA Championships; one U.S. Women's Open Championship; one du Maurier Championship; seven-time Ladies European Tour Order of Merit winner; one LPGA Player of the Year; twice Ladies European Player of the Year.

Laura is the same now as she was when she came on the scene. Doesn't like to practice. Kind of a free spirit. Loves Vegas. Loves her soccer. She's well deserving to be in the Hall of Fame, if anybody deserves to be in a Hall of Fame. She supported the European Tour when it was nothing. Loves to play golf. Hates slow play. She just doesn't get the whole slow-play thing. First person I ever saw that tees the ball up without a tee, just kind of knocks a seven-iron in the ground, builds a little tee, puts the ball on it and boom. She doesn't leave anything back, and when she hits it, she just goes and gets it. She's got really great hands. Very, very coordinated. Great Ping-Pong player, great tennis player. She's an athlete. You look at her, and you're kind of saying, no, but she is.

Meg Mallon, born 1963; one LPGA Championship; two U.S. Women's Open Championships; one du Maurier Championship.

Voted the nicest player on tour back in the early '90s. She didn't have the big credentials coming out of college and really worked hard. Kind of like a Jay Haas. Very steady. Good iron player, great putter, good thinker. Very good course management. Great Solheim Cup partner and player. Really loves the history of the game and people that came before her. Has a tremendous respect for the founders. Just a good egg.

Annika Sorenstam, born 1970; three Dinah Shore titles; three LPGA Championships; three U.S. Women's Open Championships; one Women's British Open Championship; eight-time LPGA Player of the Year; six-time Vare Trophy winner.

As far as Annika goes, she was the best player I ever played against, day in and day out. Her ball striking was unbelievable. It didn't move one way or the other. It was just a straight ball. When she was on—and she was on a lot—the only thing that would hold her back was her putting. If she putted halfway decent, she won. If she didn't putt very good, she didn't win. But her ball striking, she would hit sixteen, seventeen greens a round like it was nothing. And she was long. Her focus was golf. She always told me, "When I have kids I'm quitting. I don't know how you do it, having kids and playing golf. I can't play unless I'm number one." That's just the way she is. She couldn't be warm and fuzzy and hang out with you. It just wasn't in her DNA. Some people just have to play golf that way. It takes all different types of people. They have to do what they have to do to get ready. She could not handle being less than number one. I never played with Mickey Wright, but as far as the full game, Annika was it. Every time I played with her, I was like, are you freakin' kidding me? Do you ever miss a shot?

Karrie Webb, born 1974; two Dinah Shore titles; one LPGA Championship; two U.S. Women's Open Championships; one du Maurier Championship; one Women's British Open; two-time LPGA Player of the Year; three-time Vare Trophy winner.

Karrie burst on the scene young. One of the best golf swings I ever saw. A lot of power. She played it kind of close to the chest, didn't really give you much. Karrie was hard to get to know at the start. She said I treated her like shit when she first came out. I said, "Come on, that's a rookie. You can't give a rookie that much." I think she likes the game. I'm not sure she loves the game. She's really good at it, and she likes being good at something. She's kind of like a mini–Beth Daniel. She's a perfectionist. She wants to hit the ball good on the range. She wants to hit the ball good on the golf course. She takes her game very seriously. She works very hard at it, but I don't think she enjoys it like I enjoy it. Off the golf course, totally different person, carefree and a lot of fun. But on the golf course, she's all business.

Se Ri Pak, born 1977; three LPGA Championships; one U.S. Women's Open Championship; one Women's British Open Championship; one Vare Trophy.

Se Ri kind of busted out. She was kind of the first Korean to get out here. She was the lightning rod for everybody else to come over, with the success she had. After every round of golf, she had to talk to the press, and after every practice round she had to talk to the press. It was amazing what she had to go through. She had tons of power. Sturdy legs. I don't even think she knew what she had back then. I remember when I played with her in her rookie year, I was like, "Whoa, this girl's good." Powerful, powerful swing. Just kind of did everything great. The first year she probably would have won three or four more times if she'd had a really good caddie. I couldn't believe some of the yardages he would give her. You could just tell she was going to be really good, and she still is. We never really saw anything like Se Ri and her caddie. When we got off the golf course, our caddie went one way and we went the other way. Her caddie did everything. Took her clothes to the dry cleaners. Picked her up at the airport. It was the changing of the guard in what the caddie's responsibilities are. Now, a lot of them do all that stuff.

Lorena Ochoa, born 1981; one Dinah Shore title; one Women's British Open; four-time LPGA Player of the Year; four-time Vare Trophy winner.

Lorena Ochoa was probably the most spiritually sound person I've ever met. Golf was her way to make a difference in the world, and that was her main goal, to make a difference in the world in Mexico. She was kind of like a Lopez: you couldn't tell if she was shooting 66 or 76, very nice to everybody, just a warm, genuine person. She was one of my all-time favorites, is one of my all-time favorite people, ever. I just thought she was the greatest ambassador for women's golf that there was. As far as game-wise, she just could friggin' bomb the ball off the tee. She was like Gumby, just a rail, limber as hell, and just bomb the ball. Her putting was probably the weakest part of her game. She just had a feel for winning. But her goal in life was to make a difference, and she has. That's still her passion.

Inbee Park, born 1988; three LPGA Championships; two U.S. Women's Open Championships; one Women's British Open Championship; one Dinah Shore title; one LPGA Player of the Year; one Vare Trophy.

If you were to look at her, you'd just think there's no way she could be number one. Pretty good distance, very underrated iron player, and just a phenomenal putter. If you watch her, she never really lines anything up. Kind of gets up there, and her caddie sort of tells her generally where to hit it, and they go in. It's amazing. She might walk around and look at it, but she never gets down in a stance and lines it up. It's weird. She's just very consistent. Doesn't get too high, doesn't get too low. Very calm.

Yani Tseng, born 1989; one Dinah Shore Championship; two LPGA Championships; two Women's British Open Championships; two-time LPGA Player of the Year; one Vare Trophy.

Yani just crushes the ball. Probably became number one when she wasn't really ready to be number one, for her game. She came out early, and it was really easy for her. Then she just kind of struggled, and she's still struggling. I've played a lot with her. She's putting the ball good. She hits some good irons, but she hits her driver just off the world. She hits the ball so far, hits it like a guy. When you hear it, it sounds like a guy, the speed and the force.

Michelle Wie, born 1989; one U.S. Women's Open Championship.

Michelle can't seem to stay healthy. She hits the ball a long way. Her one fault, and this isn't any news to anybody, is her putting. She doesn't think it was a mistake, but looking back on it, I just think playing all those men's tour events, it would have done her good to just crush the juniors, then crush the amateurs, then crush the collegians, and then come out.

Lydia Ko, born 1997; one Evian Championship.

The jury's still out. She's young. She's had a lot of success early, but I think the hard part when you have success early is how do you handle it when things aren't going well? Hopefully, that will never happen, but you never know. She's been playing professional golf for a long time. She's out here all day long. She'll practice until dark. I'd play with her and think, okay, she probably shot a couple under, and I look up and it's, like, five under. I don't think she does anything great, but she does everything really good. She's a good putter, very good course management, solid ball striker, sneaky long, and a great swing.

Inkster's Best? (1) Sorenstam, (2) Ochoa, (3) Webb, (4) Daniel, (5) Sheehan. "That would be my top five," she said, "but I didn't play with Nancy in her prime, so we might need an asterisk."
One for the lady, too.

# 8

## Hidden Tiger, Crouching Dragon

I wish I had paid better attention the first time I met Tiger Woods. To be perfectly honest, it didn't mean a heck of a lot to me, and it meant even less to him. Woods, young or old, has always been a riddle. I wasn't right about how good he was going to be, and I wasn't right about how bad he would get. He's utterly obvious sometimes and, at others, an enigma with a big grin, even if occasionally there's a tooth gone missing. I try to tell myself it's not really all that complicated. "It is what it is" was his favorite threadbare phrase. To some people he's a puzzle with few pieces, an overcooked gumbo of nature and nurture. A little Earl. A little Tida. And voilà. Earl, who loved his own hyperbole, said his son could have an impact equal to Gandhi. Though he walked that back at double time, he meant most of it or was, at the very least, willing to hold out for a percentage of it. I guess we both went wide of the mark.

The first time I saw Woods was in 1994. He may have already won his first U.S. Amateur. If not, he was just weeks or days away from it. He was going to be on the cover of *Golf Digest*, a much bigger and more important voice in golf then than it is now, and

I didn't much like the idea of doing a cover shoot with a kid. To me, it was reminiscent of *Sports Illustrated* putting Gary Nicklaus on its front page at sixteen. It was a lot of pressure and for what? By then I'd already seen a string of prodigies come out of college and amateur golf and not live up to what the world thought they should be. Ben Crenshaw. Curtis Strange. Hal Sutton. Fred Couples. Bobby Clampett. John Cook. Mark O'Meara. Willie Wood. It's true, some would have Hall of Fame careers and some not. But in a game that had put out bear traps for the Next Nicklaus, the bait could lead to a roach motel.

I met the real Next Nicklaus at the Navy Golf Course in Cypress, a modest public course with a modest one-level clubhouse and a modest grill room with modest hot dogs and a modest pro shop, when he and his father, Earl, showed up for our cover shoot. Fancy was uptown. Fancy was Riviera and Los Angeles Country Club and the University of Southern California cheerleaders and movie folk and the LA Lakers. Kobe Bryant wasn't even a glimmer in Los Angeles's eye. Tiger and Earl knew fancy, though. They'd done fancy. They just weren't fancy. But they knew one day they were going to *own* fancy, or at least the mineral rights. Though I was both a writer and a photographer for *Golf Digest*, I was there to take the pictures so Tiger and Earl were less wary than they tended to be around people who were going to record conversations and repeat things. Once, at a lunch I had with J. C. Snead and his uncle Sam, at Sam Snead's Tavern in Hot Springs, Virginia, J. C. introduced me as someone from *Golf Digest*, and Sam, who was sitting in a booth by himself, glowered at me like I was a squirrel he was about to shoot and skin and bring home to Audrey, his wife, for her favorite dinner meal. "It's okay," J. C. said to him. "He's a photographer." Sam immediately relaxed. "Good," he said. "I hate writers. Writers lie." Tiger and Earl felt the same way. Tiger still does, more than ever.

I told Tiger and Earl I'd scouted out a spot for the photos, and Earl sent us on our way. He wanted to wait in the grill room or someplace where he could smoke. Off we went, Tiger and me. Most photographers have a line of chitchat that spews forth in moments like these, Cheez Whiz out of the can, the comfort food of conversation. But Tiger didn't do small talk. In fact, he didn't talk at all. No matter how hard I tried, I got little more than nods of the head or uh-huhs. Perhaps he was shy, but I've never believed that. I think Tiger already knew he was way bigger than me, for sure, and way bigger than *Golf Digest*, too. Foolishly, I had thought we were exploiting him. That was my first lesson in Tiger Woods 101.

When we rejoined Earl in the grill room, Tiger turned into a regular teenager, talkative, pleasant, a different person altogether when Pops was around. Afterward we drove to the house where he grew up on Teakwood Street, as modest in its own way as the clubhouse at the Navy GC. Most people talk about Nicklaus's records taped up in Tiger's bedroom. What I remember most was the table in the living room loaded with trophies. If he had won the U.S. Amateur, that one hadn't made it there yet, at least I don't recall it, and it's probably the most attractive piece of USGA hardware there is. There wouldn't have been room for it anyway. Big or small, the tournament didn't matter. If there was a trophy involved, it had a place on that table. This was Tida's shrine to her boy. As near as I could tell, Earl liked the dog better.

I saw Tida once at what everyone liked to call the big house in Florida after Tiger had become the world's most famous athlete and she and Earl separated. In the old days players liked to introduce the attractive young blonde having a drink with them at the bar as their "niece." Earl, it was commonly supposed, had a very large extended family. On this visit another *Digest* photographer was duplicating the Woods family photo album, and I was along as the Cheez Whiz. Tida was more talkative than Tiger had ever been. The best photo I saw was skinny-kid Tiger in his Spiderman costume. Besides the album, which was in every regard a collection of your standard middle-class family snapshots, Tida had devoted one of the upstairs bedrooms of the big house, a room far larger than any in the home on Teakwood, to nothing but framed pictures of her son. Magazine covers. Program covers. Book covers. Anything you could slap a mat on and frame. If the table on Teakwood seemed like a Buddhist shrine, this was more of a Russian Orthodox cathedral with one icon. I had even taken some of the pictures. Just above the light switch inside the door was one of those quickie prints you get at Eckerd's in a cheap frame. Easily the smallest picture in the room, it was taken the night after Tiger won his first Masters by twelve shots. He was asleep in the bed of his rented house in Augusta, hugging the green jacket in his arms like a kid with a blankie. I told her she needed to take special care of it, that it was an important photograph. She looked at me as though I couldn't begin to comprehend how important it was. She was probably right.

After Teakwood Street the next time I saw Tiger was for a feature about his first Stanford golf team, the most interesting collegiate team ever assembled. There was the freshman black/Asian superstar (Woods); the Navajo-Isleta–San Felipe Native American (Notah Begay III), who made it to the PGA Tour briefly but wound up on the Golf Channel as a talking head with earrings, the resident Woods expert/friend and, to my way of thinking, one of the smartest people in golf; a Japanese American who got as far as the Buy.com Tour and had the full-on Columbus world ranking of 1,492 when he quit playing in 2012 (Will Yanagisawa); a Chinese American who would become one of Woods's closest friends (Jerry Chang) and who replaced the team's token white guy (Steve Burdick), who had been the best player on Stanford's national championship team the year before Woods arrived but lost his swing and eventually became a youth minister; and a damn-near cripple (Casey Martin), who would be the only one of the bunch to make it all the way to the Supreme Court and, you could argue persuasively, did as much for golf as all the rest put together. Still a notch or two shy of Gandhi, though.

Years after I was in Palo Alto, I visited Martin in Eugene not too long before he quit playing tournament golf to become the golf coach at the University of Oregon. He was still trying to stick on tour when I saw him. It had been a long time since he'd been asked to do his grizzly striptease, removing the elastic wraps around his bum right leg, allowing it to swell as the blood pooled, unable to make its way back to his heart, and I didn't ask him to do it for me. I'd seen it at Stanford. As far as I was concerned, that show went dark the day he won his court battle. Martin's PGA Tour biography used to list his career record in playoffs as 0-1 (he lost to Matt Gogel in the then–Nike Tour's Cleveland Open), but it neglected to mention how he beat them like *Cool Hand Luke*, with a leg full of nothin', all the way to the Supreme Court and back. Incidentally, that's the same Matt Gogel that Tiger ran over like a squirrel crossing the road in the 2000 AT&T at Pebble Beach who would also find his way into the world of on-course commentary.

When I saw Martin he was living in a modest town house in Eugene, a first-cul-de-sac-on-the-left kind of place. Even with Klippel-Trénaunay syndrome, it was conveniently located enough that he could walk across a footbridge over the Willamette River to watch the Ducks play on Saturdays in the fall. Since the courts mandated he be allowed to use a golf cart in competition in accordance with the Americans with Disabilities Act, it was the longest walk he ever made.

There are beach rentals that look more lived in than Martin's flat did. The mostly empty living room had a baby grand piano with sheet music for Vince Gill songs and "Amazing Grace." There were two short pieces of wooden two-by-four and a police lineup of putters and chipping irons standing against the off-white wall. There was a chair in a corner for when he'd been using the clubs too long. On the mantel over the gas-log fireplace was the Ben Hogan Award given to him in 1999 by the Golf Writers Association of America, as someone who continued to be active in golf despite a physical handicap or serious illness. His office was upstairs, the Stanford diploma under glass. A letter from Senator Bob Dole and a Tank McNamara cartoon were carefully framed on the wall. There was a collage of snapshots from the long legal march that began in 1998 and ended in 2001. Robin Williams. Paula Zahn. Phil Knight. Stone Phillips. Some performer from Las Vegas whose name he couldn't remember. There was no silver trophy for beating the tour at match play. No Court TV souvenir mug or ashtray. You get the feeling that hidden in a dresser drawer somewhere Martin should have had a shirt that said: Went All the Way to the Supreme Court and All I Got Was This Lousy T-Shirt. Justice Scalia may have been the Simon Cowell of the Supremes, but Martin didn't become America's idol; all he got was the chance to fail at golf the old-fashioned way. Which was all he wanted to begin with.

Since Martin was granted access to a golf cart, there has been no avalanche of requests for similar accommodation, one of the fears of those who opposed him so doggedly, including Jack Nicklaus and Arnold Palmer, a stance both came to regret. Martin, the golf coach, even succeeded in qualifying for the U.S. Open at the Olympic Club won by Webb Simpson in 2012. If anything, at all, has become clear in the time since Martin sued the PGA Tour and won, it is that he was such a singular talent in such a flawed body that the search for the next Casey Martin would take a lot longer than the one for the next Jack Nicklaus did. Or the next Tiger Woods will.

Even among this Stanford band of the unorthodox, Woods was different. They tried to make him one of the guys, especially Begay, but he just wasn't. He was better than they were. They knew it. He knew it. The sports information department knew it, too, and handled him like the All-American quarterback of a different sort in a different sport. He was the most important part of the picture and always the last one to step into the frame.

I was there for Woods's first Masters appearance as the U.S. Amateur champion when he finished T41 and the next year when he missed the cut and at the U.S. Open in '95 when he withdrew and the following year at Oakland Hills when he finished T82. In his first U.S. Open at Shinnecock Hills Woods was carried off the golf course on a cart after five holes of the second round. He'd shot 74 on Thursday, the same as one of his playing partners, Ernie Els, whom he would come to victimize repeatedly. The other man in the group was the reigning Open and PGA champion, Nick Price, who held the opening-day lead with a 66. Woods sprained his left wrist hitting a wedge out of the rough on the third hole and aggravated it further playing out of the rough again on the fifth. After his tee shot on the sixth, he packed it in. At the time I wondered if the skinny kid from California might not have a pride problem. After making bogey on four of the five holes he'd played on Friday, a WD with an ice pack on a wrist would look better in the papers than an 80 and an MC. That year Woods had already had his first arthroscopic surgery on the left knee that would betray him. He was a phenomenon, all right, but I'd already seen too many can't-misses who missed. Put me down for skeptical.

In '96 I stopped in Stillwater, Oklahoma, to work on a piece about Mike Holder, the legendary Oklahoma State University (OSU) golf coach who would become the university's athletic director. Mike was, and still is, a tough guy, and you don't have to shoot up his ex-players with Sodium Pentothal to get them to tell you so. When Bob Tway, who holed out from a bunker to beat Greg Norman in the '86 PGA Championship, was at OSU, he and Holder got into an honest-to-God rolling-around-on-the-ground wrestling match on the practice tee when Tway had the nerve to complain about the quality of the range balls.

Holder insisted his players qualify for their spots on the team. When the Stillwater weather was particularly odious—cold and rainy with a wind that starts blowing somewhere east of Santa Fe, what they politely refer to as winter in Oklahoma—Holder would take great delight in announcing the team's qualifying scores would count double. As a direct consequence of this, any time the weather was particularly awful in a PGA Tour event the leader board would be littered with the names of Oklahoma State's alums. Willie Wood, who was at OSU the same time as Tway, once had a closed-door meeting with the coach. He had the temerity to suggest that since he, Willie Wood, was an All-American, he shouldn't have to qualify. Holder looked at him and said, "Willie, we'd be better with you, but we'll be just fine without you." He qualified.

Tiger Woods, who had already had his "hello world" moment in the Milwaukee Open, was a topic of my conversation with Holder on that trip. I hadn't been to any of Woods's U.S. Amateur victories or to his earliest carding-securing wins in Las Vegas or Orlando. All I'd seen him do was finish far off the pace or, worse yet, not at all in major championships. I asked Holder what he thought of him. "He's going to win the Masters," he said. Rookies don't win the Masters, I said, even if they've played there before. "You really think he's that good?" I asked Holder. "No," he replied. "I *know* he's that good."

For whatever reason, Woods has always had trouble getting off the first tee. Only he knows where that comes from, but long ago I decided it was because he was never quite sure who was going to show up that day and he was always just a little bit afraid it might not be Tiger Woods. It convinced me there was a Jungian persona who wore a red shirt and another opposite self altogether. Dr. Bob Rotella, a sports psychologist, has a favorite story about Sam Snead. He says Snead once told him that, in his prime, after a round he'd always take a shower at the club where they were playing because where Sam grew up, they didn't have hot showers. He'd stand in it as long he could keep getting hot water and replay his round. Any shots that hadn't gone well he'd visualize playing them perfectly. When he got out of the shower he'd forget about golf until he went to bed. In bed he'd visualize the next day's round, striking the ball just the way he wanted. At some point in his career, Sam told Rotella, he started getting in the shower after rounds and seeing only his bad shots. Sometimes at dinner he would start thinking about his bad stuff. He couldn't forget about it. In bed at night he'd see mistakes. Snead said he questioned whether he ought to keep playing, that he was embarrassing his own reputation, and that when they introduced him on the first tee, he worried whether he could live up to what they were saying about him, afraid that he wasn't going to play golf like Sam Snead. Who knows if Tiger, when he was playing like a twenty-handicapper at the beginning of 2015, got to where Snead got? Maybe he didn't or maybe he already had. Maybe it was part of the two-year-old who walked onto Mike Douglas's set. What's remarkable isn't that he had trouble on the first tee; it was that he could so overwhelm his doubt with talent and training. That was Earl. It was very Green Beret. The gym where I sweat every day in North Carolina is full of special-operations soldiers from nearby Fort Bragg. If you wonder how Woods could be so foolish as to hurt himself lifting weights, they don't. They train because they don't dare not train. The cost is too high.

In the 1997 Masters Woods hooked his opening-tee ball into the trees on the left and ultimately made bogey from a greenside bunker on his way to a front nine of 40. After the ninth Jung showed up. He birdied the tenth, chipped in on the twelfth, hit driver and six-iron for a two-putt birdie at the thirteenth, and, more remarkably, a driver and wedge at the par-five fifteenth for eagle. A wedge into the seventeenth allowed him to close with a back nine of 30. The rout was on. After Woods took the second-round lead, no one had a better seat or explained what was about to happen any better than Colin Montgomerie, who joined Woods in the final pair on Saturday.

Three shots behind, Montgomerie was anxious for the third-round match-up. After all, just the year before Nick Faldo had come from six back to dismantle Greg Norman. Montgomerie, the son of the man who at one time ran venerable old Fox's Biscuits, a company whose modern slogan is "More Yum per Crumb," imagined himself Faldo to Woods's Norman. Monty had gathered more than just crumbs on the European Tour, having already been the Order of Merit winner four times by the time he faced Tiger Woods. He would go on to top their money list four more times and would be the European Tour player of the year four times. He lost the '94 U.S. Open in a three-man playoff to Ernie Els and the '95 PGA in a playoff to Australian Steve Elkington. Though he'd never win a major championship, he'd finish runner-up in five. In '92 at Pebble Beach, in his first U.S. Open, Montgomerie shot an early two-under-par 70 the final day in howling winds to post an even-par 288, prompting Jack Nicklaus, working in a television booth, to congratulate him on winning the Open four hours before Tom Kite, who pitched in on the 105-yard downhill seventh after missing the green with a full-blooded six-iron, actually did. In the '06 U.S. Open at Winged Foot, Monty was one of the players who came to the eighteenth with a chance to win. He stood in the fairway arguing with himself like Hamlet until, unfortunately for him, he won, picking a seven-iron instead of the six- and hitting it fat, short, and right, to forfeit his last best chance at a major. In '05 he finished five shots behind Woods in the Open Championship at St. Andrews but was never really a factor. As Monty later put it, "It was great to be in contention on a course which was built for Tiger 200 years before he was born." Montgomerie would never lose a singles match in Ryder Cup competition and captained the victorious European team at soggy Celtic Manor in Wales in 2010. Woods at Augusta, however, was playing for himself, not God and Country.

After Monty shot 74 to Tiger's 65 that Saturday, he came into the Augusta National media center, sat down, and said, "All I have to say is one brief comment today. There is no chance. We're all human beings here. There's no way does Tiger Woods not win tomorrow." Woods had a nine-shot lead over the Italian Constantino Rocca, who had putted through the Valley of Sin to tie John Daly at the Old Course in the Open Championship two years before and then lost the playoff. Someone asked how Monty could be so certain. "Did you just arrive?" he shot back. "Have you been on holiday?" Someone else mentioned Faldo and Norman. "This is different. Very different. Costantino Rocca is not Nick Faldo and Tiger Woods is not Greg Norman."

It was all over but the inviting of Lee Elder, who drove 570 miles from his home in Pompano Beach, Florida, to be there Sunday. The first black man to play in the Masters came back to watch the first black man win it. Woods shot a final round of three-under-par 69 to win by twelve. He was the youngest player ever to win the Masters and set the bar for the largest margin of victory at the same time. He came off the eighteenth green, into the arms of his father, Earl. "I made history here," a tearful Elder said, "and I came back to see more history made. To have a black champion of a major is something that makes my heart feel very, very good. Tiger winning here, it could have more potential than Jackie Robinson breaking baseball's color barrier." But if Earl overshot on Gandhi, Elder whiffed on the whole Jackie Robinson thing, too. It wasn't part of the package.

Tigermania took flight. Woods knew he could overpower Augusta National with its generous fairways and lack of rough, but a U.S. Open or a PGA, with narrow fairways and thick rough, would be something else again. The thirsty young Woods wanted a game that could scoop up double handfuls from the major championship river. After all, he was chasing the number eighteen, all of them posted on his bedroom wall. He turned to his instructor, Butch Harmon, a Vietnam combat veteran whose most famous previous pupils had been the king of Morocco and Greg Norman. Harmon thought the reworking would be so dramatic that Woods might have to shut it down for a year, the way Nick Faldo had with David Leadbetter. Woods thought otherwise. Harmon, whose given name was Claude, was the eldest of the four sons of

Claude Harmon, the 1948 Masters champion. All became teaching or club pros of consequence, passing on the wisdom of their father, who had been a close friend of Ben Hogan. In Tiger's case Butch believed that because Woods's hips unwound so fast in the downswing, faster probably than anyone who ever played the game, he needed to keep his club short of parallel at the top and reduce as much as possible the amount it crossed the line. Then, if Woods could keep from getting his right elbow behind his body, he could uncoil as fast as he wanted, producing slightly less power but more accuracy. Harmon figured if Woods could play from the fairway, his towering irons and remarkable short game would make him invincible.

The transition wasn't quick. Woods won twice more in '97 but only once in '98, when he and Harmon were doing the heavy lifting. For a period of years after his Masters breakthrough, extending through his magical year in 2000, Woods devoted time to giving clinics for inner-city kids in large metropolitan areas and simultaneously raising money for what would become the Tiger Woods Foundation. Stops included Minneapolis, Cincinnati, Indianapolis, Denver, New Orleans, and Chicago, among others. Tiger would enter his clinics from the back of a driving range on a charging golf cart as loudspeakers blared Survivor's "Eye of the Tiger." Earl kicked off the clinics with his "Caring and Sharing" speech, and Tiger would follow. Sometimes there was a gathering at a neighborhood African Methodist Episcopal church in the evening. More often there was a dinner for large donors and a charity auction. As part of these clinics Tiger typically took two waves of roughly twenty-five or thirty kids, most of whom didn't know which end of the club to hold much less that there was a right way and a wrong way to do it. Before long it became obvious busing kids out of the inner city for an afternoon of laying the sod over range balls under the hot sun and then sending them right back to a life where they'd never again see a golf course except on television wasn't really helping anyone. The realization took Tiger and Earl, in particular, out of the Pied Piper mentality and pulled them into the world of bricks, mortar, and scholarships.

Because I was at more than a few of these clinics, I saw Tiger away from the pandemonium that surrounded him whenever he played a tournament. Each practice-tee session with the kids could take an hour, sometimes more. Woods spent time with every child. He'd stand behind them and watch them hit a ball or two, even the ones who couldn't dream of making contact. Then, he would step up to them, put out his hand, and introduce himself. "Hi, I'm Tiger Woods. What's your name?" One of his clinics, it may have been Indianapolis, was on a brutally hot afternoon. The ball-park had to be one hundred degrees down the right-field line and worse with the heat index in dead center. There was a small tent with iced bottled water where Tiger could take a break between sessions. I was standing outside with sweat dripping from every pore of my body. I looked at him and said, "Let me get this right. If I stroke out, you're not performing mouth-to-mouth resuscitation on me, are you?" He looked at me, smiled, and said, "See you on the other side, brother." At another clinic, in Cincinnati, Tiger was watching a black teenager, Kevin Hall, who was deaf. The kid could really hit it, a rarity at these things. Tiger watched him nail a couple of drivers and then whispered something to Hall's mother, who relayed the advice to Hall using sign language. The next drive flew twenty yards farther. Hall turned and looked at Tiger with a smile larger than Woods's own. A few years later Hall won the Big Ten Championship playing for Ohio State. In those years I saw Woods interacting with a few women, too. He was single, rich, young, and one of the most famous athletes on the face of the planet. And he behaved like he was single, rich, young, and one of the most famous athletes on the planet. Life was good.

By 1999 the changes Woods and Harmon were working on had begun to kick in. The first three majors of the season were so dramatic in their own right, they cloaked the trajectory Woods was on. At Augusta National José Maria Olazábal, who had battled back from a case of rheumatoid arthritis that, at times, had limited his ability to walk so severely he had to crawl to the bathroom, won a second Masters. "When I was at my lowest, I never thought about this," the Spaniard said of winning another green jacket. "I thought I would never play golf again." On an uncharacteristically chilly, drizzly day in June at the U.S. Open, Payne Stewart made a dramatic winning putt on the eighteenth green of Pinehurst's No. 2 Course to beat Phil Mickelson, the expectant father, by a shot. Stewart would die in a plane crash a few months later. And at the Open Championship at Carnoustie, Frenchman Jean Van de Velde took a three-shot lead to the eighteenth tee but ended up in the Barry Burn, water up to his fetlocks, and in a three-way playoff eventually won by Scotsman Paul Lawrie, who had started the day ten shots behind him. While Woods had won at Torrey Pines (the first of eight victories there, including the 2008 U.S. Open), at Muirfield Village, and at Cog Hill G&CC, his best chance at a major prior to the PGA was at Pinehurst. He'd gone into Sunday two shots out of Stewart's lead and finished that way but not before he made a birdie on the sixteenth, the converted par five, and lipped out for birdie on both the seventeenth and the eighteenth. It was the first inkling of what was to come. August and the PGA would mark the beginning of one of the greatest sustained stretches of excellence in the history of championship golf.

Going into the last major championship of the twentieth century, Woods was undeniably the number-one player in golf, yet he'd been unable to build on his historic and overpowering victory at Augusta National two years before. In Chicago at Medinah CC, the big story early in the week was the controversy brewing over payments (or, more precisely, nonpayments) to players for participating in the Ryder Cup. The host, the PGA of America, got huffy about the topic on one side, and so did Woods, Mickelson, Mark O'Meara, and David Duval on the other. A nineteen-year-old Spaniard, Sergio Garcia, took the opening-round lead with a 66 and won over the Chicago galleries with his puppy-dog enthusiasm. By Saturday night Woods was tied for the lead with Canadian left-hander Mike Weir, who would win the Masters four years later to end what would be, at the time, Woods's two-year reign. They were two shots ahead of Garcia and Stewart Cink, a lanky twenty-six-year-old American who became best known for beating a fifty-nine-year-old Tom Watson in the Open Championship at Turnberry ten years on.

Woods looked to have put the tournament away, building a five-shot lead with eight holes to play on Sunday. The last seven times he'd either led or been tied for the lead going into the final round of a tournament, he'd won, usually quite handily. This looked like just the latest in the string. Woods three-putted the twelfth to drop a shot, however, and when Garcia birdied the par-three thirteenth, the young Spaniard shook his fist at Woods, across Lake Kadijah and back up the hill on the tee. Garcia claimed it was all in good fun. Woods didn't play golf for fun. He double-bogeyed the hole, and the lead dwindled to one. That fist was the beginning of a less than beautiful friendship. In the following years their feud would escalate after Garcia's excessive celebration in a made-for-TV contest, one of the Battle at Bighorn events; grow through Woods's description of his bludgeoning of Tweety Bird after he beat the head-to-toe-yellow-clad Garcia in the '06 Open Championship; blossom into complaints of purposely distracting an opponent when Woods pulled a club out of his bag at the Players Championship as Garcia was making a stroke on the second hole; and ultimately find its way into a European Tour awards dinner with an ill-advised comment about fried chicken. But back to Medinah.

After bogeying the fifteenth to put Woods back in front by two, Garcia drove his ball between two fingerling roots of an oak tree at the corner of the dogleg on the sixteenth. The ball looked like it had nestled between the toes of a velociraptor. Closing his eyes, he launched a high, slicing six-iron at the green and went in hot pursuit after it, running up the fairway, bounding like a white-tailed deer in a blue golf shirt to see where it landed. He made par there and finished with two more. After bogeying the sixteenth Woods was up by a single shot. He made a clutch eight-footer for par at the seventeenth and closed it out with a routine four at the last. "Getting number two is definitely a relief," a shaken Woods said. There was much, much more to come.

Vijay Singh, the Fijian who had been suspended by the Asian Tour in 1985 and endured a self-imposed exile to a club job in Borneo for two years over a dispute involving one of his scorecards in the Indonesian Open, won the second of his three career major championships in the Masters of 2000. The undisputed king of the tireless ball beaters on the PGA Tour, Singh took a three-shot lead over David Duval into the final day, and while Duval closed to within a shot at one point, Singh held on for the victory. From June 1998 until October 2005, no player outside of Woods, Singh, or Duval would claim the world's number-one ranking, with Woods holding the position the overwhelming majority of the time. Trying for a second consecutive major title at Augusta National, Woods had opened with a 75 to make Singh's job easier. It would be the worst score Woods would post in any major championship until the third round of the Open Championship at Muirfield in 2002, when he got caught out in twenty-five-mile-an-hour winds and sideways rain and shot 81. Including Medinah the year before, Singh's Masters victory would be the only thing that kept Woods from winning six straight majors.

No golfer on Earth was going to beat Tiger Woods at Pebble Beach. Maybe no golfer who ever lived, at the top of *their* game, could have beaten him. Not Jones or Hogan or Hagen or Snead or Nicklaus or Palmer or Player or the lot together, though it would have been fun to watch them try. Woods won by fifteen shots. He took a ten-shot lead into the last round. That week he found just under three-quarters of the fairways and led the field in driving distance at a seal's whisker below three hundred yards. He hit a couple of tenths under three-quarters of the greens and averaged only twenty-seven putts a round on Pebble's notoriously quixotic surfaces. He was twelve under par, and Ernie Els and Miguel Ángel Jiménez tied for second at three over. Els played with Woods in the final round Sunday. When it was all over and they were in the scoring area together, Ernie jokingly cautioned Tiger with words to the effect of: "Make sure that card is correct. I don't want to have to come back here tomorrow to play Jiménez."

It was during the second round when Woods ripped a seven-iron out of the right rough from 208 yards over the one-hundred-foot blind incline to twelve feet on the sixth green that caused NBC's Roger Maltbie to utter the most famous phrase of his announcing career, "Guys, this is just not a fair fight." There were more superlatives flying around Pebble Beach than seagulls. "If I played out of my mind, I probably would have lost by five, six or seven shots," said Els. Rocco Mediate, who would lose to Woods so dramatically in a playoff in another U.S. Open on the California coastline in

2008 at Torrey Pines, said, "I actually had people asking me if anyone could catch him. Catch him? Are you kidding me? As long as he was upright, he was going to win. A lot of people have trouble with the comments some people have made about Woods but the truth is the truth."

Pebble Beach's eighteenth is one of golf's greatest home holes, and that year it was the scene of a Tuesday-morning send-off for Payne Stewart. Twenty golfers and Stewart's longtime caddie, Mike Hicks, lined up along the fairway to drive twenty-one golf balls into the ocean. Woods was not among them. The eighteenth was also the hole where John Daly, already on his downward slide, made a cozy fourteen. And it was the hole where the only person who could have prevented Tiger Woods from winning that U.S. Open—Tiger Woods—nearly did exactly that.

Because of a couple of fog delays, the finish of the second round was pushed into Saturday morning. On the eighteenth tee Woods hooked his tee shot onto the rocks, unleashing a daunting percentage of the seven words George Carlin said you can't say on TV into a live microphone. What was potentially worse was that the night before, dissatisfied with his putting stroke, Woods had taken the seven golf balls he had in his bag to his room behind the eighteenth green in the lodge for a little late-night practice. In the morning he left three of them there. After play resumed he gave a ball to a kid on the thirteenth and did it again on the fourteenth. When Woods hooked his tee shot out-of-bounds on the eighteenth, Williams offered him an iron to get the next shot in play. Woods gave him an angry stare. He took the new ball and blasted away again with his driver, eventually making double-bogey seven. Later Woods asked Williams about the iron. "Last ball," Williams said. Now, had Woods lost that one, too, he would have been allowed to borrow a ball from another player as long as it was the same make, model, and so on. The trouble, however, was that Woods was playing a new Nike ball, a prototype, and no one else had any. The only other option would be sending Williams scurrying to Woods's room to retrieve one of the balls he left there. If he delayed play for more than fifteen minutes, he'd have been out of luck. Instead, he had a six-shot lead.

"You keep hearing that he's young and he'll learn it's not that easy," Singh said, "and wait until he starts missing those six and eight footers. Meanwhile, he keeps making them. Amazing." That day would come, but not soon. Selected to the World Golf Hall of Fame that same year, Sir Michael Bonnallack, the five-time British Amateur champion who had recently retired as secretary of the Royal and Ancient said, "If Tiger doesn't win at St. Andrews, there should be a stewards' inquiry." It would not prove necessary.

Woods was one claret jug shy of the career Slam and a seemingly unstoppable force. His opponents weren't so much intimidated as they were discouraged. They were happy to concede, if Woods played his best and they played their best, Woods was going to win, maybe by a lot. This, they could accept, if grudgingly. What was so utterly demoralizing was that he was showing no signs of ever being less than his best. The door never opened, not even a crack. This was far more disconcerting than the mere fact that he was better than they were. Woods had sent people who thought Old Tom Morris was a brand of bourbon back to the days of tweed coats, silk ties, and rut irons to find dusty old records to measure him against.

Els, who had finished so far behind Woods just weeks before at Pebble Beach, led him by a shot after the first round at the Old Course. By the time the second round was finished, Woods was in the lead by three and by six after fifty-four holes in calm conditions. David Duval, nursing a bad back, cut the Woods advantage to three on Sunday but lost it in the loop, the shepherd's crook where the course turns on itself out by the River Eden and heads home to the Jigger Inn and the R&A. By the time the twosome got to the twelfth, the six-shot lead had been restored. Duval would have a disaster in the Road Hole Bunker, taking four to get out, but the issue had been long since decided when that happened. The next year the Jacksonville, Florida, native would come close to derailing the Tiger Slam, then win the Open Championship at Royal Lytham and St. Annes, validating the number-one ranking he held briefly in '99. After that he began one of the more mysterious career slides golf ever witnessed. Duval, whose voice had a quavering, breathless quality to it, was one of the more introspective players on the PGA Tour, if not always one of the most agreeable. With a thick lower body reminiscent of Nicklaus, Duval's upper body changed almost as much as Woods's, going from pudgy to ripped, then backsliding into middle-aged recliner ready. Armchair psychologists made much of the painful operation Duval endured when he was nine to extract bone marrow for what proved to be an unsuccessful donation to his older brother, Brent, who suffered from, and succumbed to, aplastic anemia at the age of twelve. But if there were emotional scars, it would seem far more likely to have had something to do with what the loss of a brother and a son can do to a family than a painful surgical procedure.

After being the number-one player in the world and winning his major championship, having bursitis, tendonitis, Achilles' problems, hip problems, and a bout of vertigo, Duval would finish in the top five in only one more major, the 2009 U.S. Open at waterlogged Bethpage Black, where he was two shots behind Lucas Glover, tied for second with Phil Mickelson and Ricky Barnes. Mostly, Duval missed cuts or didn't even qualify. Some theorized he had been to the top of the mountain and decided the view wasn't worth it. "Is that all there is?" was the phrase attached to him. He told Woody Paige for *Mile High Sports*, "Somebody asked me, 'Are you famous?' And I said, 'I used to be.' And everybody made a big deal about it, and I never quite understood what the big deal was." But for Woods, unlike Duval, the top of the mountain was the only place he could breathe.

When Woods won by eight strokes at St. Andrews with the lowest score, 269, ever shot on the most historic terrain the game has, he became the youngest player to complete the career Slam, joining Gene Sarazen, Ben Hogan, Jack Nicklaus, and Gary Player as the big five. Woods was twenty-four. Nicklaus had been twenty-six. Woods arrived not just younger but faster than the rest, too, though that was complicated by history. In Sarazen's case the Masters didn't exist for much of his career, and the late-blooming Hogan, of course, made just one trip to the Open Championship, winning it at Carnoustie and never going back. Still, Woods was a god among gods. Fittingly, the next venue would be Valhalla.

Woods had won the last two major championships by a combined twenty-three shots. His competition looked to have been rolled up like a beef burrito. Was Garcia, the teenage Spaniard, the only one capable of giving him a game? It turned out the best golf could muster was a journeyman named Bob May. But what a journeyman. Both May and Woods had grown up in Orange County, California, one the son of a gas station owner, the other the son of a special-forces lieutenant colonel. May was tough as tree bark, and he found a natural home at Oklahoma State, playing for the equally tough Mike Holder. May had been a member of the victorious 1991 Walker Cup team with Phil Mickelson. He had qualified for the LA Open at Riviera cc when he was sixteen. Woods, who was seven years younger than May, got into the same PGA Tour event at an earlier age, but it was on a sponsor's invitation. Turnabout was fair play since that was exactly how May got into the PGA Championship at Valhalla GC outside Louisville, Kentucky, in August 2000.

Valhalla is a Jack Nicklaus–designed course built under power lines and owned by the PGA of America. Louisville was the hometown of Muhammad Ali, who claimed to have thrown his Olympic gold medal into the Ohio River after being refused service at a diner, a story that's been debunked in various places—the river part, not the diner. Kentucky and Indiana, on either side of the Ohio River, shared a racial history rich in its Ku Klux Klan roots. When the wisecracking Fuzzy Zoeller misspoke at the '97 Masters with comments about the menu of the next year's champion's dinner, as unintended as the racial overtones surely were, it was also worth remembering he grew up in New Albany, Indiana, right across the river from Louisville.

Woods knew who Bob May was only too well. Before he could begin breaking Jack Nicklaus's records, he had to knock down May's. "When I grew up in San Diego, Bob May dominated," Mickelson said. "He won every Southern California junior title there was. He's also a tough competitor. Bob was one of the most difficult guys to beat head-to-head." When the two of them went into Sunday afternoon at Valhalla with Woods holding a slim one-shot lead over May, neither was surprised the fight went the distance, and then some. Tied going to the back nine, May birdied four of the next five holes, but that was only good enough to get his nose one shot in front of Woods. At the fifteenth Woods made a crucial fifteen-footer to save par, while May missed a six-footer for birdie that could have stretched his lead. Woods tied him with a birdie on the seventeenth, and they both made dramatic birdie putts on the eighteenth to go into extra holes.

The sixteenth was the first of the three-hole aggregate playoff, and Woods jumped into the lead immediately with a seven-iron to eighteen feet and a putt that tracked straight at the hole as he ran after it, pointing at the ball as it toppled into the cup. They both parred the next two, and Woods had won his third straight major, the first player to win three in a single year since Ben Hogan in 1953. "We never backed off from one another, birdie-for-birdie, shot-for-shot, we were going right at each other," Woods said. "Both of us shoot 31 on the back nine on Sunday afternoon with no bogeys. It was just as good as it gets."

It was as good as it would ever get for Bob May. His back blew out in 2003, a combination of herniated discs and a structural abnormality in his spinal canal that caused repetitive pinched nerves. He played all four majors the year after he lost to Woods in Kentucky but never got into another one after that. May had back surgery in 2004 and, after a couple of attempts to return to tournament golf, wound up with his own teaching academy in Las Vegas. Woods, on the other hand, advanced to the Tiger Slam.

The money shot from the 2001 Masters was Tiger Woods standing on the edge of the eighteenth green at Augusta National holding his cap over his face, composing himself after he'd made a birdie putt he didn't need. "I'm done. I just won the Masters," Woods said. "When I didn't have any more shots to play, that's when I started to realize what I had done and I started getting a little emotional. That's why I put the cap over my face, to pull it together, so that when Phil made his putt, I was able to shake his hand." Woods had done something no other golfer who ever lived had done—he would be the simultaneous titleholder of the four professional major championships. Purists, whatever that means in the context of an achievement that previously had never been accomplished, claimed some fanciful sine qua non that the championships had to be won in the same calendar year to be a "true" Grand Slam. You might just as well have been chuffed at Sir Edmund Hillary for dawdling his way up Mount Everest, having started in March but not reaching the summit until May. Not quite "grand" enough, it was dubbed the Tiger Slam. Bobby Jones got his first ticker-tape parade in New York City in 1926 and a second after he was halfway to his 1930 Slam, the impregnable quadrilateral. Ben Hogan got showered with paper after he stepped off the USS *United States* in 1953 following his third major victory of the year in the Open Championship at Carnoustie. While the currency of your basic ticker-tape parade devalued some over time—the 1927 Yankees didn't get one, but they were giving them to the president of Tunisia by the 1960s—Woods celebrated the Tiger Slam by getting the flu and, after that, making a video game for EA Sports.

"It's harder to accomplish a Grand Slam in one year, there's no doubt about that," Woods said. "But I think if you can put all four trophies on your coffee table, you can make a pretty good case for that, too." Indeed.

Woods entered that Masters Sunday playing with Phil Mickelson, who trailed him by a shot. They were, at the time, the number-one and number-two (if a distant number-two) players in the world. Until the Deutsche Bank of 2007 where the balance of power shifted, Woods held a decided head-to-head advantage over Mickelson, going 10-5-3 when they were paired together. It was all the sweeter this time because it was the final round of not just a major but a historic one at that. While Mickelson lost his chance when he three-putted the sixteenth after leaving his tee shot on the back-right upper shelf of the steeply sloped green, it was David Duval who nearly managed to sour what would be Woods's seminal achievement. Duval's birdie at the fifteenth tied him for the lead with Woods, but his seven-iron at the sixteenth went over the green and he fell a shot back just that fast. Missed birdie chances at the seventeenth and eighteenth allowed Woods to par the fifteenth, sixteenth, and seventeenth before making an eighteen-footer for birdie at the last for his sixth major championship overall and fifth in the last six, an edifice of dominance, a Great Wall built to keep his peers out. Mickelson would finish three back, his twelfth top ten in a major. It would be three months before Duval would break through in the Open Championship and three years before Mickelson leaped into his own green jacket. When the champion's interview was ending in the media center, Augusta National member Billy Payne, who was presiding, said, "Tiger, we are all very proud of you. Congratulations on your second Masters Championship." When Woods returned eight Aprils later and Payne was the chairman of Augusta National, the reception would be decidedly chillier.

After winning at Augusta Woods didn't play again until the Verizon Byron Nelson Classic in May. A serious student of golf history, while Nelson was alive Woods rarely passed up the opportunity to shake hands with one of golf's great gentlemen in the viewing stand at the eighteenth green of the tournament that bore his name. There was no year more appropriate for that meeting than 2001. Woods was asked to compare his Slam with Nelson's streak of eleven straight in 1945. "I just had to peak four times. He did it 11 consecutive times," Woods said. "I did mine in major championships. He only won one that year because that was the only major they held that year. Both of them are unique in different ways, his is for consistency and mine is just for peaking at the right time." Though he won twice more after the Masters, it felt as though Woods had released all the air from the balloon when he blew into his cap on the eighteenth green at Augusta. His weariness seemed to surprise even him, but it didn't last long.

The following April Woods joined Jack Nicklaus and Nick Faldo as the only players to successfully defend a Masters title. Augusta National had taken its first steps in what was euphemistically called "Tiger-proofing" the golf course by lengthening it three hundred yards. The added distance boomeranged, playing into the hands of the longest hitters, and Woods was still in the top handful, or just a hangnail shy of it. The first, seventh, ninth, tenth, eleventh, and eighteenth tees were pushed well back. Land was purchased from Augusta CC, the Donald Ross–designed course next door to Augusta National, just to build a new back tee for the iconic thirteenth. The end result wasn't Tiger-proofing the course but serving it up to him like a suckling pig in a luau. The top six players going into Masters Sunday were Woods, Retief Goosen, Vijay Singh, Phil Mickelson, Sergio Garcia, and Ernie Els. Not a bunter in the bunch. Goosen and Garcia faded fast. Els made an eight on the thirteenth. Singh did him one better, taking a nine on the fifteenth. Six shots behind with eleven to play, Mickelson could make just one birdie. It was impossible to escape the perception that the top players in the game seemed incapable of giving chase. It was Tiger Woods and the (pick-a-number) dwarfs. He coasted home three shots clear. All that was left was for Augusta National chairman, Hootie Johnson, to step into the role of the defending champion to slip the green coat on the winner. Those who one day would find fault with Woods's record of achievement claimed that, while Nicklaus had to beat Palmer, Trevino, Watson, and so on, Woods beat nobodies. If there was ever any truth to it, and there wasn't much, it was only because he scared off all the somebodies first.

Two months later Woods was equally dominant when the U.S. Open went to a truly public golf course (as opposed to "resort" courses like Pebble Beach and Pinehurst), the Black Course at Bethpage State Park on New York's Long Island. Sheer length was an even bigger factor at Bethpage than it had been at Augusta National. The weather went sour on the USGA, not quite as horrific as the deluge they encountered there in 2009 that forced a Monday finish when the course became a quagmire, but cold enough and rainy enough that a good third of the field couldn't even reach the fairway on the tenth and eleventh holes. While the raucous New York crowds were adopting Phil Mickelson, who would push his personal record to 0-40 in major championships, and ridiculing Sergio Garcia by counting out loud as he nervously gripped and regripped his club in a kind of manual dystonia, Woods led after the first, second, and third rounds and took a four-shot lead into Sunday. Mickelson provided the only serious challenge of the day, pulling to within two, but in an echo of the missteps by Woods's pursuers at Augusta, he bogeyed the sixteenth and seventeenth. Woods won by three. Not since Nicklaus won the Masters and the U.S. Open thirty years before had anyone gone into the Open Championship with thoughts of winning all four majors in the same year. "It's certainly do-able," Woods said, weary of his own four in a row being characterized as somehow flawed, "because I've done it before."

The two biggest collectors of major championship titles in the history of the game each would have hopes of a calendar Slam dashed in Gullane, Scotland, at the Honourable Company of Edinburgh Golfers. Nicklaus was pipped by Lee Trevino, who successfully defended his title when he chipped in for par on Muirfield's seventeenth, though it looked like he was making little more than a dispirited pass at the ball after going through the green in four. The hole out for par simultaneously drove a stake into the heart of Tony Jacklin, who was tied with him at the time and would three-putt from eighteen feet. It was a massive blow from which Jacklin, by his own reckoning, never recovered. The chip in kept Trevino a shot ahead of Nicklaus, who had finished ahead of him. Conversely, thirty years later, Woods was forced to hunker down under his umbrella to survive the vicious afternoon squall that blew him right off the giant yellow leader board. The early players had been spared the twenty-five-mile-per-hour winds with gusts strong enough moles could hang glide, the perpendicular rain, and bone-chilling cold, but Woods, who had started the third round just two shots off the pace, was among those who suffered the worst of it. In truth, others handled the conditions better. Destiny, it seemed, had taken a hand, and Woods believed in destiny, especially his own. The 81 he shot that day would be the worst score Woods recorded as a professional until he yipped and chipped his way to an embarrassing 82 at the TPC Scottsdale followed by a wretched 85 at Nicklaus's Memorial Tournament thirteen years later during his odyssey through humiliation and injury.

The disappointment of being blown out of contention at Muirfield was magnified when Woods, who had never won a major championship coming from behind, birdied the last four holes at Hazeltine National GC outside Minneapolis, Minnesota, to come up one stroke shy of catching Rich Beem, a bookend journeyman to Bob May, but without May's amateur résumé. If ever a player deserved the characterization of journeyman, it was Beem, whose voyage to major champion had been an odd one indeed. Days shy of his thirty-second birthday, Beem carried a card in his wallet to remind him of the time he'd spent selling cell phones at the Magnolia Hi-Fi Buy in Seattle for seven dollars an hour before he took a job as an assistant pro at El Paso CC, the Texas town where he grew up. Beem won the International, a points-based (rather than stroke- or match-based) competition in Colorado, the week before the PGA for his second victory on tour. His first came in his rookie season three years before, a year of wild living chronicled in the book *Bud, Sweat and Tees* about his exploits with then caddie Steve Duplantis. By 2002 Beem was married and had a new caddie, Billy Hein. Duplantis would step off the curb and be struck and killed by a taxi near Camino Del Mar and Fifteenth Street in Del Mar, California, just after midnight on January 23, 2008, when he was caddying in the Buick Invitational at Torrey Pines. Woods would win that tournament and come back in June to win the U.S. Open on a broken leg at the same golf course. After the 2002 PGA Championship, Beem never won again on the PGA Tour. His next most visible moment was when he made a hole in one in the 2007 Nissan Los Angeles Open on the fourteenth at Riviera CC to win a car and jumped on top of a red 300ZX behind the tee box. The year after his Hazeltine victory Beem would finish T15 in the Masters but never be inside the top twenty in a major after that. He had back surgery in 2010 and tried to play in Europe for a year. Possessing a nonchalant, almost glib, self-deprecating wit and easy manner with a microphone, he found his way into television.

Had it not been for God and Scotland and Rich Beem, Woods could well have had his calendar Slam in addition to the eponymous one. As it was he had won eight major championships in his first six years as a professional, a feat all the more remarkable because of the swing change and mini slump after the '97 Masters. By comparison Jack Nicklaus won seven majors in his first six seasons as a professional. After their great beginnings, neither Nicklaus nor Woods would win a major championship in their following two seasons. Of his quiet period in 1968–69, in *My Story*, Nicklaus says:

I realized that for much of the time from 1967 through 1969 I had been attempting to win by forcing good scores. So often during that period I would follow a minor error with a more costly mistake by taking a dumb risk or pressing my swing to produce an improbable shot. Reflecting on this, it dawned on me that there was still plenty of time. Bob Jones may have won his thirteen majors in only eight years then retired at twenty-eight, but Ben Hogan had won all nine of his in his thirties and forties . . . and look at Sam Snead for longevity. Everyone with an ounce of common sense knew golf required patience above all else.

Nicklaus's family was growing. He was venturing into course design, assisting Pete Dye at the Harbour Town Golf Links that would open in '69. Corleone-like, the Nicklauses were making the move from cold Columbus, Ohio, to warm Palm Beach, Florida. He was preparing to take over his own business affairs from Mark McCormack, something that would happen after the death of his father, Charlie, of pancreatic cancer in 1970.

For Woods, those two quiet years of 2003–4 weren't so quiet, either. At the 2001 Open Championship at Royal Lytham and St. Annes, Swedish golfer Jesper Parnevik, who might well have won the 1994 Open Championship at Turnberry had he chosen to look at a scoreboard before playing the eighteenth, introduced Woods to former Swedish model Elin Nordegren, who was the nanny to his four children. Woods and Nordegren didn't begin dating until the following year, but by 2003 they were traveling together, including a trip to the Presidents Cup at the Links Course at Fancourt Hotel and Country Club in George, Western Cape, South Africa. They became engaged on a trip to the Shamwari Game Reserve near Port Elizabeth. The wedding ceremony was held at the posh Sandy Lane resort in Barbados in October 2004. Such was Woods's worldwide celebrity that the wedding attracted the kind of paparazzi who ordinarily have grander things to do, pursuing misbehaving Hollywood stars or corrupt government officials. One photographer, undeterred by the hot tropical sun, camped out for days inside a pump station on the golf course in an attempt to get a few precious frames of the couple. Still others rented a house with a view (with the help of telephoto lenses) into the resort's front entrance. They were thwarted by a crane hoisting a giant panel to block their shots like Hakeem Olajuwon defending the rim of the basket from point guards driving the lane.

From his "hello, world" moment on, Woods had a healthy contempt for anyone he believed was exploiting his, Woods's, fame for their own enrichment, his own colossal and highly lucrative business relationships notwithstanding. When his first caddie, Mike "Fluff" Cowan, who carried his bag during his twelve-shot victory in the 1997 Masters, parlayed his bushy mustache and famous boss into a commercial for Choice Hotels International, he was quickly switched out in favor of the dour and more tight-lipped Steve Williams, a New Zealander who had previously worked with both Raymond Floyd and Greg Norman. "Tiger was just a kid when I worked for him," Cowan said years later. "He enjoyed having a really fun time. Just wholesome fun. Video games. Telling jokes. We played some pool together." Not after Cowan cashed in.

Woods's relationship with swing instructor Butch Harmon was deeper and more difficult to break off. They had been together through all three of Woods's U.S. Amateur victories and his eight major titles, including the Tiger Slam and the impeccable run in 2000. The blunt and gregarious Harmon was likewise viewed as cashing in, including a gig as commentator for Sky TV in Great Britain, his teaching center in Las Vegas, a magazine deal, and his own product endorsements. By the 2002 PGA Championship Woods said he wanted to be alone on the practice ground rather than have Harmon standing a post behind him. The son of Claude and, like Woods's own father, a Vietnam combat vet was being slow-walked out the door. By the next year's U.S. Open, the rift had become a tear. In March 2004 Woods called Hank Haney, the instructor of one of his closest friends, Mark O'Meara (though they, too, would drift apart), and asked Haney to help him. With Haney his swing would become flatter, but the prime directive was to protect Woods's left knee following a second surgery in 2002. By swinging more around himself, Woods hoped to eliminate some of the violent snap of the knee that had been a power generator for the twenty-year-old Woods. During the transitioning phase Vijay Singh passed him as the number-one player in the world. He went 0-10 in the majors. Tongues wagged. Egos were bruised. Second guessers second-guessed.

Worst of all, the health of Woods's father, Earl, deteriorated badly.

By the time Woods's swing changes were sufficiently ingrained to allow him the freedom to really contend again in a major championship, Earl was too sick to come to them. Plagued by rain and stoppages in play, Woods nonetheless took a three-shot lead over Chris DiMarco, Woods's journeyman du jour, into the final eighteen holes at Augusta National in April 2005. Woods had never lost a major with a lead on the last day and never won without one. DiMarco, who was born in New York but grew up in Florida after the age of seven, was a thick-hipped player as famous for his devotion to his alma mater, the University of Florida, as he was his golf. He had a tendency to pick the club up on the backswing and finish high. What he lacked in power, he made up in grit. He was one of the first tour players to resort to the claw grip to steady his stroke on the greens. DiMarco had only three tour victories to his credit, but along with the '97 Open champion, Justin Leonard, he'd taken Vijay Singh to extra holes in the PGA Championship at Whistling Straits in Wisconsin the year before. The Masters would be the second major he'd lose in a playoff in as many years, and he would push Woods all the way to the finish in the '06 Open Championship at Hoylake the following year, Woods's tearful first victory after the death of his father in May 2006.

Holding a one-shot lead over DiMarco on the par-three sixteenth, Woods pulled his eight-iron tee shot left of the green. DiMarco had a fifteen-footer for birdie. Faced with a delicate chip, Woods remembered the way Davis Love III, the son of a teaching pro who won his only major championship under a rainbow at Winged Foot, had played his shot from nearly the same spot, chipping it up the large ridge in the green and allowing the ball to feed back down and toward the hole. Woods decided to ride the same roller coaster. His chip went up, turned, and started back down. On the edge of the cup, the ball paused. Then, as if the gathering roar of the crowd was like a pinball champion bumping the green with their collective hips, the ball dropped into the cup. It was certainly the stroke that tilted the competition. DiMarco missed his birdie, and the lead was two. Woods celebrated with such enthusiasm, he nearly cost himself a fourth Masters title. The only shot on that hole that equaled it in timing and drama was when Nicklaus made his forty-foot putt in 1975 and danced around the green with his putter raised as Johnny Miller and Tom Weiskopf looked on from behind him. Where Woods lost his concentration and bogeyed the next two holes, Nicklaus managed to gather his. Then again, Nicklaus had Miller and Weiskopf breathing down his neck. The biggest challenge Woods was facing was getting his new swing back up the hill to the antebellum clubhouse.

Woods's tee shot on the seventeenth sailed right into the trees that had been planted between the fifteenth and seventeenth holes to narrow both landing areas. He couldn't reach the green and gave the shot he'd gained at the sixteenth right back. Then, even more inexplicably, his eight-iron from the fairway on the eighteenth found the greenside bunker, and he bogeyed again. When DiMarco's birdie chip lipped out, they went to sudden death. Woods and DiMarco returned to the eighteenth tee for the playoff, and this time Woods was flawless, hitting three-wood and another eight-iron to fifteen feet and made the putt to end his frustration in the majors and the high dudgeon over his new swing and new coach. When Retief Goosen shot 81 to squander a three-shot lead on Sunday of the U.S. Open at Pinehurst No. 2, only New Zealand's Michael Campbell, doing eye exercises in Port-o-Lets for calmness and concentration, prevented Woods from winning back-to-back majors. The number-one player in the world was back.

At St. Andrews Woods would join Nicklaus, who was that week waving good-bye to competitive golf from the top of the Swilcan Bridge, as the only players of the modern era to win the Open Championship twice on the Old Course. Prior to Jack, James Braid was the last to double up there, and he did it the year Mark Twain died, 1910. Woods's five-shot victory over Colin Montgomerie would also give him two laps around the career Slam, something only he and Nicklaus had done. And Woods had done it before his thirtieth birthday.

Unlike 2000 Woods found a couple of bunkers this time at the Old Course, but the real difference was his putting. He hadn't putted well at Pinehurst, and he wasn't much better at St. Andrews, but his ball striking was nearly flawless. If his swing hiccuped down the stretch at Augusta, it hummed at St. Andrews. He led after every round and played the kind of conservative, just-enough-to-win, style of golf Nicklaus had ascribed to himself going into the 1970s. "To have the opportunity to get to 10 already this soon in my career, it's very exciting to hopefully look forward to some good years in my 30s and, hopefully, into my 40s," said Woods. As it turned out, that might have been too much to hope for.

By April of the following year Earl Woods was losing, and cancer was winning. No amount of Tiger's cursing of his father's smoking, which he'd done for years, was going to change the outcome now. The mines had been laid. Woods knew the '06 Masters would be the last major his father would watch, even hazily. Playing championship golf for yourself is too difficult for most. Playing it for someone else is damn near impossible. Woods wanted to call his shot but couldn't force it to happen. Phil Mickelson won his second Masters, and it was Woods who put the green coat on him. By the time the two of them got to Winged Foot for the U.S. Open, Mickelson was going for three majors in a row, and Earl Woods had passed away. The son was a mess. From Deacon Palmer to Arnold, from Charlie Nicklaus to Jack, from Earl Woods to Tiger, there is a father-and-son dynamic that runs through golf the way the Colorado River runs through Arizona. Ben Hogan carried the brooding scars of his father's suicide his entire life. To jump off the Jungian cliff one last time, despite his assertions to the contrary, Earl remained too much the guarantor of Tiger's existence, to his mortal end and beyond. Woods missed the cut in a major championship for the first time. On Sunday there was more carnage on Winged Foot's eighteenth than the chariot race in *Ben-Hur*, and Mickelson was the main casualty. Geoff Ogilvy, the articulate Australian, ambled away with the title the way John Wayne walks off at the end of *The Searchers*. Or maybe that was Bill Murray.

In July the Open Championship was returning to Royal Liverpool GC, known as Hoylake, for the first time since Roberto de Vicenzo won there thirty-nine years before. What they forgot this time was the rain. A thirty-minute commute from Liverpool by train, the old links was harder, drier, and browner than the leather on the soles of Bernard Darwin's shoes. At St. Andrews in 2000 Woods took all the bunkers out of play by flying them. Hoylake would be the counterweight. "When I saw the rough on the other side of the bunkers, even if I drove it over the top, I couldn't hold the green," says Woods. "So, that's when my whole strategy changed. I was pretty aggressive in practice rounds but adopted a different philosophy once I realized I just can't spin the ball out of the rough. The ball was rolling sometimes up to 100 yards. I couldn't control my ball on the ground because it was too fast, so I decided to lay back where I felt like I'd have a little more spin and a little bit more control." Woods was playing a strategic rather than overpowering game yet again and produced a virtuoso long-iron demonstration. He took the lead by a shot at the halfway point and stayed there, finishing two ahead of Chris DiMarco. If Woods was healing, DiMarco barely had time to begin. His mother, Norma, had died of a heart attack at the age of sixty-eight on vacation in Colorado just a couple of weeks before. He forced his father, Rich, to come with him to Hoylake, to forget, and to remember. After sinking the last putt a sobbing Woods embraced his caddie, Williams, and then his wife, Elin. "It just came pouring out," Woods said. "All the things that my father has meant to me and the game of golf, I just wish he would have seen it one more time." He had gone into the last round one shot ahead of Sergio Garcia, who turned up for their game, as the R&A calls its pairings, dressed head to toe in yellow. Afterward, Woods recovered sufficiently emotionally to send a text message to a friend, "Just bludgeoned Tweety Bird." His father was gone, but the feud with Garcia carried on.

Woods returned to Medinah, where he held off Garcia in '99 to cement his first big swing change and to deliver further evidence, as if any was now needed, that his second alteration had achieved its goals. After a third-round 65 Woods was tied for the lead with Luke Donald. His Sunday success rate from that position in major championships remained unblemished, and this day would be no different, even if Donald was something of a favorite son. A native of Hemel Hempstead, England, the quick-witted Donald attended Northwestern University in Evanston, where he studied art, dabbled in oil painting, won the '99 NCAA individual title—breaking the scoring record held by Tiger Woods—and still called suburban

Chicago home. He was a short hitter but a deadly mid- and long-iron player and magical out of the bunkers. Five years later Donald would become the number-one player in the world, holding the spot for forty straight weeks before he and Rory McIlroy began swapping it back and forth. Altogether, he was the world's top-ranked player for fifty-six weeks. He was also a member of four winning Ryder Cup teams with an imposing 10-4-1 individual record. But the Luke Donald of 2006 was no match for a thirty-year-old Tiger Woods in full command of his swing. Woods putted like a demon and by the twelfth hole held a five-shot lead, which would be his eventual winning margin over Shaun Micheel, the first golfer out of Memphis, Tennessee, to win a major championship since Cary Middlecoff, sometime-resident John Daly notwithstanding. The centerpiece of Micheel's career was a seven-iron from 175 yards out of the semirough to two inches on the eighteenth hole at Oak Hill CC in Rochester, New York, to win the PGA three years earlier. At Medinah Woods became the first player to win two PGAs at the same course, a curiosity more than a distinction since the PGA of America didn't have the kind of dependable rota the two Opens had. He tied his own scoring record and became the first player to go four-for-two, that is, multiple major championships in back-to-back years. That, of course, is if you don't want to count Bobby Jones, which is like talking Barry Bonds and leaving Babe Ruth out of the conversation.

The winners of the year's first three majors of 2007 were among the most interesting trio golf had produced in a long time, if not among the better known. Zach Johnson, from Cedar Rapids, Iowa, would lay up on every par five at Augusta National and make eleven birdies on them to win by two over two South Africans, Rory Sabbatini and Retief Goosen, and Woods, who led briefly in the last round but, ultimately, could do no better than even par on Sunday. At five-feet-eleven (and that's generous) and 160, the deeply religious Johnson was, pound for pound, the toughest player on the PGA Tour. "I don't hit it very far, I don't overpower a golf course," Johnson said. "I think I'm mentally tough." No one would have disagreed. Ángel Cabrera, the Argentine who would win the first of his two major titles in the U.S. Open at Oakmont by a shot over

Jim Furyk (who had more disappointing Opens yet to come) and Woods (who made just one birdie the last day), grew up in the kind of poverty the average American touring pro couldn't begin to understand. Cabrera spoke mostly through his coach and interpreter, Houston's Charlie Epps. "I never thought this was possible," said the man they called El Pato, the Duck, because of his wobbling gait. It had been a very long time since anyone from such meager beginnings had accomplished so much. The winner of the Open Championship that year at Carnoustie was Padraig Harrington, joining Fred Daly as the only Irishmen to have won the championship or, for that matter, any major, doing it sixty years apart. The meticulous Harrington, a trained accountant, barely escaped the numbers game that felled Jean Van de Velde there eight years earlier. Playing Carnoustie's eighteenth with a three-shot lead, the Frenchman was famously photographed barefoot in the Barry Burn. He would eventually lose a three-way playoff to the Scot Paul Lawrie. Harrington found the burn off the tee, dropped, then found the burn again with his five-iron. He managed to get up and down from forty-seven yards to fall just one shot behind Sergio Garcia. "I didn't want to take seven," he said. "It crossed my mind that he (Van de Velde) made seven to lose the Open and I was slipping down that slippery slope." Garcia needed to par the eighteenth to win but couldn't manage it, hitting his three-iron second into the greenside bunker. Never breaking concentration, the disciplined Harrington won the four-hole aggregate playoff for the first of his three majors. For his part, Garcia felt he'd been iced by bunker rakers on the last hole of regulation and doomed by the Fates when his approach on the second hole of sudden death hit the pin and spun away. No one felt worse for Sergio than he did for himself.

Going for three straight Open Championships, Woods was never a factor at Carnoustie. In the second round he duck-hooked an iron off the first tee into the Barry Burn, an almost inconceivable mistake, even for someone with notorious first-tee jitters. A new father, Woods's first child, Sam Alexis, was born a month earlier. Woods chose the name Sam because that's what his father had called him at golf tournaments. Anyone who has played a team sport knows, regardless of the crowd noise, the human ear and brain allow you to pick out the voices of your teammates. Earl called Tiger "Sam" because he could yell to him from a crowd, and Tiger could pick out his voice. Besides, Earl teased him, "You look like a Sam." Worse than not factoring in the outcome, Woods damaged his anterior cruciate ligament (ACL) running. He took the injury with him to Tulsa and the PGA, the last major of 2007, where he made it worse—and won.

With Woods putting for a 62 on the eighteenth hole of Southern Hills CC in Tulsa at almost seven o'clock Friday evening, casting a shadow across the green as long as the one he had cast over the game in the ten seasons since his first major victory, on the adjacent ninth green Steve Stricker and Brett Wetterich stopped to watch. No one had ever shot 62 in a major championship. The ball hit the hole, swirled halfway down, and popped out the other side. Wetterich pointed his index finger at the ground and gave the swirling symbol for power lip out. Woods would have to be content to be just one of twenty-three (at the time) to have a 63. It gave him a two-shot lead that he stretched to three going into the final round on a week when sweat was the coin of the realm and temperatures flip-flopped on either side of one hundred degrees. When it was over Woods would be a perfect thirteen for thirteen with the lead going into the last round of a major, but it was far from a carefree romp.

He was pursued by Ernie Els, who got within a shot until his bogey at the sixteenth finished him off, and Woody Austin, who also got within a shot when Woods bogeyed the fourteenth. Austin grew up in Tampa, Florida, and learned to play on the municipal Babe Zaharias Golf Course. He attended the University of Miami and made a living, off and on, as a teller at the GTE Federal Credit Union in Tampa before finally earning a spot on tour. The piece of video that surfaced every time Austin was in contention was of him beating himself in the head with his putter shaft in '97 at Harbour Town. Austin was gifted with remarkable hand-eye coordination, but it didn't transfer to the greens. That bit of self-flagellating business would be replaced at Royal Montreal in the Presidents Cup when he went totally submerged after tumbling backward into a water hazard on the fourteenth hole. He showed up the next day for his singles match with a pair of swimming goggles.

Of his bogey at Southern Hills' fourteenth, Woods said, "I just felt like, I got myself into this mess, I need to get myself out." After a birdie on the eighth Woods had led Austin by six and Els by five. From there through the fourteenth, he was two over par. Austin birdied the eleventh, twelfth, and thirteenth to threaten. Woods responded with a birdie at the fifteenth and iced it with strong pars on the way home. As he came off the golf course he was greeted by Elin and Sam. "It's a feeling I've never had before," he said. "Having Sam there and having Elin there. . . . [T]his one feels so much more special than the other majors." More ominously, on the eighth hole, Woods made birdie from the fringe and unleashed a fist pump that brought his left leg down awkwardly on the sidehill of the green. While the how and why and how much of the knee injury he sustained in England were open to question, what was not was that the knee had become a career-threatening problem. It wasn't the only one.

Woods was as dominant as ever opening the 2008 season. He won three times in America and once in Dubai before the Masters but came up three shots shy of catching Trevor Immelman at Augusta National. Immelman would become the second South African, after Gary Player, to win the Masters. In the previous two years Immelman had battled an intestinal parasite that caused him to lose twenty-five pounds and undergone an operation to remove a tumor from his diaphragm. After Augusta Woods announced he'd undergo surgery to clean up issues in the knee. Not even he knew the extent of the damage. The ACL had ruptured. The U.S. Open was going to be held at Torrey Pines GC, a municipal facility just north of San Diego. Woods had won there six times, including that winter, since turning professional. No way would he miss an Open there. Surgery to fix the ligament would have to wait.

Comparing Woods's U.S. Open victory at Torrey Pines with Ben Hogan's at Merion in 1950 is a breathless exercise in overstatement. Hogan had very nearly died when his Cadillac hit a Greyhound bus in 1949. He'd broken his ankle and his collarbone and fractured his pelvis in two places. He'd had surgery to tie off a major vein feeding blood from his lower extremities to his heart. In the second round at Merion, either Cary Middlecoff's or Hogan's caddie took the ball out of the hole for him because Hogan couldn't do it himself. One thing Hogan and Woods did share, however, was a lousy left knee. The greatness of Hogan's performance at Merion doesn't diminish the fact that Woods's feat at Torrey Pines was the single most heroic effort the sport had witnessed in fifty-eight years. If it wasn't a Hogan, it was at least a Willis Reed, the inspirational leader of the New York Knicks in the 1970 NBA finals.

For someone who guarded the secrecy of his aches and pains better than the Central Intelligence Agency protected its watch list, Woods had always been oddly comfortable publicly showing just how much pain he was in. He could die better, and longer, than Dickens's Little Nell. So bad was the knee and, as it turned out, the two stress fractures of the tibia that Woods couldn't play prior to the U.S. Open and could barely practice. At Torrey his warm-ups before play seemed routine, but as every round wore on, his condition deteriorated. His trainer and physical therapist, Keith Kleven, was keeping him upright. Woods didn't wince or double over with pain on every shot. He could never be certain when it would come. But come it did. "I just kept telling myself that if it grabs me and if I get that shooting pain, I get it. But, it's always after impact, so go ahead and just make the proper swing," he said. "If pain hits, pain hits. So be it."

His first-tee weakness was as pronounced at Torrey Pines as it had ever been. Three times Woods made double bogey on the opening hole, including Sunday, wiping out the one-shot lead he took into the final round. By the second hole he was two shots behind Rocco Mediate, the refreshingly candid son of Italy from Greenburg, Pennsylvania, who would become the next journeyman to push Woods into overtime in a major championship. Mediate was a fast-talking son of a barber who attended the '91 Ryder Cup at Kiawah Island as a spectator and often preferred to change his shoes in the parking lot instead of the clubhouse. He had five tour victories and two heroes, Arnold Palmer and Tiger Woods; a round body; a rapid gait; an even faster tongue; and a back that was nearly as weak as Woods's knee. He also had the bloodless nerve of a con artist and put it on display in the 2005 World Series of Poker.

England's Lee Westwood, who once dropped from number 4 in the world to number 256 and then climbed all the way back to number 4 again, would have the first of his seven top-three finishes in majors at Torrey. Mediate, watching on a television by the scoring area off the cart barn underneath the clubhouse, had posted 283 and held a one-shot lead over Westwood and Woods, who were playing the reachable 527-yard eighteenth. Both drove into bunkers and were forced to lay up. Westwood left himself a twenty-five-footer for a tying birdie but missed. Woods was twelve feet away. The putt rolled across Torrey's Poa annua green as smoothly as a frog jumping down a brick staircase. It caught the right edge of the cup, and gravity gathered it in. Woods roared much like he had on Augusta's sixteenth when his chip in shook the earth. "I knew he would make it," Mediate said. "That's what he does."

In the Monday playoff Woods got three shots ahead, but Mediate refused to go away. The winner of thirteen major championships began giving shots back. By the time they reached the eighteenth, Woods needed another birdie to keep the match alive. This time he reached the green in two and, when the eagle putt missed, left himself a four-footer. Mediate had a twenty-foot putt for a winning birdie but missed. Woods converted. They would need a nineteenth hole, the seventh. Mediate drove the ball into a bad spot in the fairway bunker and couldn't make par. The most courageous performance golf had seen in decades ended with a whimper and a four. "Great fight," Woods said as he hugged Mediate at the green. Afterward, calling it his greatest victory, Woods said, "I'm glad I'm done. I really don't feel like playing anymore." Unintentionally prophetic words. In a week he'd have the ACL repaired. Even so, no one knew how truly done he was until it all came tumbling down.

When Woods came back in '09 he played well but putted poorly, both in the Masters and at the U.S. Open, which returned to soggy Bethpage. He missed the cut for just the second time in a major at Turnberry when Tom Watson nearly won a sixth claret jug at the tender age of fifty-nine. In the PGA at Hazeltine Woods took a two-shot lead into Sunday along with his fourteen-for-fourteen streak of major closeouts. He also brought his balky putter with him. Y. E. Yang, the son of a farmer and a veteran of the South Korean army, didn't blink. He did the opposite, chipping in for an eagle on the fourteenth, complete with the Korean version of Woodsian fist pumps, and closed it out with a hybrid from 210 yards to twelve feet on the eighteenth. If you don't count Tiger's Thai heritage, Yang became the first Asian to win a major. Woods had taken thirty-three putts and shot 75. He'd won the last tournament he played going into every one of the Grand Slam events and came up empty in the only tournaments he really cared about. The knee was fixed, but the putter was broken. And it was about to get worse.

Approaching his thirty-fourth birthday Woods was well aware that Tom Watson had won his last major at thirty-three and struggled with his putting from then on. Palmer won his last major at thirty-four before his putter up and wandered off. Watson had won all his majors in a nine-year span. Palmer's ticket was good for a seven-year ride. Nick Faldo got his six in ten seasons, the last bit gift-wrapped by Greg Norman. Hogan's late-in-a-sporting-life run lasted eight years. Jones went early, scooping everything up in eight and quitting. Player, the fitness pioneer, and Nicklaus were the exceptions. They kept winning big titles for nineteen and a ridiculous twenty-five years, respectively. Woods had won fourteen majors in eleven. No one knew better than he did the damage he'd done to his body. And no one knew better than he did that putting was a mysterious gift that could be repossessed as quickly as it was given. So, what exactly was the cause and effect? Did his double life lead to a diminution of his game, or was it the other way around? According to the *National Enquirer,* he'd been caught on film in a parking lot back in '07 with someone other than his wife.

On the Friday morning following Thanksgiving of 2009, shortly after two o'clock, Tiger Woods came running out of his house barefoot, jumped into his Cadillac Escalade, pulled out of his driveway, and hit a fire hydrant and then a tree on Deacon Circle in Orlando's Isleworth, one of the toniest enclaves in one of

Florida's tackiest cities, or the happiest place on Earth, take your pick. When help arrived, the back window of the suv had been smashed, Woods was drifting in and out of consciousness, Elin was there, Tiger was bleeding from his mouth, and a nine-iron was handy. Apparently, that's the standard club selection for such occasions, since it's the same one Brenna Cepalek chose for Nick Faldo's Porsche.

According to a *Wall Street Journal* story that would run later that year, Woods had traded access to a men's fitness magazine for silence from one of its sister publications, the *Enquirer*, two years earlier. Hush money, in whatever form, rarely stays hushed long. When the police and the public record get involved, privacy becomes a quaint notion. After he hit the hydrant, so many trollops shot out, it was like a hot August day in Brooklyn except the kids playing in this unsavory gusher were a slew of suddenly voracious reporters many of whom wouldn't have known a V-groove from a v-8. As much as they might have liked to, not even the golf guys could ignore it. Bobby Jones had Grantland Rice, who aspired only to create legends. Tiger Woods had TMZ, which was interested only in destroying them. And he had passed out ammunition like Tootsie Rolls at Halloween.

Steinway didn't make enough baby grands for all the whorehouse piano players in Woods's entourage. There may have been something going on back there, but they couldn't imagine what it was. The handlers manned the barricades like the Wicked Witch's flying monkeys. There was a financial empire that needed safeguarding. Woods managed to do overnight what seemed like an absurdity for the better part of a dozen years: he'd transformed his narrative into farce. He became low-hanging fruit for late-night comedians and easy prey for satirical shows like *Saturday Night Live* or *South Park*, the animated show that specializes in crudity. Defeat was not nearly as hard to swallow as humiliation. That went down in a bowl of Fruit Loops as he hid on his couch. "I don't know how he got out of bed some days," said the third swing instructor of his professional life, Sean Foley.

Though there's little point in contemplating a counternarrative, one suspects had his father still been alive, Tiger Woods would have handled the scandal differently, and better. Earl was no choirboy. He could dance the flamenco every bit as passionately as his son. But Earl was one of those guys who believed the value of a man is less what he has than what he leaves behind, and Tiger was his marker. At business meetings when chief executive and financial officers would file into a conference room and toss millions of dollars at the feet of his son like frankincense and myrrh, Earl was as likely to take a siesta as count the zeroes. He liked money; he just didn't think much of it. It was a way to keep score. Chances are Earl would have laughed out loud at Crisis Management 101 when the first thing they started hunting for was a twelve-step program to put on Tiger's résumé. And if they'd tried to hold a mea culpa in front of a velvet curtain and an audience of horse-faced undertakers, Earl would have called in an air strike. He fought the Vietcong. He could have run off a platoon of flunkies. Without Pops around Woods was never more timorous than when he was called to account.

Of course, if you took all the halls of fame in all the sports in all the world and limited membership to just the saints, you could hold a meeting of the inductees in a tool shed. Young, wealthy athletes behaving badly wasn't much of a scoop. That Woods was black while all of golf's other sinners, some of whom were in the World Golf Hall of Fame while others were merely contemporaries, were white didn't escape notice, either, particularly in a sport with a decidedly discriminatory history. In the end Woods was felled not by racial animus but rather by the grandiosity of the target and the hypocrisy of his polished image. And the fall was breathtaking, digitally propelled by text messages and voice mails. As one of Faldo's exes, Melanie, wrote in the *Guardian*, "Monogamy and professional golf do not happily co-exist. . . . At the time, I felt that the very characteristics that make a sportsman great are the ones that can destroy a marriage. And like Tiger's wife, Elin, when things went wrong, I felt the weight of the corporate machine bear down as it moved into the most personal of spaces in my life to protect its charge." They tried to circle the wagons in Isleworth, but there were more bimbos than Conestogas.

One of the first sponsors to drop Woods was Accenture, a management consulting and technology behemoth. When he announced his hastily arranged, and nationally broadcast, mea culpa in February 2010, he did it the same week as the Accenture Match Play Championship in Tucson, Arizona, one of the PGA Tour's showcase events. The sudden announcement of his public reappearance sent the media scurrying to accumulate frequent-flyer miles getting to Florida. Accenture had closely interwoven its flashy advertising campaign with the Woods persona, it's backlit airport displays posing the question "What Would Tiger Woods Do?" They got their answer—he'd get even, that's what. So while PGA Tour commissioner Tim Finchem handed Woods the keys to the tour's headquarters 1,979.99 miles away, Woods's colleagues were left to face the music. Rory McIlroy, just twenty at the time, delivered, only half in jest, the one-liner that was on the tip of everyone's wagging tongue who was left in Tucson: "I suppose he might want to get something back against the sponsor that dropped him."

When Woods returned to competitive golf at the Masters in April, he was greeted by a lecture from the dais in the media center delivered by the very man who had been so proud of him just a few years before, Billy Payne, now the chairman. Said Payne:

We are not unaware of the significance of this week to a very special player, Tiger Woods, a man who in a brief 13 years clearly and emphatically proclaimed and proved his game to be worthy of the likes of Bobby Jones, Jack Nicklaus and Arnold Palmer. As he ascended in our rankings of the world's great golfers, he became an example to our kids that success is directly attributable to hard work and effort. But, as he now says himself, he forgot in the process to remember that with fame and fortune comes responsibility, not invisibility. It is not simply the degree of his conduct that is so egregious here; it is the fact that he disappointed all of us, and more importantly, our kids and our grandkids. Our hero did not live up to the expectations of the role model we saw for our children.

With what seemed like a security guard behind every Georgia pine, Woods putted poorly but still finished a respectable fourth, as Phil Mickelson won his third Masters, enjoying a tearful embrace with wife, Amy, weakened by her breast cancer treatments and barely strong enough to make it to the golf course. The sweetness of the Mickelson moment and the memory of Tiger's embrace of his father thirteen years before, juxtaposed against the five-month plummet into disgrace, were commingled in teardrops behind the eighteenth green. Woods played next at Quail Hollow CC in Charlotte and shot a desultory 79 in the second round, missing just the sixth cut of his career. It was the worst Woods had ever looked on a golf course, to that point. Resembling an actor who had forgotten his lines, fumbling with the curtain trying to get off the stage, he seemed more a candidate for the NFL's concussion protocol than a challenger in a golf tournament. In the 2004 PGA Woods said, "I tee it up with the intent of giving it everything I've got. I think that's one thing I'm most proud of is that I've never bagged it. I've never dogged it." After that day in Charlotte, that was no longer the case.

As if to cue the future, the tournament was won by Rory McIlroy, his first on the PGA Tour, shooting a remarkable 62 the final day. Rumors were also flying that Woods had split with his instructor, Hank Haney, who had taken over for Butch Harmon in 2004. In fact, Haney was being slow-walked to the exit, just as Harmon had been.

The following week Woods withdrew from the Players Championship with a bulging disc in his neck. He played in the year's remaining major championships, but his best finish in them was a T4 in the U.S. Open at Pebble Beach, the course where he had been so dominant ten years earlier and a place where Haney, in particular, was not looking forward to what would be another round of the Harmon-versus-Haney scales of justice. The neck, however, was just the beginning of a tsunami of injuries that would roll over Woods in his middle and late thirties. The neck forced him out of the Players in '10. In the following year's Masters he would damage his Achilles' tendon playing a shot from underneath the Eisenhower Tree on the seventeenth. He showed up for the Players in May, but the Achilles, along with what was purported to be a sprain of the medial collateral ligament of that delicate left knee, sidelined him after shooting 42 on the front nine. In 2012 he was carted off the Blue Monster at Doral when his Achilles tightened during the Cadillac Championship, and by August he was feeling pain in his lower back at the Barclays, claiming it was caused by a bad mattress, of all things. He hurt his elbow at the 2013 Players, and it caused him visible pain during the U.S. Open at Merion a month later. His back problems returned at the PGA Championship, and at the Barclays back spasms drove him to his knees. The all too believable rumor was that he'd hurt his lower back lifting weights. In March 2014 he had to withdraw from the Honda Classic because of back spasms, and though he finished his round with a 78 a week later at Doral, he played through obvious lower-back pain there, too. He withdrew from the Arnold Palmer Invitational in Orlando because of the back and had surgery in Utah for a pinched nerve in March. He returned in time to play at Congressional CC in the tournament that benefits the Tiger Woods Foundation but looked weak and missed the cut. He finished sixty-ninth when the Open Championship returned to Hoylake, withdrew from the tournament at Firestone, missed the cut in the PGA Championship at Valhalla, then called it quits for the year. That was the pupil Sean Foley inherited on the practice range of the PGA Championship in 2010 after Haney beat Woods to the punch, telling him that May he was done being his instructor.

Woods would leave Foley before he returned to competition in Scottsdale in 2015, seeking the advice instead of a little-known teacher, Chris Como. While working with the diminutive Foley, a Canadian who got his start on tour teaching a swing that helped his countryman Stephen Ames (whom Woods would beat by a vengeful 9 and 8 in the 2006 Match Play Championship) overcome serious back issues, Woods won eight tournaments, a pittance compared to either Harmon or Haney. And none of those titles were going to help Woods match Jack Nicklaus's total of eighteen major championships. Woods's work with Foley was often criticized, particularly by Brandel Chamblee, an announcer on the Golf Channel. Chamblee had been an All-American at the University of Texas and played the PGA Tour for fifteen years, winning once—the Greater Vancouver Open in 1998. "I'll give Sean Foley his due. He teaches a very pretty, efficient golf swing but it's not imaginative and it's not versatile. I'm amazed at Tiger's ability to incorporate three drastically different golf swings and bring them to some level of excellence. Nobody's ever done that in golf, ever," said Chamblee. "Tiger, doing what he's doing now, in my opinion, will never get anywhere near as good as he was in 2005–6–7–8 and he won't sniff getting as good as he was in 2000." Gene Sarazen lost four years in his prime when he went down the wrong swing path. Time was the one thing Woods didn't have. Foley was benched.

Golf instructors, particularly the ones who work with touring professionals, are businessmen in addition to teachers and know how to promote their product, themselves. Neither Harmon nor Haney nor Foley was immune from it, and all benefited from their association with Woods. But Haney, in particular, never seemed to rise above looking at Woods's record as his own. It was a never-ending competition between himself and Harmon. And in the only measure the world really cared about, major championships, Harmon won 8 and 6—and that didn't include the three U.S. Amateurs. After Woods began working with Haney and they bridged the early struggles, as Woods got better and better and won more and more, Haney was like the Nate Silver of golf statisticians, able to dial up comparisons between Woods-Haney and Woods-Harmon at the drop of a three-putt. Haney's exploitative book, *The Big Miss*, appeared in early 2012. It's most interesting revelation may have been what it didn't include—in fact, what it specifically excluded—and that was the use of steroids when Woods's name was associated with a Canadian doctor, Anthony Galea, who'd been associated with transporting human growth hormone across the Canadian-American border. The unvarnished truth is, if it were ever proved that Woods had been taking steroids or human growth hormone during his glory years, it would hurt his legacy more than all the porn stars in California.

Haney also writes in his book:

In the 127 official PGA Tour events that Tiger played as a professional with Butch as his coach, he won 34 times—just under 27 percent of his starts . . . . For the entire six years that I was officially his swing instructor from Bay Hill of 2004 through the Masters of 2010, Tiger played 91 official PGA tour events. He won 31 of them—34 percent. . . . I was surprised. As measured by victory percentage, Tiger had performed better with me than he had with Butch. My respect for Butch would keep me from gloating. But I felt good that in the future those numbers would empower me when answering my critics.

What Haney could never seem to wrap his mind around, and to some degree it applied to all Woods's instructors, was that they were the hired help. It was never about Butch or Hank or Sean. It was always all about Tiger Woods.

As the forties beckoned, Woods was playing the closing holes of his career into a three-club wind of bad karma. America is the land of second chances. For Woods to reignite his pursuit of Nicklaus's eighteen major championships, he would have to avoid further injury, he would have to rediscover the swagger his scandal had robbed from him, and he would have to beat a new generation of players, led first by Rory McIlroy, who was going into the 2015 Masters looking to complete a career Slam of his own and seconded there and at the U.S. Open at Chambers Bay by Jordan Spieth. In all sports, even one you can play into your dotage, time is the ally of the young. "What people fail to realize," Woods said of his dominance in his prime, "it was not over just because I pulled in the parking lot. Just because I show up doesn't mean they're going to give me the trophy. I had to earn it. It's still the same thing now, I have to out-perform everybody."

If Nicklaus was the target, he was also the template. "When you have been out of golf for awhile, and you've gone through some sort of trauma—as I experienced with my hip surgery—you've got to relearn, mentally, how to play again," Nicklaus wrote in *Golf & Life: Jack Nicklaus*. "And when you haven't shot decent numbers for a while it's hard to get a round going and keep it going. That's not nerves. It's nerve. You have to regain your nerve and that's hard to do. It's being able to stand there, look at that flag, stare it down and shoot at it. Sometimes it takes a little bit more nerve to do than before, when it was second nature."

Patched on the inside and out, Woods sought nothing more, nothing less, than curing the hangover of his humiliation with the pick-me-up of more major championships. Hogan got hit by a bus, but it couldn't stop him from being Hogan. If Woods was truly able to reignite his quest, it would surely become the most fascinating stretch run any golfing career had ever known. The record of eighteen major championships would emit radioactive pressure the closer it got, competing against players who didn't fear his destiny, with a body that seemed as fragile as Baccarat crystal.

Nicklaus's accumulation of titles of consequence decelerated after he reached thirty-eight, picking off four more in eight years to set the bar. When Watson left Royal Birkdale with his fifth Open Championship at thirty-three, who would have thought it would be his last? When Woods was carried out of Torrey Pines State Park on his shield at thirty-two, who would have predicted his most courageous major might be the exclamation point at the end of the sentence?

As many superlatives as Woods accumulated in his first twelve years or so as a professional, after he hit the fire hydrant, his stat sheet became littered with worst-ofs. "That's pretty much what pro sports do, try to beat you up and convince you you're not as good as you used to think you were," says Dr. Bob Rotella, the sports psychologist. "At some point it starts to affect people's dreams. If you want to separate yourself from everyone else on the planet Earth, you have to do stuff that's hard to do."

Working with Como, his new coach, at the start of 2015, Woods showed up at Torrey Pines and in Scottsdale playing as embarrassing a form of golf as any great player ever put on public display. It was so ugly even he couldn't bear to look at it, and he took himself out of play until Augusta. His golf was so bizarre, stories about it could have started, "A Florida man . . ." It was one thing to make swing changes and suffer the consequences, but it was quite another to watch one of the best players to ever play the game scrape it around like a common weekend chopper, alternately stubbing or skulling the simplest touch shots around the green. Real improvement was illusive. His major championship record ran to 0-24 since Rocco Mediate and Torrey Pines, and he'd dropped to 292nd in the world. By the time he turned forty, it would be 413. Making a cut was an achievement. In an effort to qualify for the PGA Tour's year-end quadrilateral, the FedEx Cup, he recorded his only top ten of 2015 in Greensboro, the tournament where Sam Snead—the only man to have won more tournaments in a career—had been victorious as often as Woods had at Bay Hill or Firestone, eight times. The pit seemed bottomless. Woods had a second back surgery in Utah in September, ending a season that, for all intents and purposes, had ended already. A month later the doctors went in again. He said he'd come back from injury before and was confident he would again. Then, in an interview at his own tournament in the Bahamas, he said he just didn't know. Woods was morphing into golf's Mickey Mantle, an athlete of profound ability, blessed with brilliance on the field, who limped away bandaged in irrelevance.

The great ones always seem to take one last lap around the track, and Woods might still get his. The distance between the achievements of Jack and Tiger grew even as Nicklaus's collapsing vertebrae were shrinking him physically and Woods's were being surgically repaired. The record reveals a simple reality: Woods streaked faster across the universe of championship golf than anyone ever had, but it was still Nicklaus who burned the brightest and the longest.

# 9

## Change of Fortune

The two greatest comebacks in the history of the Ryder Cup Matches happened in America, thirteen years and a thousand miles apart. The first went to the Americans, the second the Europeans, and only an exorcism could have prevented either one. Ben Crenshaw, the captain of the U.S. team in 1999 at The Country Club, kissed the seventeenth green where Francis Ouimet had turned back the British eighty-six years before Justin Leonard holed the putt that made the Americans lose their collective minds. At Medinah in 2012 European captain José Maria Olazábal, who was standing on the seventeenth green with a putt to halve the hole the day the Americans lost their minds, dressed his team in blue and white as an airplane spelled Seve Ballesteros's name in the sky sixteen months after the death of Europe's greatest champion. There are times when the game isn't won, it's written.

Once the Ryder Cup expanded to include all of Europe in 1979, it became competitive in just four years, the amount of time it used to take to get a college undergraduate degree. In the following thirty years or so, the Europeans would go on to get a doctorate in kicking America's ass. With Ballesteros, Nick Faldo,

Bernhard Langer, Sandy Lyle, and Ian Woosnam as the core, and two-time major champion Tony Jacklin as the captain (a position he would hold in four straight Ryder Cups), the visiting Europeans nearly beat U.S. captain Jack Nicklaus and his Americans at PGA National in West Palm Beach in '83. Ominously, one supposes in hindsight, as Lanny Wadkins was polishing off the challengers, bolts of lightning discharged on the horizon. Two years later Europe won the Ryder Cup for the first time in twenty-eight years at The Belfry, and two years after that they won for the first time on American soil, dealing the U.S. captain, Nicklaus again, a defeat on *his* own soil, too, Muirfield Village in Dublin, Ohio. From the '83 matches until '99 at The Country Club, the Europeans won the cup four times and the United States won it three times, and once the matches were halved, though, that tie was as good as a win for Europe since they already had it and got to keep it. Only '85 was a blowout, with the Euros winning by five. Four times the margin was a single point.

The Age of Nicklaus was waning, though Jack had one more spectacular curtain call in '86 at Augusta National, and with it names like Lee Trevino, Raymond Floyd, Tom Watson, Lanny Wadkins, and Hale Irwin were aging out, too. The best players in the world hailed from Europe, just as they had in Ouimet's day. In the seventeen Aprils from '83 through '99, the Masters was won by a European player ten times. America reclaimed the golden cup it had lost in '85 in the lamentably jingoistic atmosphere of Kiawah Island with its tableau of sea oats and desert camouflage. America then successfully defended its title in Europe but was upset two years after that when the Europeans came from behind in the singles at Oak Hill in Rochester, New York, as two old foes, Faldo and Curtis Strange (who had won the second of his back-to-back U.S. Opens at Oak Hill after beating Faldo in a playoff at The Country Club for his first), took turns throwing up on each other's golf shoes, with Faldo managing to keep enough bottle to win a crucial point. At the closing ceremony Strange buried his face in his hands. Two years after that, with Ballesteros as captain, wildly driving his cart around Valderrama GC like it was the Monaco Grand Prix while U.S. captain Tom Kite politely chauffeured Michael Jordan to good vantage spots, Europe won again. And so it was that the United States, swallowed up in the black hole of defeat in a contest it had once dominated, sought to reclaim the Ryder Cup at the course where the amateur Ouimet became the totem of American golf, defeating the best professionals in the world, the invading Brits Harry Vardon and Ted Ray, in the 1913 U.S. Open.

Ouimet grew up at 246 Clyde Street, across from The Country Club's seventeenth hole. He was the second of four children born to an immigrant Quebecois, Arthur, and his second wife, Mary, a daughter of Irish immigrants. The Ouimets had no attachment to the club or the game, other than as a place for young Francis and his older brother, Wilfred, to earn money caddying or for their father to obtain the kind of odd-lot work that allowed him to scrape together a modest living. At first the golf course was nothing more to Francis than the shortest distance between two points—a shortcut to the Putterham School. He became obsessed with the game, and by the time the U.S. Open rolled around to The Country Club, the twenty-year-old Francis had already won the Massachusetts Amateur Championship and had gotten as far as the quarterfinals in the U.S. Amateur, losing to Jerome Travers. It was a fine résumé for someone barely out of the caddie yard, but Vardon, forty-three by then, had already won the Open Championship five times (he'd win it the next year, too), and Ray, seven years Vardon's junior, had won it once. The task of keeping the British stars from dominating America's National Open attracted another twenty-year-old, a young professional from Rochester, New York, named Walter Hagen, whose florid taste in clothing would have made a clown fish look like a cod. As self-effacing as popping a champagne cork, Hagen announced to anyone in the locker room who might be interested, including Johnny McDermott, who was going for his third U.S. Open title in a row and had just dusted both Vardon and Ray to a fare-thee-well in the Shawnee Open, that he'd made the trip from upstate New York to help them stop the British. And until he made a double-bogey seven on the fourteenth in the final round and slipped out of contention on the soggy closing holes, he'd been in a position to do it, too. His day would come. This one belonged to the excaddie from the other side of the street, who didn't drink, smoke, swear, or rattle.

Ray and Vardon both finished the fourth round ahead of Ouimet, posting dueling 79s and a 304 total. To catch them Francis would have to play the last six holes in two-under par, a daunting task with his opponents already on the veranda with their feet up. He chipped in on the thirteenth for a birdie; parred the fourteenth, where Hagen had come undone; and saved par on the fifteenth when he got up and down from a tough lie. He still needed one more birdie. At the sixteenth Ouimet had to make a nine-foot putt to save par. On the seventeenth he played his approach, what writer and historian Herbert Warren Wind described as a jigger-shot (a club between a midiron and a mashie), to the back level of the green, twenty feet beyond the pin. In *The Story of American Golf*, Wind wrote, "The ball took the roll nicely, slipped rapidly down the slope, struck the back of the cup hard, and stayed in. The keyed-up spectators crammed around the seventeenth green could not control themselves. They yelled, pummeled each other joyously, swatted their friends with umbrellas, and shouted delirious phrases they had not thought of since boyhood. Jerry Travers, the icicle himself, jumped three feet in the air." The only things the American Ryder Cuppers left out in their '99 celebration were the umbrellas and Jerry Travers, who'd been dead for nearly a half century.

Ouimet, with a one-shot lead over Vardon and five on Ray, would birdie the seventeenth again in the playoff when Vardon was forced to take a bogey five after driving into the fairway bunker at the crook in the dogleg. It put Ouimet three ahead with just the eighteenth to play. Vardon doubled the last. Ray birdied it. Ouimet's 72 was five shots better than Vardon, six ahead of Ray. The deed was done. It's fair to say Ben Crenshaw and Herb Wind, if not quite pen pals, enjoyed a robust mutual bond. Ben was a lover of golf history and an admirer of Wind's telling of it. Wind, one of golf's gentlest souls, was fond of Crenshaw and appreciated his abiding love of the game. He encouraged the young player's interest in golf course architecture. There is a group photo taken after the 1913 playoff with the four-foot ten-year-old caddie Eddie Lowery in the foreground and Francis, holding a horseshoe, perched on the shoulders of some spectators. After Crenshaw kissed the seventeenth green following Justin Leonard's make and José Maria Olazábal's miss in '99, Lanny Wadkins, one of Crenshaw's assistant captains, turned to Ben as they walked to the eighteenth hole and said, "You've always had a horseshoe up your ass." The double meaning, intended or not, would not have escaped Crenshaw.

Lowery, the caddie that day and the son of Irish immigrants himself, moved to California and became wealthy in the automobile business. He was the main benefactor of Ken Venturi and Harvie Ward, two of the finest amateurs of the 1950s, even as amateurism faded from the game in favor of Arnold Palmer hitching his pants and charging into the lead on television. Ward won the British Amateur in '52 and would win the U.S. Amateur back-to-back in 1955–56. Venturi would finish second in the Masters in '56, but his crowning achievement was his brave victory in the stifling heat at Congressional CC in the '64 U.S. Open. In January 1956, however, after Ward and Venturi had spent a rather long evening carousing about the Monterey Peninsula in a fashion very similar to the way Robert Louis Stevenson spent half of 1879 chasing Fanny Osbourne there, Lowery knocked on the door of their hotel room and told them to get out of bed; he had arranged a money game for them at the Cypress Point Club. After clearing the previous evening's cobwebs out of their young heads, they learned their opponents would be Ben Hogan and Byron Nelson, who won by a shot in one of golf's most celebrated private four-balls.

British Airways supersonic jetliner Concorde was retired from service in 2003, but it was still the preferred mode of transport for the European Ryder Cup team in '99. When Jacklin first accepted the captaincy offered by the European Tour, he insisted on first-class treatment for his team, something it had lacked previously. Concorde was the tip of that spear. The flight from London to Boston would take just over four hours. Normally, because of noise concerns, Concorde was not allowed to land at Boston's Logan Airport except in the event of an emergency. Of course, there are rules and, then, there are rules. In '89 Concorde transported French president François Mitterrand from Paris to Boston so he could deliver the commencement address at Boston University. According to the *Boston Globe*, a similar exemption was granted the European Ryder Cup team, because "there's a dignitary at the head-of-state level traveling in the aircraft and that makes it a military aircraft. Therefore, it's not within Massport's authority to deny it access." And besides, whether Prince Andrew was on board or not, it's the freakin' Ryder Cup for godsakes.

Crenshaw came to Boston by limousine after spending time with the Bush family at their compound in Kennebunkport, Maine. Former British prime minister John Major was there, too, along with Jimmy Patino, one of Spain's richest men and the owner of the Valderrama GC, where Ballesteros had led the European team two years before. At the PGA Championship at Medinah CC in August, a controversy over whether players should be compensated for representing the United States in the matches oozed out of the locker room and into the media. Ever the traditionalist, Crenshaw was appalled. If the flag is on the bag, money should have nothing to do with it. It's for honor and country and golf. The PGA of America, the sponsoring entity on the U.S. side of the Atlantic, was, to be sure, making money with both hands, like one of those game shows where they stuff a contestant in a glass box and blow bills of various denominations around inside as the person greedily, and unbecomingly, snatches as much out of the air as they possibly can in sixty seconds. The issue was eventually put aside when the PGA of America promised to address it after The Country Club, which it did. The end result was that team members were allowed to designate substantial sums—it has grown over the years—to the charities of their choice. It's a formula the Presidents Cup adopted as well.

Still, the Americans had the taint of avarice about them. That didn't diminish the way they were received in Boston one bit, however. In one of the country's great sporting cities, the U.S. side was cheered from their first public team meal at the Union Oyster House, where they were outfitted with Ryder Cup lobster bibs, right up until the privacy of the team room Saturday night at the Four Seasons Hotel, when it looked to all the world as if they'd been rolled up like crabmeat in a tortilla.

Ryder Cups, all Ryder Cups, have more undercurrents than the Colorado River rapids, and Brookline was a class 6 in two twelve-man rafts. While the Americans were trying to avoid being labeled rapacious, pampered, and spoiled, the Europeans were wondering why on earth their captain, Mark James, had left aging stalwarts Nick Faldo and Bernhard Langer (both forty-two at the time) off the side, picking a surprising rookie, Andrew Coltart, and the more defensible Swede Jesper Parnevik instead. When Faldo sent a letter to the European team expressing his best wishes for their success, rather than pass along the message, James tossed it in the trash. In the coming years as the results mounted in favor of the Europeans, they were often portrayed as a more cohesive unit, a team of jovial, backslapping colleagues, rather than a collection of entitled individuals, as the Americans were accused of being. The truth, however, is that the picture of victory is as pretty as a Renoir portrait, while failure resembles an oil painting of two dead pheasants hanging from a nail. When things didn't go right, a European locker room could get just as testy as an American one, and losing captains were excoriated on both sides of the Atlantic. The European "system" was a lot like Hogan's secret. It helped them for others to believe it helped them. Who would have known the "system" better than Nick Faldo, who was berated as the worst English captain since Bligh after the Euros lost at Valhalla in '08? Well, the worst since James, that is.

On Saturday night of the 1999 Ryder Cup, James's captaincy looked as much like a fiasco as the discovery of penicillin. While the payoff doesn't come until the twelve singles on Sunday, the essence of the Ryder Cup is forged in the foursomes and four-balls when players who ordinarily spend their entire careers hunting as lone wolves find themselves stalking their quarry in pairs. In the first two days at The Country Club, the Europeans fed on American lamb. Leaping uninhibitedly into the arms of his partner, Parnevik, Sergio Garcia, who had given Tiger Woods such a run at the PGA Championship just over a month earlier, helped deliver two points for Europe the first day, defeating Woods and his partner, Tom Lehman, in the morning and following that with a meal of Phil Mickelson and his partner, Jim Furyk, in the afternoon. Colin Montgomerie, the best of all the Europeans and one of the all-time-great Ryder Cuppers, and his partner, Paul Lawrie, contributed another point and a half. Of the Americans it seemed as though only Hal Sutton was rising to the occasion, but it wasn't close to being enough. Europe had blitzed the Americans and taken a four-point lead.

The United States knew it needed to cut into that advantage on the second day—no team had ever come back from four points down in the singles to win—but they couldn't do it. The foursomes were halved 2–2, as were the four-balls. Parnevik and Garcia were the stars again. They were unbeaten in their four matches, bringing Europe three and a half points and propelling the side to a 10–6 advantage at the end of Saturday. The Fat Lady was apparently singing for the Boston Pops. Europe needed just four of the twelve points in the singles to retain the cup. The Americans would need pitons and pickaxes to climb this Bunker Hill.

James was asked about the chances of Europe winning. "I think it would be a disappointment if we didn't," he said. "I came here with the objective of getting 100 percent out of this team, the most points I could. I feel we've gone about it the right way. Time may prove me wrong." Indeed, it did.

While the European team was justifiably confident, the Americans were staggering like a heavyweight fighter pinned against the ropes, absorbing a terrible beating. None seemed punchier or more dazed than Captain Crenshaw.

Crenshaw had won the Masters twice, in 1984 and then eleven years later just a few days after the death of his longtime instructor, Harvey Penick. He and fellow Texan Tom Kite were at Penick's funeral the day before play began in Augusta. As one longtime golf writer, Tom Callahan, put it before the Masters even started, "I'll take low pallbearer." Crenshaw was acknowledged to be one of golf's all-time-great putters with a low, silky stroke that fanned the blade open on the way back and closed it on the follow through. It was a motion that could be devilishly untrustworthy from just a few feet, but no one holed more putts of distance than Crenshaw. Though he did win those two Masters, the world of golf had expected much more from a man who, with his longish blond hair, was in that police lineup of Next Nicklauses whose records would never be mistaken for Jack's. Perhaps it was the Graves' disease he struggled with through much of the '80s that held him back. In his amateur days Crenshaw was a force majeure. He'd won three NCAA individual titles, one in a tie with Kite. He had a reputation for showing up minutes before his tee time, pulling his clubs out of the trunk of his car, scraping his shoes on his feet as he hurried to the first tee, and then breaking par like it was the glass covering on a fire alarm. At one amateur event a fellow competitor named George Haines, who was nicknamed the Mapper for his unique depictions of golf holes, was asked how he reckoned the distance of a particular par three that was all carry over water. "I wait until Crenshaw walks across and I count his steps," he said. Crenshaw's nickname, Gentle Ben, was the most comical thing about him because his rage on the golf course could run hot enough to peel the paint off a Ford pickup. He was a legend even before he won in his professional debut in the Texas Open in 1973 but would, ultimately, become better known for his contributions to simple, elegant golf course design than even his two Masters titles. With his team trailing by four points and only the singles to play, Ben sat in front of the media and, more or less, babbled.

As gracious a fellow as Crenshaw was, when it came to the art of oratory, he would never have been accused of being the Texas Churchill. This, however, was like putting a microphone in front of someone with a grade-2 concussion. He rambled. He paused. He strayed. He blathered. The team had already left to return to the sixth floor of the Four Seasons Hotel. His assistant captains and old friends Bruce Lietzke and Bill Rogers were watching Ben on the television in the locker room. They looked at each other and quickly agreed they needed to give him the hook, get him off the stage. They bolted to the interview room to save Crenshaw from himself. Before they could get there, though, Ben began wagging his finger.

"I'm going to leave you with one thought. I'm a big believer in fate. I have a good feeling about this. That's all I'm going to tell you," he said, then rose quickly from his chair and left the dais as if he'd delivered Macbeth's soliloquy. It was a stunning moment, as likely to be interpreted as a nervous breakdown as a prophecy.

Pairings in the Ryder Cup, as opposed to the Presidents Cup, are done by blind draw, but the only option for the Americans couldn't have been more manifestly apparent. Crenshaw would have to front-load his singles order, get all his best players out on the golf course as fast as possible, trust that they would do what they were supposed to do, and hope that they could build enough momentum to pull the back end along. Trailing by such a large margin, this gambit would be about as surprising as the sun rising in the east.

Though he could dangle his feet from the catbird seat, James had two problems of his own making. He'd chosen not to play three members of his team, Andrew Coltart, Jean Van de Velde, and Jarmo Sandelin, at all until the Sunday singles. Would they be ready for the pressure? And the pairs of Sergio Garcia and Jesper Parnevik, Colin Montgomerie and Paul Lawrie, and Lee Westwood and Darren Clarke had played in every session. Would they tire, emotionally or physically? There had been a time when Europe tried to hide players. The greatest European captain, Tony Jacklin, had similarly held Gordon Brand Jr. out of the matches until the singles in the '83 Ryder Cup. That was the only time Jacklin did it, however, and he never held out as many as three.

Van de Velde was the Frenchman who had lost the Open Championship that summer at Carnoustie in one of the greatest one-hole collapses the game had ever witnessed, rivaled only by Sam Snead's triple bogey at Spring Mill in the 1939 U.S. Open. Van de Velde took a three-shot lead into the eighteenth of the final round but wound up losing in a playoff with Justin Leonard and the eventual champion, Paul Lawrie. Van de Velde's collapse began at the tee when he hit driver into the right rough rather than taking less club and putting the ball safely in play. He compounded the error when his second shot caromed off a grandstand to the right of the Barry Burn. The ball landed in knee-deep rough, and from there, he dumped it into the burn. Van de Velde took off his shoes and socks, rolled up his pants legs, and climbed down into the shallow water to see if he could play it, but it would have been impossible. Instead, he elected to take the penalty drop. His fifth shot found one of the greenside bunkers, where he managed to get up and down just to tie. Sandelin, another rookie, was born in Finland but grew up in Sweden and earned his way onto the European team with victories in the Spanish and German Opens, while Coltart, a Scot, had been one of James's captain picks over the more experienced Faldo or Langer. His sister Laurae was Lee Westwood's wife.

Back at the Four Seasons, the Americans dined on P. F. Chang's carryout, railed at the acerbic commentary of NBC's Johnny Miller, and watched a video that was a mixture of poignant personal moments and film clips like George C. Scott's opening speech in *Patton* and John Belushi in *Animal House* saying, "What? Over? Did you say 'over'? Nothing is over until we decide it is! Was it over when the Germans bombed Pearl Harbor? Hell no!" The evening featured George W. Bush stopping in the team room to read William Barret Travis's letter from the Alamo. "I am besieged by a thousand or more of the Mexicans under Santa Anna," it says.

I have sustained a continual bombardment and cannonade for 24 hours and have not lost a man. The enemy has demanded a surrender at discretion, otherwise, the garrison are to be put to the sword if the fort is taken. I have answered the demand with a cannon shot and our flag still waves proudly from the walls. I shall never surrender or retreat. Then, I call on you in the name of Liberty, of patriotism and everything dear to the American character, to come to our aid with all dispatch. The enemy is receiving reinforcements daily and will no doubt increase to three or four thousand in four or five days. If this call is neglected, I am determined to sustain myself as long as possible and die like a soldier who never forgets what is due to his own honor and that of his country. Victory or death.

Of course, Bush no doubt skipped Travis's postscript about bushels of corn and heads of cattle, beeves as he called them.

Benching 25 percent of a twelve-man side, even if they were all rookies—particularly because they were rookies—was an extraordinary gamble by James. The risk was highlighted when the pairings came out. He sent Westwood out first, putting a heavy burden on the tough Englishman to get a quick lead, since he was being followed by two of the three players who had yet to see action. Westwood would face Lehman. Perusing the lineup, the Americans suddenly saw a glint of hope. If Lehman, who had won the Open Championship three years before at Royal Lytham and St. Annes, could capture his point against Westwood, and if the Americans could take advantage of Van de Velde and Sandelin in the next two games, three points of James's four-point lead would be gone right out of the blocks. Suddenly, it looked to the Americans like they had a chance after all.

Following the two rookies, James installed Darren Clarke and Jesper Parnevik as his firewall. If the Americans knew they had to seize momentum, James knew they had to keep that from happening. It couldn't have gone worse for the Europeans. Lehman did, indeed, beat Westwood. Unsurprisingly, Davis Love III steamrolled Van de Velde, 6 and 5, and Mickelson beat Sandelin, 4 and 3. Sutton beat Clarke. David Duval swamped Parnevik, 5 and 4. As he closed out the Swede, Duval, who previously had referred to the Ryder Cup as "just an exhibition," stomped around the green with his hand up to his ear, pleading for all the noise the rowdy Boston crowd could deliver. Tiger Woods beat the last uninitiated player, Coltart, 3 and 2, while Steve Pate defeated Miguel Ángel Jiménez, 2 and 1. The United States had won the first seven matches. A tie would be good enough to keep the cup, but Europe needed four of the last five points to get it.

Padraig Harrington, the Irishman who would win three major championships in 2007–8, the last two while Woods was nursing his damaged left knee following his U.S. Open win at Torrey Pines, put Europe's first point on the board against O'Meara. Crucially for the Americans, Furyk beat Garcia, who had been the emotional star of the first two days. Lawrie, the Open champion, gave Europe a second point. That left just José Maria Olazábal playing Justin Leonard and Colin Montgomerie playing Payne Stewart still on the golf course. America needed a half point. If Europe won both, they would keep the cup.

Leonard, a Dallas native, had been an All-American at the University of Texas, just like Crenshaw. He'd won both an NCAA title and a U.S. Amateur. He was small, with an unusually rigid lower body in his setup that seemed to rob him of whatever power he might have been able to produce. He made up for it, however, with a controlled iron game and sheer tenacity. He hadn't played particularly well the first two days, though he had managed two half points, the first paired with Davis Love III and the second with Hal Sutton, who had both played well, particularly Sutton. Crenshaw had paired Leonard with Sutton on a hunch. Johnny Miller, in the booth for NBC said, "My hunch is that Justin should go home and watch on television." Through eleven holes of his singles match, Leonard was four down to Olazábal. If O'Meara couldn't pull it out against Harrington (he hooked his tee shot at the eighteenth, pulled his second into the greenside bunker, and lost the point when he couldn't get up and down), it could well come down to Europe's best, Montgomerie, against Payne Stewart, who had won the U.S. Open in June on Pinehurst's No. 2 Course.

Olazábal, however, had been struggling with his driver all week, and the weakness resurfaced at the worst possible moment, as he bogeyed the eleventh through the fourteenth holes. When Leonard rolled in a thirty-footer for birdie on the fifteenth, he'd won four straight holes and evened the match. They halved the sixteenth and came to Ouimet's seventeenth. They both hit the fairway. Leonard's approach spun fifty feet back down the slope of the green from a pin tucked on the upper shelf. Olazábal was half that distance away for his birdie. Putting from the opposite direction Ouimet had faced, when Leonard's ball hit the back of the cup and dropped, the Americans lost their minds. Leonard turned and ran to the edge of the green. Players, caddies, wives, even a stranger or two, ran after him. Olazábal stood frozen behind his marker, watching them. If he made it, they would halve the hole. Among the spectators was thirteen-year-old Keegan Bradley, the nephew of LPGA Hall of Famer Pat, who was up on the shoulders of his father, Mark. The Americans regained their composure. Olazábal missed. The United States was guaranteed the half point that would win the cup. Crenshaw kissed the green. Later, the Americans were accused of stampeding across Olazábal's line. Though what did happen was an appalling breach of etiquette, that didn't. "That kind of behavior is not what anybody expects," Olazábal, known as one of the game's true gentlemen, said. "It was very sad to see. It was an ugly picture to see."

With the matter now truly decided, Olazábal and Leonard played the eighteenth. Behind them Montgomerie and Stewart were finishing a match that, as it turned out, didn't matter. All day Montgomerie had been treated in the most reprehensible way by the Boston crowd. It was so abysmal that his father couldn't bear to remain on the golf course. At one point Stewart had a fan removed from the gallery. All even, when they reached the eighteenth green, Stewart picked up Montgomerie's coin and conceded the match to him. "That's it," Stewart said. The gesture, and in fact the way Stewart had tried to blunt the crowd all day, was not lost on Montgomerie, who remained forever grateful.

When it was over a cadre of victorious Americans made their way through a storage room above the pro shop and out onto a seldom-used balcony to spray champagne on each other and the crowd below. After the closing ceremonies the party moved to the Four Seasons. By the time Crenshaw got there, Stewart was already in full celebration mode in his chili-pepper lounge pants. A month later he was dead.

In the ensuing months, years in fact, a parade of apologies for the scene at Ouimet's seventeenth, a scene everyone on both sides viewed as unacceptable, never seemed to mollify the Europeans. In the Ryder Cup even small slights are magnified in defeat but forgotten in victory. Conspiracy theories blossom like Augusta National's flowering shrubs. Gamesmanship becomes a hanging offense, alleged as if a capital crime had been perpetrated against either the Crown or Congress. And, in just two years, they were quite prepared to do it all over again.

If the comeback at The Country Club momentarily blunted the ascendance of the Europeans, its effects didn't last long. Four of the next five Ryder Cups fell into European hands, including back-to-back blowouts at Oakland Hills outside Detroit and the K Club outside Dublin. The first matches after The Country Club were scheduled to be played in September 2001, but the terrorist attacks of 9/11 in New York, in Washington DC, and on United

Airlines Flight 93, which crashed near the Diamond T coal mine in rural Pennsylvania after a courageous uprising of its passengers, forced a postponement for a year.

In 2002 at The Belfry, the fourth time the matches had been staged there, the Americans and the Europeans went into the Sunday singles tied 8–8. In a bit of serendipity peculiar to the blind draw, the European captain, Sam Torrance, put his strength out first, while the American captain, Curtis Strange, put his strength out last. Torrance's team was able to get four and a half out of the first six points and held on down the stretch, with the decisive blow being struck by little-known Philip Walton, who beat the world number two, Phil Mickelson, 3 and 2.

Two years later the landslides began. The Americans were beaten on their home soil by a staggering nine points, 18.5–9.5. The U.S. captain was Hal Sutton, who had been the backbone of the team at The Country Club. A product of Shreveport, Louisiana, Sutton had a square jaw, square smile, and forearms as thick and hard as sandbags. He won the 1980 U.S. Amateur at the Country Club of North Carolina in Pinehurst, and his father, Harold, a wealthy Louisiana oilman, wanted his son to be the next Bobby Jones. Instead, after winning the 1983 PGA Championship at Riviera CC in Los Angeles, Sutton was yet another brawny blond nominated—though not elected—to be the Next Nicklaus. He went through wives with Nick Faldoian dispatch, eventually piling up four divorces. At Oakland Hills Sutton showed up in a black cowboy hat, a stylistic faux pas in its own right, but his strategic misstep was pairing Phil Mickelson, who had changed his equipment company on the very brink of the matches and practiced off by himself, with Tiger Woods, putting the world's number-one and number-two players, who were none too fond of one another, together. This, in and of itself, wasn't a sin. In 1977 Tom Watson and Jack Nicklaus were paired together in foursomes, and in 1981 they played two foursomes matches and a four-ball together and were unbeaten. But when you put your two biggest names together in the morning four-ball and they lose, with the team gaining only a half point out of four, well, you don't send them back out in the afternoon. Sutton did. They lost again, and the

Americans were five points down after the first day. The rout was all but accomplished.

Two years later at the K Club it was all about Darren Clarke. A burly (except when he would succumb to the occasional bout of fitness and lose enough stone to build a cathedral), cigar-smoking, Guinness-drinking Northern Irishman, Clarke had the reputation for being jovial one minute and bilious the next. His wife, Heather, was diagnosed with breast cancer in 2001 and again in 2004. She succumbed to the disease six weeks before the matches at the K Club. Ian Woosnam was the European captain, and following Heather's death Clarke called the stout Welshman, a former Masters champion with a taste for the brown stuff himself, to tell him he'd be ready if he wanted him on the side. Clarke later said it had been Heather's dying wish that he play. Woosnam picked Clarke and Lee Westwood and paired them twice in four-balls, and twice they won. They each won their singles. The Europeans took a four-point lead into the final wet, sloppy day and dominated, winning eight and a half of the twelve available points. When Clarke closed out his opponent, Zach Johnson, there were tears in his eyes as Woosnam raised his arm high like a referee at a prizefight. Europe had now won five of the last six Ryder Cups, with its only loss coming in the largest comeback in the history of the matches.

At Valhalla GC in 2008 America was on the verge of Ryder Cup irrelevance. Paul Azinger was the captain, and he grouped his players into four-man units he called pods. The idea was that these semi-self-contained groupings would be invested in the captain's picks, in the foursome and four-ball pairings, and, ultimately, in each other. It was team building based on a military model, the navy SEALs. Meanwhile, the Europeans were being led by Nick Faldo, who seemed the walrus to America's SEALs. While Faldo had played more matches and won more points than any other European player, he stumbled with names and with pairings. Two of his best seemed out of sorts. Sergio Garcia had not recovered from the breakup of his relationship with Greg Norman's daughter, Morgan-Leigh, and Padraig Harrington had won two major championships that summer and seemed physically and mentally spent. Azinger's team was bolstered by two native Kentuckians,

Kenny Perry and J. B. Holmes, who helped draw out the crowd, and a rookie, Anthony Kim, whose enthusiasm was able to draw out Phil Mickelson's. With a good ol' boy dash of Boo Weekley, the Americans took a two-point lead into the singles and stretched it to a five-point victory. America was back.

It didn't last long. Out-twitted, outdressed, outinterviewed, and, in the end, outplayed by a distance no greater than the gap between the *f*s in *Cardiff*, the United States left the Ryder Cup behind in Wales but got to keep their pride and the rain suits they had to buy to replace the ones they brought with them that weren't Wales-proof. Pushed into Monday by a monsoon that turned the Usk Valley into the Mekong Delta, the Americans needed a Boston-size rally to climb out of the quagmire they found themselves in after being very nearly shut out in the third session of foursomes and four-balls. Trailing 9.5–6.5, the United States rallied in the singles, pressing the issue all the way to the final match, the first time the fate of the cup had come down to the final twosome since Kiawah Island nineteen years before. The same man who took America's national championship home from Pebble Beach took their golden trophy, too, when U.S. Open champion Graeme McDowell coaxed in a downhill fifteen-footer on the sixteenth hole to go two up on Hunter Mahan and then closed him out on the seventeenth to reclaim the Ryder Cup, 14.5–13.5. Following his U.S. Open triumph, McDowell expressed his desire to find a proper pub to celebrate. He was taken to Brophy's Tavern in Carmel, a known caddie hangout. His autograph from that night is still under Plexiglass on the wall. He added a pelt in Wales.

No one strides with as much purpose as Montgomerie when he's stalking the Ryder Cup. There's a harrumph in every step, as though someone had run Seve through the Ministry of Silly Walks. Yet the brilliance of the man in the event, as a player and, then, a captain, went undisputed, even by him. "There was method in everything I've done here, from the moment I've been selected as Ryder Cup Captain. There's been method in what I've been doing here, all right," he said confidently before the rain-delayed singles when the United States nearly snatched his method away.

Having now lost in upstate New York, Spain, England, Detroit, Ireland, and Wales in the previous seventeen years, winning convincingly in Kentucky and fortuitously in Boston, the Americans were set on reclaiming the Ryder Cup they'd left on the soggy fields of Wales at the Medinah CC outside Chicago. In discussing America's first golf boom and its country clubs, Herb Wind wrote:

> The clubhouse, of course, was the assistant that became the star of the show. Starting as Stanford White's modest lounge and locker-room at Shinnecock, the clubhouse had now become the center of the social life of America's middle-middle, upper-middle, and upper classes. At the clubhouse you lived with the people you wanted to associate with, played your bridge, drank your gin-and-tonic, ate your guinea hen, danced your foxtrot, traded your tips on stocks, and gave your daughter away in marriage. . . . In Chicago, a thousand Shriners, building the Medinah Country Club at a cost of $1,500,000, planned to have the whole works, plus toboggan slides and ski runs.

With the possible exception of Royal Birkdale's sprawling white edifice that resembles a supersized Tastee Freez, the Shriners produced a clubhouse of such singular character that it ranks as the most eccentric in all of championship golf. This Baghdad on the Lake, designed by Richard Schmid, is sixty thousand square feet of redbrick, spires, arches, minarets, and a sixty-foot-high rotunda fit for a faux sultan of the most incomprehensible taste. So it was that after two PGA Championships and three U.S. Opens, the world of golf was, at long last, able to figure out a suitable use for the byzantine structure. It made a perfect mausoleum for the hopes of the 2012 U.S. Ryder Cup team that was bagged, stuffed, and mounted by captain José Maria Olazábal's European squad, 14.5–13.5, in the most breathtaking bushwhacking in the history of hugs and high fives.

Thirteen years earlier it had been Olazábal who stood stone-faced as a herd of fashion-don't Yanks wearing their wretched sepia-toned shirts depicting team photos of Ryder Cuppers gone by bounded like mindless gazelles across the seventeenth green on their way to what was the previous greatest comeback in Ryder Cup history. This time instead of Francis Ouimet, it was the spirit of his late friend and partner Seve Ballesteros who guided Europe to a Boston Tea Party of its own, spraying magnums of champagne all over the northwest suburbs of Chicago. The European team rebounded from the very same 10–6 deficit the Americans faced in '99 at The Country Club and won by the identical final score, only they did it in front of a U.S. crowd on American soil dressed in Seve's trademark navy-on-navy with his silhouetted figure stitched on their sleeves. It happened, in some measure, because both sides remembered that it could but only one believed that it would, and in a place where there was no enchanted green for Olazábal to drop to his knees to kiss. He would have to kiss the sky.

All those years ago Ben Crenshaw wagged his finger and said he believed in fate, but so did Ollie, and he had one important bit of flesh going for him, too, Ian Poulter. On Saturday morning, before the first foursome match went out, a skywriter spelled out "Do It for Seve—Go Europe" in white dashes against a crisp, blue autumn sky. The United States believed it had a thirteenth man in the crowd. Europe's was watching from another place altogether. Halfway through the day's afternoon four-balls, the United States had built a commanding 10–4 lead. It couldn't have looked much worse for the visitors. First, Chicago resident Luke Donald and Sergio Garcia managed to hold off the rally of Tiger Woods to gain a point for Europe. Then, as Rory McIlroy looked on in grinning wonderment, Poulter made five straight birdies, finishing in the dark on the eighteenth with his double fist pump and his singular facial contortions that made him look like Cujo was inhabiting the body of a spiky-haired shih tzu. From that moment on it was as if the entire European side was possessed.

When the Euros fell behind 5–3 on Friday, Olazábal tore into them in their team room. After Poulter's heroics Saturday, it was unnecessary. "I said last night if we had lost any of those two matches, today would have been mission impossible but thanks to what Poulter did, well, the trophy goes back to Europe," said Olazábal, as he stood in the middle of the celebrating throng on the eighteenth green after Europe had won eight and a half of the twelve singles to retain the cup they'd brought with them from Wales and, frankly, thought for the longest time they'd lost. "When we got together last night I made it clear to the players we still had a chance. That the most important thing was believing in it."

But overcoming the largest lead America has held going into the Sunday singles in more than thirty years was a big ask, particularly on U.S. turf, and especially if they'd had to do it without the number-one player in the world. In what was certainly the first time in Ryder Cup history the United States ever got its ass handed to it by police escort, McIlroy very nearly missed his tee time when he confused eastern for central and pulled up to the Medinah clubhouse at 11:14 a.m. for an 11:25 match in the front seat of a state police car with a trooper as his chauffeur. "At least I wasn't in the back," said McIlroy. "He said, 'Have you got motion sickness?' I said, 'I don't care if I'm sick just get me to that tee.' It's my own fault, but if I let down these 11 other boys and vice-captains and captains this week I would never forgive myself." McIlroy had been slated to play Keegan Bradley, who had been the American counterbalance to the pop-eyed Poulter with his own screaming fist pumps. When it became clear McIlroy was running perilously late, Bradley informed the officials that if the number-one player in the world should miss his tee time, it wouldn't matter. Their match would simply go off when he arrived. No harm, no foul—and certainly no penalty.

It was no secret the Europeans would have to go out fast on Sunday, but lights and sirens? Really? Just as Crenshaw had done when he was in the same hole, Olazábal put his best out early. Unlike James, U.S. captain Davis Love III thought he had countered with his hottest players, too, only the heat they'd generated in the first two days flickered and died in the singles. The Euros delivered the first five points, twice winning the seventeenth and eighteenth holes. Luke Donald beat Bubba Watson convincingly; Poulter won the last two holes to beat Webb Simpson; without so much as a good-morning waggle, McIlroy played his best golf of the week, making six birdies to take out Bradley; Paul Lawrie, in his first Ryder Cup since Brookline, trounced Brandt Snedeker; and Justin Rose birdied the seventeenth and eighteenth holes to cut the legs out from under Phil Mickelson.

"The last two holes were as good putts as I've ever holed in my life," said Rose. "Seventeen was just a beautiful moment but 18 was a real clutch putt. That's where I was shaking. I said to myself, 'Rosie, this is the moment. Win, lose or draw your Ryder Cup comes down to this putt.'" Rose, an Englishman born in South Africa, would win the 2013 U.S. Open at Merion GC, playing his approach on the eighteenth hole from very nearly the exact spot Ben Hogan had played his famous iron shot in his 1950 comeback. Hogan's finish, framed by the gallery on each side of the fairway, was captured in Hy Peskin's well-known *Life* magazine photo. While it's usually written that Hogan played a one-iron, others maintain it was a two-iron. Golf writer Charles Price was on the ground right beside Peskin and always insisted it was a two-iron, as did another writer, Dan Jenkins, who was even closer to Hogan personally. "I only know what Ben told me," Jenkins would say. When Rose won at Merion, he pointed to the sky, a gesture to his father who had passed away. The sky in Chicago had already been filled with Seve's blue.

Mickelson and Bradley, who was the emotional spark for the Americans all week, had been 3-0 in foursomes and four-ball, and U.S. captain Davis Love III sat them out Saturday afternoon—at Mickelson's insistence—to be fresh for Sunday. The theory was, why risk two points to chase one? As it turned out the United States had taken a pass on winning the point that could have put the Ryder Cup out of Europe's reach only to come up empty in the singles. Live by the plan, die by the plan. It was second-guessed as much as Mark James's strategy of sitting three in Boston.

Dustin Johnson, who was best known for his long drives and his missed opportunities in a PGA at Whistling Straits and U.S. Opens at Pebble Beach and, later, Chambers Bay; Zach Johnson, who had won the 2007 Masters with a magnificent wedge game into Augusta National's par fives; and Jason Dufner, who won the 2013 PGA Championship at Oak Hill with an equally impressive iron game, kept American hopes alive at Medinah. Lee Westwood had been in poor form all week, but he beat Matt Kuchar to nudge the Euros closer. That meant the golden trophy would rest in the hands of two of Love's captain's picks—forty-two-year-old Jim Furyk and forty-five-year-old Steve Stricker—and Tiger Woods, who was the U.S. team's anchorman just as Montgomerie had been in Boston. Furyk became the third American of the day to lose the seventeenth and eighteenth holes, both with bogey, and fell to Garcia. Stricker went one down to Martin Kaymer when he, too, bogeyed the seventeenth. Kaymer's par on the eighteenth secured at least a tie, which meant Europe would retain the cup. And, yes, as he stood over the eight-footer, he thought about his German countryman Bernhard Langer and his miss at the Ocean Course at Kiawah Island in '91. "I sat down with Bernhard and talked to him a little bit about the Ryder Cup because my attitude wasn't the right one," said Kaymer of their Saturday-morning meeting. "But now, after that match today against Steve, I know how important the Ryder Cup became and is." Kaymer had won that PGA Championship at Whistling Straits when Dustin Johnson grounded his club in a hazard—every grain of sand on the course beside Lake Michigan was defined that way. He had been going through a swing change for much of 2012, and had he not made the team on points, his form was so poor he said he wouldn't even have picked himself, let alone expected Olazábal to do it. Kaymer's swing adjustments, developing a dependable right-to-left shot along with his usual left-to-right ball flight, propelled him to a dominating performance in the U.S. Open at Pinehurst No. 2 two years later.

After Kaymer made the cup-clinching putt, bedlam ensued on the eighteenth green. Woods lost the last hole to Francesco Molinari, adding an otherwise meaningless half point to Europe's total. "It was already over," said Woods. "This is a team event and the cup was already retained by Europe, so it was over." The prize is the cup, not a 14–14 tie. As the victorious European team draped themselves in flags on the eighteenth, Love shook McIlroy's hand. "Glad you could make it on time," the U.S. captain said with a smile before talking about his team's loss. "I don't have a reaction yet, we're all kind of stunned. We know what it feels like now from the '99 Ryder Cup. It's a little bit shocking."

Stricker was 0-4-0 on the week and the only U.S. player who was completely shut out, though Woods came close with just a half. Furyk's disappointment cut far deeper. He'd been tied for the lead at the Olympic Club in San Francisco with a good chance to win a second U.S. Open when he snap-hooked a three-wood off the sixteenth tee, failed to birdie the par-five seventeenth, and staggered home on the last. "I'll be honest," said Furyk. "It's been a very difficult year."

The singles may be the decider, in the words of Bush 43, who was in the Chicago gallery along with Bush 41, but the four-balls and foursomes are just over 57 percent of the points and about 80 percent of the spirit of any Ryder Cup. It's where most of the hugging, knuckling, fist pumping, chest bumping, and backside slapping goes on. Mickelson could be excused for giving Bradley a friendly swat on the behind in the first day's afternoon four-ball because, after all, he owns part of a baseball team in San Diego, or a Padre or two anyway. For two days in Chicago they were the majority owners of the Euros.

Bradley was the valedictorian of the 2012 class of the University of Phil, a traveling series of seminars involving practice rounds and enough cash to pay off student loans, all done just to get ready for weeks like the Ryder Cup. At twenty-six and a PGA champion, Bradley approached his golf ball with the kind of decision-making resolve of a squirrel crossing a busy street. His cha-chas behind the ball before stepping in to hit it were only the beginning. When he lined up his putts with his long belly putter, he cocked his head as if preparing to cut the eight-ball into the side pocket. Four years previously at America's last victory at Valhalla, Mickelson drew energy from another rookie, Anthony Kim, but comparing that to Bradley's ardor was like saying a AAA battery puts out the same wattage as Vermont Power and Light. Bradley was the American who could go fist pump to fist pump with Poulter. After winning their last foursomes match Saturday morning by a record-tying 7 and 6, and taking into account Phil's advancing years and Keegan's rampaging adrenal glands, Love parked his two-seater Ferrari in the garage for the afternoon.

While the dream team formerly known as Stricker and Woods was going 0-3 on Friday and Saturday—even if there were mitigating circumstances, that is, the stunning play of long-hitting Nicolas Colsaerts—it was the American rookies who largely staked the United States to its 10–6 lead heading into the Sunday singles. Bradley accounted for three points, Jason Dufner and Webb Simpson two apiece, and Brandt Snedeker one. Bubba Watson, the Masters champion, and his rookie partner, Simpson, were a pairing forged the previous year in the Presidents Cup. They lit up both their four-ball matches, making nineteen birdies and winning each 5 and 4. Snedeker, fresh from winning eleven million dollars and pocket change in the FedEx Cup, was the only first-timer not to get a point on Bring a Rookie to Medinah Day. He and Furyk got three down to the Northern Irish twosome of McDowell and McIlroy but managed to pull even before Snedeker's drive sailed wide right on the eighteenth, leading to the loss of a full point. They came back in day-two foursomes to beat the Irish one up. In essence, they had played Europe's most celebrated team over two days and thirty-six holes and gotten a push out of it.

Meanwhile, Olazábal was relying on the considerable heroics of two individuals, Colsaerts and Poulter. With Westwood holding his cape, the Muscles from Brussels made a once-in-a-generation Ryder Cup debut, with eight birdies and an eagle to beat Stricker and Woods all by himself in four-ball, one up. Though Colsaerts may have made every putt he looked at Friday, he hit more rims than a Belgian cyclist on Saturday and was shut out. Before Poulter gave his teammates the breath of life, it seemed as though the most important stroke of the day was going to be the long putt Dustin Johnson made for birdie at the seventeenth followed by his par at the eighteenth that gained the United States a full point, putting them up 10–4. But that was the last time anything good happened to America on Medinah's seventeenth.

"Yeah, we carried Seve on the arm for Sunday for a reason," said Poulter.

In the European team room there was a picture from another Ryder Cup of Olazábal leaping up behind his partner, Ballesteros, his hands on his shoulders, trying to get a glimpse of something in the distance. Turned out, it wasn't a flag he was looking for but Medinah. In the scrum on the eighteenth green someone asked Ollie what it all meant to him. He couldn't get through the answer. "It means everything," he said, turning away. "For him and for me, yes, everything."

Olazábal and Ballesteros had been the greatest partnership the Ryder Cup had ever known. In Chicago Jake and Elwood are the only pair that could ever give them a run, with or without a police escort. There were those who criticized Olazábal for not prevailing on Molinari to pick up Woods's coin, à la Stewart at The Country Club, declare it a tie, and walk off into the sunset. But the man who had stood on the seventeenth green thirteen years before in Boston, icily watching the Americans celebrate while he still had a putt to tie, was never, ever, ever going to allow that.

Two years later at the Ryder Cup at Gleneagles, on the first shot off the first tee of the first match of the first day, Ivor Robson, the elfin-toned starter who has launched a thousand foozles in Open Championships, introduced Webb Simpson as Bubba Watson, and it was more or less downhill from there for sixty-five-year-old U.S. captain Tom Watson, who had been recruited by PGA of America president Ted Bishop specifically to resuscitate America's lifeless Ryder Cup fortunes. Watson, after all, had captained the '93 team that won at The Belfry. Success didn't strike twice. With the European victory of 16.5–11.5 in the Scottish midlands, the United States had struck out in eight of its last ten at bats, relegating America to a golfing status of all field, no hit.

All along Watson maintained he was going to opt for the hot hand, but when push came to shove he sat rookies Jordan Spieth and Patrick Reed, who had won their match in the opening four-ball, 5 and 4. One thing Watson wasn't going to do was go with the cool ones, something he proved by benching ten-time Ryder Cup-per Mickelson and his chosen partner, Bradley, all day Saturday. It led to a very public revolt at the U.S. team's media postmortem.

When Tony Jacklin first agreed to be Europe's captain, his initial act was to go see Seve Ballesteros, who'd been left off the 1981 team in a dispute over appearance money. "I knew I couldn't do it without him, so we met. He felt slighted and hurt by what had happened, and boy was he angry," Jacklin said. "I said, 'I can't do it without you and it's as simple as that—as far as I'm concerned you're the best player in the world.' He agreed to come on board and, by God, did he help." Thus was formed one of the greatest partnerships in the history of the matches and its most enduring rivalry: Seve versus All Things American.

Jacklin had gotten the buy-in of the man who would be the heart and soul of his team just as Paul Azinger had gotten it at Valhalla. You can believe in pods or not, but once you've lost your team, you've lost the Ryder Cup. Tom Watson was a great champion, a word Seve wouldn't have used lightly. But Watson's solution to America's Ryder Cup weakness was to just be tougher. It's the well he drew from after he'd lost a pair of U.S. Opens, simply deciding he would never let it happen again. It turned out his mettle didn't split twelve ways.

For better or worse, Phil Mickelson has frequently found the bully pulpit of a microphone to be his chosen avenue to advance what he thinks ought to be done, from taxes in California to cell phone cameras in Ohio. Mere moments after Europe's victory, Mickelson delivered his indictment of Watson. "No, nobody here was in any decision," he said.

Paul McGinley, the European captain, gave the world's best player, Rory McIlroy, his comfort food when he paired him with Garcia. Then he gave him the job of pulling up an out-of-form Poulter because McGinley knew he'd need the Englishman's passion in the singles. Finally, he put McIlroy out third on Sunday, essentially saying to him, if it all begins to go wrong, you're the firewall. You're the number-one player in the world. Your job is to put blue on the board. Full stop. Any potential U.S. rally doesn't get by you. McIlroy, who had become so much more comfortable with his place atop the game than he had been just two years before, took all of it on and then ruthlessly took out his good friend Rickie Fowler in singles, 5 and 4. To whom could Watson turn? If the groundwork goes undone, no one is going to answer that text.

After yet another loss, where could the United States turn? The Americans reached back, too, all the way back to Medinah to give Davis Love III a curtain call in the hopes that, the second time around, it will be written for him at Hazeltine the way it was under a rainbow at Winged Foot, on a green in Boston, or in the sky over Chicago.

# 10

## Everybody Wants to Rule the World

Arguably the greatest feat of legerdemain performed by Tim Finchem during his twenty-plus-year tenure as commissioner of the PGA Tour was shepherding his collective through the Great Recession, partly by clinging to the pants legs of his sponsors as they were elbowing each other in a race for the exits. When the subprime mortgages swirled around the drain and the credit default swaps sucked down the world's developed economies in 2008–9, every financial institution that had its name on a golf tournament was showing up for work with a paper bag over its head. America's car companies, another traditional supporter, arrived in Washington, DC, by private jet but with their hats in their hands. It wasn't a good time to be relying on the kindness of friends, much less strangers. Finchem managed to hold the thing together when this tsunami slammed into his rainy-day fund. It was an impressive feat of stewardship that ought to be taught in a business school somewhere.

But money has a short memory. What likely will survive longer than the steroidal hacienda-style clubhouse he built behind the eighteenth green of Pete Dye's Stadium Course is the tournament he helped birth, the Presidents Cup. It wasn't entirely Finchem's idea—his predecessor, Deane Beman, was pivotal in the early discussions, too—but it was Tim's baby, played for the first time just a few months after he became commissioner.

"I was the chief operating officer, Deane was commissioner. We sat down and kicked around the general idea and notion of it," says Finchem. "We determined that we would give it a shot. We didn't sort of run around and take a poll."

The PGA Tour is in the uncomfortable position of being in control of exactly none of the most significant events in the game, not the Masters, or U.S. Open, or the Open Championship, or the PGA Championship, or the one that had enjoyed the biggest revival in the 1980s and '90s, the Ryder Cup. "It just seemed like there were a lot of players, and members of our tour, from outside the United States, who were not in the Ryder Cup," says Finchem. "The Ryder Cup had really started to go at that point. I think the driving thinking was just, isn't it too bad that we have so many top players from outside Europe that don't get on that stage." It was a vacuum, potentially a consequential one, that the PGA Tour decided it could fill. And it may just turn out to be Finchem's single most lasting contribution.

"Commissioners are administrators, they manage the situation," he says. "I'll say this, I put the Presidents Cup very high on the list of things I've enjoyed working on. Over the years, it's been a collaborative effort with the players and working to build something pretty cool."

Between February 6, 1994, and the arrival of Tiger Woods, with the exception of a single week, the number-one player in the world was either Australian Greg Norman or Zimbabwean Nick Price. When the first Presidents Cup was played, Price had just knocked Norman off the perch he would hold for the next forty-four weeks. The Europeans had already thoroughly demolished the notion of American dominance in the post Nicklaus-Watson world with cudgels wielded by Seve Ballesteros, Sandy Lyle, Nick Faldo, Bernhard Langer, Ian Woosnam, and José Maria Olazábal. The rest of the former British Empire—plus some—was rising up behind Norman and Price, Price's countrymen Ernie Els and Retief Goosen, Fijian émigré Vijay Singh, and Argentina's Ángel Cabrera.

The number-one ranking was nothing new for Norman. His first stretch there was in 1986, and with a few interruptions, he would trade it back and forth with Faldo and Ballesteros for eight years. Even with Price and Els ascending, Norman remained the big kahuna going into the first Presidents Cup. It would have been difficult to envision such an event without him. Besides, he'd been brandishing his World Tour saber, something he would officially declare the existence of in November '94 with Fox Television as his media partner—Rupert Murdoch's first foray into golf until locking down the USGA for twelve years beginning in 2015 and, in turn, hiring the aging Norman to sit in the announcers' booth for, as it turned out, one year. While the entire point of the Presidents Cup was to give the newly named Internationals a Ryder Cup–like stage to strut across, Norman's concept of a tour for just the top-thirty players was swirling in the background. When the Australian withdrew early in the week of the inaugural matches because of a stomach illness, the swirl became more of a vortex.

David Graham, the flinty Australian who won the PGA Championship in 1979 in a playoff against Ben Crenshaw and then won the 1981 U.S. Open at Merion with one of the great final rounds ever played in that championship, was the Internationals first captain, and he and Norman didn't exactly see eye to eye on much of anything. "He (Norman) wouldn't come to the dinner at the White House and I thought that was very disrespectful and I publicly stated that," says Graham.

And then he didn't want to arrive until Thursday morning and the whole team was going to be there for two or three days without him and I didn't think that was very respectful. Then, on Wednesday, he announced that he was sick and he was going to withdraw. Then, he showed up on Saturday on the first tee. He said, "I'm going to do television." I said, "Well, if you could be here Saturday and Sunday, it looks like you could have been here yesterday." I told the press I thought this was the Presidents Cup and not the Greg Norman Invitational. I didn't choose my words as politically correct as I would today, I think.

Or perhaps not. Graham nixed Norman's participation on CBS, and two years later Norman, with an assist from Steve Elkington, nixed Graham's repeat captaincy.

In 1994 if Shark Enterprises represented the brand for the Internationals, he was also thirty-nine years old. He'd won the Players Championship that year when he and Fuzzy Zoeller reprised their U.S. Open–Winged Foot white-towel waving on the eighteenth hole of the Players Club. But Norman had already won his two Open Championships and done most of his Shakespearean dying, sometimes at the hands of others and sometimes by his own, on all those other big occasions, with perhaps the most ignominious demise still in front of him in Augusta two years in the future with Faldo. Norman would go on to play in three Presidents Cups and captain the International side twice. He had a 7-6-1 career record, including 3-1-0 in '98 when the Internationals won at Royal Melbourne. And though he may have missed the maiden voyage, he did, eventually, help get the thing away under full steam. Truly, however, it was others, some of whom had the most interesting biographies in golf, who would ultimately make it sustainable.

One of those was Norman's good friend Nick Price, who would play on five teams and captain another. Born in Durban, South Africa, Price grew up in Zimbabwe when it was still Rhodesia. His father, a World War II veteran who served with the British in India, died of cancer when Nick was just ten. He was introduced to golf by his brother, Kit, who gave him a left-handed five-iron. In the 1970s Price served for eighteen months in the Rhodesian Air Force, including a sixteen-week deployment installing radio equipment in forward combat positions, an experience that gave him a perspective on life, death, and survival few of his colleagues possessed.

It seems like every generation of golfers has one or two players of immense talent who are thought to be "too nice" to win in the big moments. As wrongheaded as the entire concept may be, Price was nominated to be that man. When he was being inducted by the air force, at the end of his physical, the doctor asked Price if he had any complaints. He replied that, as a matter of fact, he did have a skin condition. Surprised, the doctor asked what the nature of the problem was, and Price told him, "Bullets go through it." There was never a time when you saw Price on a practice ground that he didn't have a joke for you, guaranteed to be one you'd never heard, and this was long before the days of Internet search engines and social media. Once, when I'd gone to Price's house at Lake Nona in Florida on a photo session, we suggested we get him water skiing on his boat behind his lakefront house. After slaloming back and forth a little, he dropped into the water. Needing just a few more pictures, we circled to pick him up and asked him to take one more run. "Sure," he said, "but be a little quicker coming around next time, mates. There are alligators in here." After we'd finished our attempt to serve one of the finest golfers in the world as a reptilian hors d'oeuvre, he invited us inside for a cold beer. This was not unusual. This was Nicky.

In his first opportunity to challenge in a major, Price allowed the '82 Open Championship to slip through his fingers at Royal Troon, dropping the claret jug into the lap of Tom Watson, a man who knew as well as anyone that cutting the head off the major championship Medusa usually took a swing or two with a battle ax. Price was three shots ahead with six holes to play in the same Open that Bobby Clampett, a skinny, curly-haired, and much-heralded amateur from Brigham Young University in his first year as a professional, held a five-shot lead at the midway point, stretched it to seven but finished 78-77, and never did much professionally thereafter. Price hadn't exactly been a juggernaut coming into the Open, having pocketed less than two thousand dollars that season on the European Tour. Troon's homeward holes had been brutal all week, but after birdies at the tenth, eleventh, and twelfth, coupled with Watson's bogey at the fifteenth, Price found himself three clear. He three-putted the thirteenth and doubled the fifteenth, then came up short on the seventeenth, chipped eight feet past, and missed coming back to fall a shot behind. He left himself a thirty-footer at the last to tie Watson but missed. Afterward Watson said it would be a learning experience for both Price and Clampett. "I cried and I'm sure they'll cry a little, too," said Watson. One of them learned enough to make it all the way to the Hall of Fame.

In '83 Price joined the PGA Tour and won the World Series of Golf at Firestone. He wouldn't win again in America until 1991. In '86 he shot a 63 at Augusta National and, playing alongside Norman on Sunday, finished fifth in Jack's Miracle at the Masters. He had top tens in major championships in '85, twice in '87, and came second behind Ballesteros in the Open Championship at Royal Lytham and St. Annes in '88, where he held the lead after both thirty-six and fifty-four holes. He was the nice guy who just couldn't seem to finish first. It mattered not at all that among his peers he was considered the best iron player in the world.

Price finished six shots behind in both the Masters and the U.S. Open in '94 and finally broke through in the PGA Championship at Bellerive CC in suburban St. Louis. At thirty-seven it would be the first of three major championships Price would win in three years. At Bellerive he picked up the pieces when Gene Sauers, a Savannah, Georgia, pro who led after each of the first three rounds and, later, Jeff Maggert faltered. After halving the sixteenth with birdies, Price and John Cook, another one of the "too nice guys" who was once one of the many blond Next Nicklauses and who'd had a couple of close calls in majors himself, knew the tournament was coming down to just them. "We both knew what each other was thinking," said Cook. "We walked up to the 17th tee and kind of snickered at each other." Price finished par-par to Cook's par-bogey. While it was Price's first major, it was back-to-back PGA Championships for his caddie, Jeff "Squeaky" Medlin. With his wife, Sue, due to deliver their son, Greg, Price had withdrawn from the previous year's PGA Championship at Crooked Stick in Indianapolis. He was replaced by John Daly, who needed a caddie, and Squeak, who passed away from leukemia in 1997, picked up the bag and the souvenir flag from the eighteenth hole.

Price burnished his record with a Players Championship in '93 and then took the final two majors of the 1994 season. The Open Championship at Turnberry will be remembered primarily for two things, the first is Price, who finished birdie-eagle-par, holing a fifty-footer on the seventeenth, jumping off the ground, and sprinting around the green. Tumbling just over the edge of the hole, the putt gained him a share of the lead with Swede Jesper

Parnevik. Years later Parnevik would become known as the man who introduced Tiger Woods to his then nanny, Elin Nordegren. On this week, however, Parnevik went down in infamy as the man who refused to look at the leader board. Playing in front of Price and thinking he needed a birdie at the eighteenth, the Swede took a risky chance with a wedge that came up short of the green in a thick lie. He dropped a shot, and it cost him the championship, or at least a chance to play off for it. "In 1982 I had my left hand on this trophy," said Price. "In 1988 I had my right hand on the trophy. Now I finally have it in both hands." Weeks later he followed Turnberry with a second PGA Championship at Southern Hills GC in Tulsa, Oklahoma, with a dominating wire-to-wire exhibition, beating his closest pursuer, Corey Pavin, by six shots to become the first player since Walter Hagen in 1924 to win the British and the PGA in the same season. This was truly Price at the very top of his game, and it was the game, emotionally exhausted as he might have been, that he brought with him to the first Presidents Cup.

If Price was a darling of the media, Vijay Singh, another member of that first Presidents Cup International side, was certainly not. His backstory, much like Price's, was one of the most fascinating in golf. It was, however, not a story Singh enjoying sharing because, when he did, he felt burned by the result. He'd learned the game on Fiji's Nadi Airport Golf Club. He had to run across the airport's single runway to get to the course. He didn't just dig his game out of the dirt, the way Hogan advised; he tunneled. Singh got off the island of Fiji faster than Gilligan got off his, though, one supposes, Vijay looked back with less fondness. Not everyone who comes up the hard way comes out hard, but there are some who do and Singh is one of them. And then some.

The basis of his adversarial relationship with the media was his suspension from the Asian Tour in 1985. Accused of changing his card to improve his score in the Indonesian Open, he was first disqualified and then suspended. He went into what amounted to a self-imposed exile in Borneo for two years, just the sort of place where wounded pride reaches its boiling point. After Borneo he joined the Safari Tour, then the European Tour, finally coming to America. Because *l'affaire* Jakarta was murky, at best, and precisely because Singh never wanted to talk about it, the subject refused to die. Singh found it far more to his liking to not speak with anyone who wanted to talk about "it." Instead, he plowed his energy into practice, becoming the most tireless ball beater in golf. He could wear the tread off any caddie who ever lived. In 2013, in an ironic flashback, Singh was temporarily suspended by the PGA Tour, though it had nothing to do with scorecards, erasers, or making cuts. In a *Sports Illustrated* article, Singh admitted using deer-antler spray, a substance on the PGA Tour's banned list after the tour began a drug-testing regime in the run-up to golf reentering the Olympics of 2016. The amount of growth hormone contained in deer-antler spray was so minimal it was considered inconsequential enough for WADA (the World Anti-Doping Agency) to subsequently remove it from its list of banned substances. When that happened, Singh's suspension was lifted, too, but that didn't appease him. Motivated, one suspects, by the residue of his perceived slights of the past—on the other side of the coin, he'd already been inducted into the World Golf Hall of Fame—he sued the tour, seeking redress for damage to his reputation caused by the chain of events his own comments to *Sports Illustrated* had set in motion. Until then he'd always been popular among his peers, if not the press, but this was not the way to win friends and influence people, two things Singh never seemed particularly interested in doing anyway.

Singh's single-minded devotion to hard work finally bore fruit at the PGA Championship among the soaring lodgepole pines and claustrophobic chutes of Sahalee CC outside Seattle. It was the first time a major championship had been played in the Pacific Northwest since Ben Hogan won the PGA Championship at match play at Portland GC in 1946, and it would be the last until the U.S. Open returned to the some fescue, some Poa annua, mostly dirt greens of Chambers Bay in 2015, where Jordan Spieth would win his second straight major championship. Singh went into the final round tied with Steve Stricker, a Wisconsin native renowned for his wonderful putting stroke, benign midwestern temperament, and the fact that he would be named the tour's comeback player of the year not once but twice. Having shots fly off into the woods that pinched and shaded Sahalee's fairways wasn't exactly unprecedented. To have the ball spit back out was serendipitous. To have it rejected like Kareem Abdul Pinetree and then land on the green near the hole, well, that's just the kind of good fortune that leads to a major championship. Singh's three-wood second shot on the par-five eleventh sliced into the trees and caromed onto the green, leaving him a twenty-five-footer for eagle and an easy two-putt birdie. Still holding a one-shot lead, Singh and Stricker found themselves together in a greenside bunker on the par-three seventeenth. The Fijian made his fifteen-footer for par, while Stricker missed from three feet inside him. Singh parred the eighteenth in a dreary Pacific Northwest downpour to win by two.

In 2000 Singh won the only major championship Tiger Woods didn't, the Masters, allowing him the distinction twelve months later of slipping the green jacket onto the shoulders of the Tiger Slam. Though heavily favored, Woods opened with a 75 and spent the rest of that week trying unsuccessfully to catch up. Singh's relationships with his putters were just as frosty as his ones with golf writers, and this Masters was not won on the greens. With a downsized and buff David Duval, who had already been number one in the world but had yet to win a major, leading at the halfway mark and Singh, Ernie Els, and Phil Mickelson a shot behind, the weather on Saturday turned as miserable as any day ever has in Georgia in April. There was sideways rain, cyclonic wind, biting cold, and, inevitably and thankfully, darkness. When the third round was eventually completed on Sunday morning, Duval and Els had shot 74, Mickelson 76. Singh, among the later twosomes who saw the worst of the weather until play was halted Saturday, concentrated on hitting the ball solidly and beneath the tree line. His two-under-par 70 was good for a three-shot lead. The issue was decided on the eleventh, twelfth, and thirteenth holes Sunday afternoon. Two shots ahead of, and playing alongside, Duval, Singh hit his second into the pond on the eleventh and bogeyed. His seven-iron on the twelfth was headed for the pine straw, azaleas, and yellow forsythia on the bank behind the green, but the ball hit and dropped into the back bunker, from where he managed to get up and down for par. Then, on the thirteenth, with

Singh already on the green in two, Duval hit into the creek fronting the green. Game and set. Match point came after Els drew
within two following his birdie on the fifteenth, but Singh equaled
it for a three-shot victory.

A second PGA Championship title came in an even more unusual
place than Singh's first, this time on a stretch of land that was
virtually treeless. Whistling Straits, on the western shore of Lake
Michigan north of Sheboygan and south of Green Bay, was built
on a combination of flat Wisconsin farmland and a former military training base known as Camp Haven. Owned by the plumb-
ing magnet Herb Kohler, more than thirteen thousand truckloads
of sand were dumped on the site for architect Pete Dye to play
around in. What came out of this doodling by the cubic yard was
either a terrifying midwestern faux links or the largest single sand
bunker ever created, take your choice. (Six years later Dustin Johnson would fail to grasp the distinction and miss the sudden-death
playoff between Martin Kaymer and Bubba Watson.) No one had
the slightest clue what it would play like in a championship, and
it wasn't until the wind blew on Sunday that Dye's course showed
exactly how cruel it could be.

Singh took a one-shot lead over Justin Leonard into Sunday, a
day when only two players managed to shoot in the 60s, the same
number who shot 80. Singh never made a birdie in regulation and
shot 76, the highest final-round score ever by a PGA Championship
winner. He finished tied with Chris DiMarco, who had started the
day five behind and made it all up with a one-under 71, and Leonard, who had a chance to win outright with a par on the last hole
of regulation but took one club less than he should have, came
up short of the green, and couldn't make a four. DiMarco, who
the following year would push Woods to extra holes at Augusta
National, had a fifteen-footer for a birdie at the last but missed,
too. Leonard had won the Open Championship at Royal Troon
in '97 and lost the '99 Open at Carnoustie in the Van de Veldean
playoff that shouldn't have been. He felt, with some justification,
like he'd thrown away the PGA Championship at Hazeltine two
years before with a final-round 77 that opened the door for both
Tiger Woods and, ultimately, Rich Beem. Leonard surely must have

felt this playoff shouldn't have happened, either, after holding a two-shot lead with three to play and bogeying the sixteenth and eighteenth. On the first hole of the three-hole aggregate-score playoff, Singh went for broke, taking out driver on the tenth, an uphill 361-yard par four. He left himself a thirty-yard pitch to the green and made his first, and only, birdie of the day. It proved to be the winning margin. DiMarco and Leonard picked up on the eighteenth after the forty-one-year-old Singh made his par putt to close them out.

The victory at Whistling Straits was Singh's eighth in his forties, a number that would eventually climb to twenty-two, eclipsing Sam Snead's record for success among the aged. Singh would play on the first eight Presidents Cup teams, making it nearly impossible to conceive of an International side without him. His career record was a respectable 16-15-9, but the odds are he litigated himself right out of a captaincy. Those odds were just as good that he wouldn't care, or at least act as though he didn't.

In addition to Norman, the other star who was missing in action in that first Presidents Cup was Ernie Els, at the time the twenty-four-year-old reigning U.S. Open champion, who played in the Dunhill British Masters instead. "Els decided not to play," says David Graham. "He already had a commitment which I kind of had a go at him about publicly when I said maybe the day will come when you'll regret not playing in the Presidents Cup. If I had to say that over again, I'd choose my words a little more carefully." One suspects, in the case of Els, that's true. "It had to have all the best International players, that's why we're doing it," said Tim Finchem. "These guys go different directions so, yeah, that was a concern."

Els had grown up just outside Johannesburg, the son of a man, Neels, who built his own trucking business. The son was six feet three, with broad shoulders, the disinterested gait of a plow horse, and a golf swing as smooth as smoke. Oakmont in '94, the site of the U.S. Open, was as hot as the Gobi Desert. Players didn't need caddies; they needed camels. The temperature didn't hover around one hundred; it surrounded it on all sides. Arnold Palmer bid an emotional farewell to the U.S. Open and tearfully adjourned to the air-conditioning. It was also the year of the quizzical ruling. With Colin Montgomerie already in the clubhouse at five under par, it looked very much like the trophy would go to either Els or Loren Roberts, the American who was such a deft putter he was tagged with the moniker Boss of the Moss. On the seventeenth the short, uphill dogleg-left par four, Els hit driver, a bold but not unprecedented play. In 1962 Phil Rodgers's drive lodged in a little pine tree near the green, and a couple of baseball swings later, he'd missed the Nicklaus and Palmer playoff and was set on the path to discovering a career as a short-game guru. In '94 Els's drive hooked a little too much and came up short behind a grandstand. As the USGA had allowed all week, line-of-sight relief from the stand took him to a drop area about fifteen yards closer to the hole—a rules conundrum—and he saved his four. But that was nothing compared to the ruling Els got on the first hole of the following day's playoff after both he and Roberts bogeyed the eighteenth Sunday to fall into a three-way tie with Montgomerie. Monday playoffs for the U.S. Open are generally ugly affairs, though Tiger Woods versus Rocco Mediate at Torrey Pines in 2008 stands in stark relief to that rule of thumb. At Oakmont, however, the rough was an extra day longer, the heat an extra day hotter, the greens an extra day harder, the players hopped up on an extra day's adrenaline and mentally wobbly from nervous sleep. This was a playoff that lived down to expectations. The ruling on the first was the famous Trey Holland/walking official/immovable-movable camera crane, from which Els was allowed to drop out of deep rough. He uncomplicated the misstep by making bogey anyway. The playoff went seriously downhill on the 342-yard par-four second. Els was unplayable in a bush and made seven. Montgomerie made a six, and Roberts took the honors with a bogey. By the time they'd finished eleven holes of this not-so-sudden death march, Els and Roberts were three over par and Montgomerie eight over. After eighteen holes the black-shirted and sweat-soaked Montgomerie had mercifully dropped out, with Els and Roberts going two more holes before Els closed it out, sweatingly, with a par.

Like everyone else in golf in 1997, Ernie Els had seen the future. With the thunder of Tiger Woods's twelve-shot Masters victory ringing in his ears and the hoof beat of Tigermania galloping across Congressional CC, Els had a sense of you-better-get-it-while-you-can on his way to a second U.S. Open. This time Tom Lehman was the designated American battling Els and Montgomerie. Lehman had won the '96 Open Championship at Royal Lytham and St. Annes by two over Els (and Mark McCumber) after Els had bogeyed the sixteenth and eighteenth holes coming home. As Ernie watched Lehman through Lytham's ground-floor windows overlooking the last green, he was approached by Tiger Woods asking advice about turning professional. Els must have felt like singing the Simon and Garfunkel lyric "Every way you look at it you lose." Going into Sunday's last round at Congressional, Lehman had led or shared the lead in the last three U.S. Opens. This one wouldn't turn out any better for him than the previous two. Boosted by a pitch-in birdie from off the front of the tenth green, Els was tied with Montgomerie and Lehman after all had cleared the fifteenth hole. Lehman bogeyed the sixteenth to fall a shot behind. At the seventeenth the downhill par four that now plays as the eighteenth, Montgomerie lost his approach right onto the bank of the greenside bunker. Els followed that shot by launching a 212-yard five-iron that hung in the sky and turned left at the pin, stopping fifteen feet from the hole on a green treacherously bordered by water behind and left. Montgomerie couldn't get up and down, and the twosome went to the par-three eighteenth with Els a shot clear of both pursuers. Behind them, knowing he needed to make up a shot coming in, Lehman had 190 to the seventeenth green. The moment he hit his seven-iron, he knew it was in the water. "Oh, no," he said. Els's two-putt three at the last closed out Monty.

Finishing in Tiger Woods's rearview mirror was something that had become fatalistically familiar to Els. In 2000 he was second to Woods at Pebble Beach, fifteen shots back. A few weeks later at St. Andrews, he'd be second to Woods again, eight shots behind. Having already completed the Tiger Slam, two years later Woods came into Muirfield with the calendar Slam still alive, having won both the Masters and the U.S. Open. Only Ben Hogan had succeeded in winning three straight, completing his triple at Carnoustie in 1953. Palmer had had the chance in '60 and lost by one to Kel Nagle. Nicklaus had the opportunity in '72 and lost by one to Lee Trevino's chip in at Muirfield's seventeenth. In 2015 Jordan Spieth would get a shot at it at St. Andrews and miss the playoff there by a single stroke. Woods would lose his bid in a sudden, barbaric Scottish gale on Saturday, shooting 81. The leaders bore the brunt of the wretched weather, and Els was among them, too. In the end his 40-32, the second-nine score made possible when the conditions improved almost as quickly as they had deteriorated, may have won him the claret jug. For once against Woods, fortune had picked him.

Els took a two-shot lead into the final day. Playing an hour before him, Australian Stuart Appleby, whose wife, Renay, had been killed in a freak traffic accident while unloading luggage outside Waterloo Station in London four years previously, shot 30 on the final nine for 65 to post six under par. Frenchman Thomas Levet joined him, followed by another Australian, Steve Elkington, the '95 PGA champion who had been forced to qualify to get into the field. Els got to eight under par on the back but couldn't hold it. He bogeyed the fourteenth from a fairway bunker and then doubled the par-three sixteenth after missing the green and scuttling his pitch shot. He reached the par-five seventeenth in two and two-putted to climb back into the four-way tie, which is where it ended. The aggregate playoff was set for three holes, the sixteenth, seventeenth, and eighteenth. Els parred them all. Elkington and Appleby played them one over. Levet had birdied the sixteenth, but when he bogeyed the eighteenth, he and Els returned to the tee for a do-over. Levet bogeyed again when he drove into one of the fairway bunkers, and Els pulled it out by getting up and down from the greenside bunker for his par. Afterward Els said of the claret jug, "If I hadn't got it this year, I don't think I'd have made it."

He would have been wrong. But before he was right, everything changed, yet again. Els had become accustomed, if unhappily so, to living in the time of Tiger, but there were other disappointments. He cast a lonely figure on the putting green of Augusta National in '04 as Phil Mickelson birdied the eighteenth just yards away for his first Masters and again at the Open Championship that year when he lost a playoff at Royal Troon to Todd Hamilton, an American player best known for his success on the Japanese Tour, who bunted his way around with a utility club that nowadays (and very likely then, too) could be found only on eBay or at a garage sale. Els struggled with his putting. He struggled with his drinking. More poignantly, he and his wife, Liezl, discovered that their son, Ben, who was born in October '02, was severely autistic. "We suspected for a few years that something was wrong," Els has written. "I mean, there's a process that every kid goes through. Crawl at nine months, walk at 12 months, and then start talking and so on. With Ben we started thinking: 'Why is he not crawling? Why is he not walking? W'1y is he not looking me in the eye?' Things like that. We soon discovered he was quite profoundly impacted by autism." At first Els blamed himself. As time went on he found himself. Els and Mickelson, the two boys who'd competed against each other in the 1984 Junior World Championship in San Diego, had each been overtaken by real life. In Mickelson's case it was the cancer diagnoses of his wife, Amy, and mother, Mary. For Els, it was Ben.

Just when he thought the window on his golf had slammed shut, the sash was thrown open for Els one more time, on the same course, Royal Lytham, where he'd booted away an Open of his own. After three utterly harmless days, when the wind finally arrived at Royal Lytham in 2012, Els towered above the rest. Already in the Hall of Fame, the forty-two-year-old South African played an astonishing back nine of four-under-par 32, better than anyone else who set foot on the course that Sunday. Ignited by a bogey on the ninth, Els pulled out driver on the short tenth and left himself just eighty-seven yards to the hole for a birdie. His six-iron to five feet at the twelfth got him to five under par, at that point still miles behind the leader, Adam Scott. He birdied the fourteenth to reach six under, then missed a chance at the drivable sixteenth. Coming down the last looking for one more, Els pulled driver again, avoided the treacherous bunkers, and followed with a sand wedge twelve feet left of the hole. When he picked the birdie putt out of the cup, he flung the ball into the huge grandstand, triumphant without having won. "I always felt that I wanted to get back to where I felt good about myself. I promise you walking up 18, I was fine with second again," said Els, who'd finished second and third in the previous two Opens at Lytham. His thoughts were of Ben back in their London home. "I know he was watching today," said Els, "and I was trying to keep him—because he gets really excited—I wanted to keep him excited today."

Instead of Els crumbling at the end as he had in '96, it was his good friend Scott who wilted. Resurrected from a slump initiated by the unhappy end of a seven-year love affair with his girlfriend Marie Kozjar, and trying to ride the broomstick putter to his first major championship, the thirty-two-year-old Aussie with the GQ looks, the jet-set life, and the gee-whiz demeanor, who once had Tiger Woods's coach (Butch Harmon), a reasonable facsimile of Tiger Woods's golf swing, and now even Tiger Woods's old caddie (Steve Williams), fell apart, well, like Tiger Woods had after his Thanksgiving Day fender bender. Scott went into Sunday with a four-shot lead. When you've previously won sixteen of eighteen times when you're ahead going into the final round, it's yours to lose, and Scott knew it. With no one applying any pressure until Els made his back-nine charge, a birdie at the fourteenth got Scott back into double digits under par, and it seemed the claret jug was going down under for the first time since Norman won in '93. Then Scott bogeyed the fifteenth from a greenside bunker. Plenty of breathing room left. The first body blow came at the short sixteenth when he lipped out a four-footer for par. Gasp. At the seventeenth he missed a six-iron left in deep rough and dropped another shot. Coupled with Els's birdie at the eighteenth, the breathing room had become a vacuum. Another bogey at the last from a fairway bunker that required a sideways escape was his fourth in a row. As Northern Irishman Graeme McDowell, Scott's playing partner, putted out on the eighteenth, you could see the Aussie mouth one word, *Wow*. Afterward he said, "I know I've let a really great chance slip through my fingers today. Hopefully, I can let it go really quick. I mean, look, Greg was my hero when I was a kid, and I thought he was a great role model, how he handled himself in victory and defeat. He set a good example for us. I can't justify anything that I've done out there. I didn't finish the tournament well today. But next time—I'm sure there will be a next time—I can do a better job of it." He couldn't have been more right.

The original Big Four of the Internationals—Norman, Price, Singh, and Els—was quickly reinforced by Retief Goosen in 2000, Scott in 2003, and Ángel Cabrera in 2005, adding their own compelling biographies to the list. Goosen won the 2001 U.S. Open at steamy Southern Hills—there is no other way to describe Tulsa in June—in another playoff that shouldn't have been. A few months older than his compatriot Els, Goosen was struck by lightning on the Pietersburg Golf Club when he was fifteen, his clothes singed, his watch burned into his wrist, his shoes knocked off his feet, the soles melted. Mercifully, he remembered nothing. Driven hard by his father, Theo, Goosen had a black temper as a junior that settled into a robotic mien as a mature player. While he manifested a machinelike appearance on the course, Goosen was actually a feel player with natural gifts and a swing nearly as musically attuned as Els's own. With the blue eyes and good looks of a leading man, he nonetheless gave the impression of someone without a functioning heartbeat. At Southern Hills he either led outright or was tied for the lead after each of the first three rounds. Mark Brooks, a chain-smoking Texan who had won the '96 PGA Championship, had shot an even-par round of 70 on Sunday, good for what he thought would be no better than third, and was emptying his locker when he found out he just might be in a Monday playoff. Goosen and Stewart Cink were playing the eighteenth all tied, both a shot ahead of Brooks. Cink missed the green with his second and the ball buried in the Bermuda rough. Goosen put his six-iron approach twelve feet past the hole. It seemed over and done with. Cink gouged his chip out, then missed his par putt. In a hurry to get out of Goosen's way (the issue was now presumptively decided), Cink missed the tiddler to make a double-bogey six, falling one shot behind Brooks.

It wouldn't have mattered much except for what Goosen did next. He ran his twelve-footer past the hole, then lipped out the two-footer coming back. Goosen made a white-knuckle three-footer just to get into the playoff with the Texan, who was hastily putting everything back into his locker. The playoff wasn't much for drama. Putting his previous day's blunder behind him, Goosen came back cold-bloodedly the following day and built a five-shot lead after ten holes, finished bogey-bogey, and still won by two. And what of Cink, who'd hurried his way right out of a shot at the U.S. Open? "I honestly believe with all my heart that things happen the way they're meant to happen," he said. "This time it wasn't my turn. My turn is coming soon." Soon turned out to be eight years away when he drove a stake through the heart of romance, denying fifty-nine-year-old Tom Watson a sixth Open Championship title at Turnberry.

If Goosen fell into a playoff with some questionable putting in Tulsa, his second U.S. Open Championship was the exact opposite. Taking a two-shot lead over Phil Mickelson and Ernie Els into the final round at Shinnecock Hills, the day settled into a back-nine back-and-forth between Goosen and Mickelson, who had broken through for his first major championship that April in Augusta. One of America's famed golf courses, Shinnecock's remote location near the tip of Long Island among the mansions where the Manhattan moguls congregate in the summers had kept it off the rota until Ray Floyd won there in '86. Its clubhouse was designed by Stanford White, the celebrated red-haired, flamboyant New York architect who was murdered in 1906 by the jealous, mentally unstable husband of a chorus girl White had once plied with champagne in the mirrored room of the Twenty-Fourth Street Manhattan apartment he kept for just such purposes. The husband, Harry Thaw, the son of a wealthy Pittsburgh coal and railroad tycoon, walked up to White during the finale of *Mam'zelle Champaigne* on the rooftop restaurant of the old Madison Square Garden—also one of White's architectural designs—and shot him three times in the head.

The "crime" of 2004, however, was what the USGA did to the seventh green, effectively shooting themselves in the foot. A facsimile of North Berwick's par-three Redan, the seventh was baked, mowed, and hardened to the point of making it unplayable. When the USGA finally grasped what they had wrought, they began watering it at various gaps between groups. As a result not all players were playing the same course. Did you get to the seventh just after they'd syringed it with water hoses or just before they decided they needed to do it again? Ham-handedly, USGA officials tried to lay the blame at the feet of Shinnecock's superintendent when the grounds staff had done nothing more in preparing the course than what they had been instructed to do.

Mercifully, Mickelson and Goosen got through the seventh without incident that Sunday. After a bogey at the twelfth, Mickelson was three behind. He birdied the thirteenth and fifteenth, however, and with Goosen's one-putt bogey on the fourteenth, they were tied. Mickelson birdied the sixteenth to take a one-shot lead. Two more holes, and back-to-back major championships would be his. Goosen, playing behind Mickelson, equaled Lefty's birdie on the sixteenth, and they were tied again. On the seventeenth Mickelson missed the green with his six-iron, finding a bunker. He blasted out to eight feet and stunningly three-putted. Goosen's par-par finish slammed the door. The South African who had nearly given away an Open by missing a two-footer had one-putted six of the first eight holes on the back. This would be the third of Mickelson's six seconds in a U.S. Open. Goosen had a wonderful chance the next year to successfully defend his title at Pinehurst. In an effort to become a Hale Irwin–like three-time collector of U.S. Opens—and, among the majors, only U.S. Opens—he took a three-shot lead into the final round over a lightly regarded leader board. The best résumé among the top ten was Tiger Woods, six back. Goosen shot 81, however, and the championship fell into the arms of New Zealander and native Maori Michael Campbell, who spent the day ducking into Port-o-Lets to do eye exercises designed to maintain focus. Goosen and his playing partner, the barrel-chested American Jason Gore, who shot 84, ended up playing the last three holes for a five-dollar side bet just for something to do. "I played rubbish at the end of the day," said Goosen, who nonetheless won the bet.

The Southern Hemisphere class of '69 also included Ángel Cabrera, born the same year as Goosen and Els. While he was a little late to the Presidents Cup party, he carried the scars— inside and out—of a personal story nearly as traumatizing as being struck by lightning and surviving. Abandoned by his parents at the age of three and raised by his father's mother, Pura Concepcion, Angel grew up in the dirt streets of Mendiolaza, scratching out a subsistence and fighting for what he wanted. He has three visible scars on his face earned in barrio brawls and a deeper hidden one from his abandonment. He began caddying at the Cardoba Country Club when he was ten and dropped out of school by the sixth grade. The older caddies called him El Pato, the Duck, because he waddled like one, but he learned to play with controlled fury. Cabrera became a star of the South American tour, then upgraded to Europe. In addition to the Argentine Open, he'd won twice in Europe before he broke through in the 2007 U.S. Open at Oakmont.

Cabrera became the fourth straight player from below the equator—and fourth straight International, of course—to win the U.S. Open, following Goosen, Campbell, and Australian Geoff Ogilvy. Thin and sinewy as a strip of beef jerky with a slowpoke gait reminiscent of Don January, Ogilvy had been the beneficiary of a four-car crash in the final turn at Winged Foot in '06. Mickelson's collapse (his fourth second) is the most memorable, but Colin Montgomerie, who couldn't make up his mind between a six-iron and a seven-iron in the middle of the eighteenth fairway, also double-bogeyed when a par would have won it. Padraig Harrington bogeyed the last three holes to lose, and Jim Furyk needed a four on the eighteenth to win but couldn't make one. Having another International player win in the wake of Winged Foot wasn't much of a surprise. That it was Cabrera was a shock to anyone at Oakmont who didn't already know him.

By then the Argentine was thirty-seven. He was rarely seen without a cigarette. He had a fondness for food and drink and a profound apathy toward the kind of athletic training Tiger Woods had supposedly imposed on the modern golfer. Cabrera didn't have six-pack abs; he had a pony keg. Raising an Italian fernet was as close to heavy lifting as he was inclined to get. But on the inside, as he would sometimes say, "La maquina est listo." The machine is ready.

Going into Sunday Cabrera was four behind the leader, Australian Aaron Baddeley, but more important, two behind Tiger Woods, the world number one who was already the winner of twelve major championships, including two National Opens. Cabrera birdied the fourth and fifth holes and made a distance-defying two on the three-hundred-yard par-three eighth to take the lead. Woods could do no better than tread water all day, making just one birdie against a double bogey on the third and a bogey on the eleventh. He blamed his putter, but in truth, he hadn't struck the ball well enough to give himself makeable chances. Furyk had the best shot at catching Cabrera with three straight birdies on the thirteenth, fourteenth, and fifteenth holes. Driving the ball fearlessly, Cabrera birdied the fifteenth with a massive tee shot and a nine-iron to three feet. He gave back shots on both the sixteenth and the seventeenth, but his five-over-par 285 proved good enough when Furyk also dropped a shot at the short, treacherous uphill seventeenth. Two years later Cabrera added a Masters green jacket to his U.S. Open trophy with a little help from Kenny Perry, who was trying to win his first major championship at the age of forty-eight. Perry, a Kentuckian with habits as modest as Cabrera's were insatiable, had had one previous chance at a major in the '96 PGA Championship when he was second-guessed for sitting in the TV tower beside Valhalla Golf Club's eighteenth hole instead of focusing on the potential playoff with Mark Brooks, where he would, in fact, struggle. "I was young at Valhalla," Perry said. "Here, I thought I had enough experience. Great players get it done, and Angel got it done. This is his second major he won. I've blown two, but that's the only two I've had chances of winning." Perry had come to the last two holes with a two-shot lead but skulled his chip on the seventeenth to make bogey and bunkered himself off the eighteenth tee. It dropped him into a three-way playoff with Cabrera and Chad Campbell, a Texan with a flat swing (some liked to compare it with Hogan's, though the results belied the similarity) who had been in or near the lead from the tournament's beginning.

The first playoff hole was the eighteenth, and Campbell went out after hitting his second in the greenside bunker. Cabrera nearly followed him except for the all-universe par that kept his hopes alive. After hitting it right into the trees that form the chute off the eighteenth tee, he clipped another when he tried to slice his recovery shot at the green. With 114 yards remaining for his third, Cabrera put his wedge 6 feet from the hole and made it to equal Perry's par. On the second extra hole, the tenth, Perry missed the green down the slope to the left and couldn't get up and down to match Cabrera's routine four. El Pato would have another chance at a Masters, this time losing in a playoff in 2013 to one of his International teammates, Scott.

Once bedeviled by self-doubt, then tempered by the disappointment of his loss to Ernie Els at Royal Lytham, Scott found a green jacket in that playoff in the dwindling light of Augusta National's cathedral hole, becoming the first Australian to win the Masters. It was his first major and their first Masters, the dreams of one man and one nation intertwined. "We are a proud sporting country, and like to think we are the best at everything, like any proud sporting country," said Scott. "Golf is a big sport at home. It may not be the biggest sport, but it's been a sport that's been followed with a long list of great players, and this was one thing in golf that we had not been able to achieve. So it's amazing that it's my destiny to be the first Aussie to win, just incredible."

Scott was at one of the lowest points of his career when Greg Norman, a man haunted by his own ghosts of Masters past, made him a captain's pick for his '09 Presidents Cup team. It was more than a pick; it was a lifeline that couldn't be severed even by the disappointment of Royal Lytham. Scott went into the final round of the '13 Masters a shot behind Cabrera and Brandt Snedeker, a fast-talking American from Nashville, Tennessee, who grew up working part-time in his mother's pawn shop. Playing in the twosome directly in front of Scott was another Australian, the then twenty-five-year-old Jason Day, who started birdie-eagle to quickly join the final pair at eight under. Two years previously Day had finished birdie-birdie in the Masters only to be overrun at the end by Charl Schwartzel, a sinewy South African who was fond of big-game hunting and piloting his single-engine plane back into the bush country on camping trips, who closed with an unheard of 4-2-3-3, four straight birdies. The 2013 masters would prove to be the second close call in a major for Day (he finished a distant second in the 2011 U.S. Open that Rory McIlroy ran off with at Congressional CC), and there would be more before his breakthrough at Whistling Straits in 2015 when he shot twenty under par, the lowest score ever in a major championship.

Pelted by the on-again, off-again rain, Cabrera took the lead after Day bogeyed the sixth and got to nine under par, three clear of the two Aussies at the turn. El Pato bogeyed the tenth, but even worse, he played the two par fives on the back one over, while Scott birdied them both, rescued when his second to the thirteenth remained mysteriously suspended on the bank above the fingerling stream that trickles down into Rae's Creek. It was Day who seemed outfitted to be the Aussie of destiny, making three straight birdies on the thirteenth through the fifteenth to lead by two, but he gave those shots back when he hit it through the green on the sixteenth and came up short in the front bunker on the seventeenth. Failing to get either up and down, he dropped a shot behind Scott and Cabrera.

Scott came to the eighteenth at eight under and hit his eight-iron twenty-five feet right of the hole. The putt caught the left side and, in an homage to the Southern Hemisphere, swirled clockwise on its way to the bottom of the cup as Scott yelled loudly enough to be heard over the screaming patrons, "Come on, Aussie!"

With Scott in the clubhouse at minus nine, Cabrera hit a big drive and a brave seven-iron inside three feet to force the playoff. Neither player held the front of the green on the first playoff hole, the eighteenth, but Cabrera very nearly chipped in. Scott managed to get his up and down to send the twosome down the tenth. Both hit the fairway, and Cabrera had another good run at birdie, leaving his putt sitting on the right edge, before Scott swept his in with the broomstick putter to upend all of down under.

If the nucleus of the Presidents Cup International teams since that very first one in '94 features players of unquestionable pedigree, they haven't been alone. Robert Allenby and Stuart Appleby, the two Australians who are sometimes confused for one another by the virtue of a single consonant even though they don't look alike, don't act alike, and don't play alike, have been on six and five teams, respectively. Mike Weir, the Canadian who became the first left-handed-playing golfer to win the Masters, was on five teams before he lost his game. Trevor Immelman, the '08 Masters champion from South Africa, made only two teams after a benign tumor attached to his ribs and, later, suffering wrist and elbow injuries. Louis Oosthuizen, who dominated the Open Championship at St. Andrews in 2010, lost in a playoff there in 2015, and lost the Masters in a playoff the year after his friend and countryman Schwartzel won it, has one of the most elegant swings in golf but bad fortune with injuries, too, and has missed more teams than he's made.

From the moment of its announcement the Presidents Cup was destined to be portrayed as Ryder Cup Lite. Its most dramatic moment was probably in 2003 at Fancourt in South Africa when, after tying 17–17, the United States and the Internationals opened the envelope—sealed before the matches began—to reveal the names of Tiger Woods and Ernie Els as the players selected by their captains to represent their teams in a playoff for the cup. Going forward, putting the full weight of a team event on the shoulders of two men was deemed to have been a bad idea. In the fading light in South Africa, however, Els and Woods gamely went back out, lasting three extra holes, all pars, with both of them making lengthy putts to halve the third playoff hole before it was too dark to continue. In negotiations between the captains, Gary Player and Jack Nicklaus, and the PGA Tour commissioner, Finchem, the competition was declared a tie. The cup was held jointly for two years. In retrospect, it was as splendid a moment of sportsmanship as the game had seen in a very long while, second-guessed almost exclusively by people who weren't there. If there has been any surprise in the first two decades of Presidents Cups, it's been the mostly favorable outcomes for the Americans, coming at precisely the same time the United States couldn't seem to buy a victory against the Europeans in that more famous competition. Such things, no doubt, run in cycles. One ought to, at the very least, take seriously the admonition of Franz Kafka, "In Man's struggle against the world, bet on the world."

# 11

## Parting Is Such Sweet Sorrow

If it was possible to go back to read the transcripts from the 1868 Open Championship, there is no doubt Old Tom, the defending champion, would be explaining to the assembled quill pushers at Prestwick that, even at the ripe old age of forty-seven, he'd never struck his guttie any better. It is the final irony of great champions. They've conquered the flight of the ball at roughly the same time they lose the ability to play the game. In the natural progression of things, the outgoing tide will sweep their muscularity out to sea like flotsam, or maybe jetsam. But in that twilight stretch when they are still powerful enough, it's not swing path that betrays them but the synaptic neurons. To borrow from the movie *Bull Durham,* golf is a game played with fear and arrogance. In the final analysis arrogance never outlasts fear. In their prime, though, in those resolute moments when the fate of their world rested in the gentle pressure of their own grip, they were able to squeeze off shots with a stomach full of razor blades as if it meant nothing more than picking up their dry cleaning. There is something about the heart of a champion, something that isn't distributed among us in equal measure like ten fingers and ten toes. And, whatever that thing is, it seems to demand one last summoning from the host body, a curtain call of last rights to drain the pool dry, proving to themselves they've used up every last smidgen of the majesty they discovered within.

There may have been more words written about Ouimet at The Country Club or Hogan or Jones at Merion—pick one—but for sheer volume, the chronicling of Nicklaus's 1986 Masters victory takes a back seat to none of them. He was not the oldest man to win a major championship. That remains Julius Boros at forty-eight years, four months, and eighteen days in the 1968 PGA Championship at Pecan Valley GC in San Antonio. Boros did everything late. One of six children of Hungarian immigrants, he didn't turn professional until he was twenty-nine, working instead in the accounting firm of the man who owned Rockledge CC in West Hartford, Connecticut. "One day in December of 1949, I looked out the window of my office at all the snow and decided to turn pro," he said. Boros played in the North and South Open at Pinehurst, North Carolina, won by Sam Snead, then went down Midland Road to play a one-day pro-am at Mid-Pines CC. He won it and became the club's professional. His first victory was the U.S. Open in 1952, a title he'd win again eleven years later in a play-off at The Country Club against Jackie Cupit and Arnold Palmer. Boros lived with a cardiac condition that led to quintuple bypass surgery in his early sixties. A heart attack killed him at seventy-four while he was sitting in a golf cart parked in the shade of his club in Fort Lauderdale, Florida. In tournaments he walked the golf course with the urgency of a man window-shopping for a hat. Over the ball Herb Wind described him as someone "as relaxed as a bowl of Jell-O." He was in constant motion, never took a practice swing, and wielded the club in a buttery back and through that looked as natural as Picasso signing his name. That such a velvety swing remained dangerous late into its competitive life surprised exactly no one.

Nicklaus, on the other hand, was a bear of a different sort. When he won the Masters at forty-six years, two months, and twenty-three days, edging out Old Tom's 1867 Open Championship for the number-two spot on the old-guy spectrum, Nicklaus was widely believed to be pretty much washed up, even by his own reckoning. "At that point in my career, I wasn't having much success," he said. "I didn't expect to win, the press didn't expect me to win, the players didn't expect me to win." Yet it happened. The Masters of '86 wasn't the last time Nicklaus would appear on the tournament's oversized, old-school, hand-operated leader boards, as iconic as the scoreboards in Wrigley Field or Fenway Park. In 1990, at fifty, he was paired with Nick Faldo in the next-to-last group, chasing forty-seven-year-old Raymond Floyd, who was in the process of draining his own reservoir of competitive vigor. Faldo caught Floyd and won their sudden-death playoff when Raymond hit his second shot into the pond fronting the eleventh green. "This is the most devastating thing that ever happened to me in my career," Floyd said afterward. That's the way it usually ends, abruptly and badly. But not for Jack. In 1990, chasing Floyd and Faldo, Nicklaus shot 74 and finished sixth. Make no mistake about it, though, his personal stockpile of excellence, the largest the game has ever known, was used up in '86, in a week, in a day, on a back nine, that took everything he had that he hadn't already given.

When doesn't destiny show up with its pockets full of tiny omens? The '86 Masters was the first Nicklaus's mother, Helen, had attended since his inaugural trip to Augusta in 1959. It was the first time Jack's sister, Marilyn, had been to the tournament. And on Sunday Nicklaus wore a yellow shirt in memory of a young boy, Craig Smith, the son of their church minister who died of cancer at thirteen and once told Jack he liked it when he wore yellow because the color seemed to bring him luck. Jack's son Jackie, by then a pro himself, was on the bag just as he had been at the U.S. Open at Pebble Beach in 1982 when, had it not been for the heroics of Tom Watson, his father would have become the first man to win five National Opens. And then, of course, there were the other bits and pieces. Nicklaus had suffered business setbacks. Not enough to ruin him financially but enough to keep any chief executive officer of a mom-and-pop empire up nights. He was using a strange new black putter, the MacGregor Response ZT, with a head the size of a Polish kielbasa. He hadn't won a major championship since his magical Jack Is Back 1980 season when he won both the U.S. Open at Baltusrol and the PGA Championship at Oak Hill. In fact, he hadn't won anything at all since his own tournament, the Memorial, in a playoff against the big Floridian Andy Bean, a man who could bite the balata off a golf ball, two years before. He was coming off a missed cut in the Tournament Players Championship and had withdrawn from the event before that after an opening round of 74 in New Orleans. His best finish in the seven tournaments he'd played was T39. And he'd been publicly written off in a couple of throwaway lines by the *Atlanta Journal-Constitution*'s Tom McCollister, who, in his pre-Masters advance, portrayed the five-time Augusta champion this way: "Nicklaus is gone, done. He just doesn't have the game anymore. It's rusted from lack of use. He's 46, and nobody that old wins the Masters." John Montgomery, a longtime Nicklaus friend who enjoyed a practical joke, was only too happy to post the article on the refrigerator of Jack and Barbara's rented house. "I was between things in my life," Jack has said. "I'd play some golf, 12 to 14 tournaments a year, not enough to keep me sharp but enough to be somewhat competitive. I was neither fish nor fowl. I wasn't really a golfer." And then, somehow, some way, he was again.

Despite having spent some time prior to the Masters with Jack Grout, his instructor since boyhood, it didn't seem particularly promising at the outset. Nicklaus opened with a 74. His ball striking was satisfactory for the first time all year, but he couldn't score. That's the way it is as the end approaches. Early in the week Ken Venturi, the 1964 U.S. Open champion who was a commentator for CBS, said it was time for Jack to start thinking about when to retire. Nicklaus had a locker-room conversation about just that with his old nemesis and friend Lee Trevino, also forty-six. "It makes it difficult to cope when people think we're as good as we were 10 years ago," Trevino said.

The opening-round lead was held jointly at four-under-par 68 by Billy Kratzert, an Indiana boy who, when he had trouble getting his tour card in his first two tries, held down a job as a forklift operator, and Ken Green, who was playing his first round in his first Masters. Green, a good friend of Mark Calcavecchia, was something of a golfing iconoclast and all-around loose cannon.

His sister, Shelley, was his caddie. He liked to wear a shamrock-green glove with matching shoes and, as the years went on, could be seen putting with a cut-down Bullseye so short a dwarf would have to kneel on the ground to use it. Twenty-three years later at age fifty-one, Green would be involved in a deadly accident on I-20 in Mississippi when his RV pitched down an embankment, demolishing its front end. His girlfriend, Jeannie Hodgin, and his brother, Billy Green, who was driving, were both killed, along with his German shepherd, Nip. Green survived but sustained numerous injuries, some resulting in the loss of the lower part of his right leg. Though he tried to play a few senior events after he recovered from the accident, the ghost pain in the limb and the disability itself proved too much.

By the end of the second round, Seve Ballesteros had moved to the top of the leader board with rounds of 71 and 68, a stroke ahead of Kratzert. Green had disappeared with a 41 on his front nine. It was just Ballesteros's third tournament of the year in America. He'd been kicked off the PGA Tour for failing to enter the required fifteen tournaments the season before. In his customary response to anything he believed to be disrespectful, Ballesteros elevated the suspension to a personal feud between himself and Deane Beman, the short-of-stature commissioner who had won the U.S. Amateur twice and the British Amateur once and tied for second in the '69 U.S. Open, a shot behind Orville Moody. Ballesteros said Beman was "a little man trying to be a big man." A four-time major champion, including two Masters, Seve had been allowed by Beman to defend his title in New Orleans. The only other event he played in the United States was on a mini tour in Lake City, Florida, where he tied for twenty-second. Between New Orleans and Augusta, Ballesteros returned to Spain to be at his father's side when cancer claimed his life in March. Rusty as he was, Ballesteros was determined to claim the tournament in memory of his father, Baldomero, and to spite his nemesis, Beman.

Nick Price, a twenty-nine-year-old Zimbabwean with a quick, compact swing capable of producing iron shots that fell out of the sky like yard darts, took advantage of Saturday's benign conditions to set the Augusta National course record with a theretofore unimaginable 63, equaling the low score in any major. In contrast, Ballesteros struggled on the greens and managed nothing better than level par for the day. He came to the seventeenth a shot ahead but was unable to hang on to the lead, finishing bogey-bogey when he three-putted the seventeenth and drove poorly at the last. The shoddy finish left him a shot behind Australian Greg Norman and tied with Price, Bernhard Langer (the defending Masters champion), and Donnie Hammond, an American who had won the Bob Hope Desert Classic in Palm Springs that winter. Three Toms—Kite, Watson, and Nakajima—were another stroke back. Nicklaus was tied, and would be paired in the final round, with the Scot Sandy Lyle, the reigning Open champion who would win the Masters two years later, highlighted by a monumental seven-iron shot out of the first fairway bunker on the eighteenth. Jack was four shots off the lead, but between him and Norman were four major championship winners. Leapfrogging all of them seemed a big ask.

Through eight holes on Sunday, no one was even entertaining the notion that what did happen could.

Norman birdied the sixth. Ballesteros birdied the seventh to stay within a shot. On the uphill par-five eighth, Kite holed his third from 80 yards for an eagle, and Ballesteros pitched in on top of him from half that distance. Just that quick, the dark-haired and quick-striding Ballesteros, with his brother Vicente on the bag, was in the lead at eight under par and ready to take Augusta National, its back nine, and Deane Beman by the scruff of the neck to honor the memory of the farmer and oarsman from Santander he'd just buried. Standing on the ninth green, Nicklaus was now six shots behind. It would take him roughly two hours to fashion one of the greatest narratives not just in golf but in any sport, producing more teary eyes than Old Yeller along the way.

As the roars descended from the eighth green back up the hill, Nicklaus turned to the crowd seated around the ninth and said, "Okay, let's see if we can get a roar up here." They laughed. He smiled. It all seemed harmless enough. He was too far behind too many good players. Nicklaus holed his eleven-footer. The patrons obliged by manufacturing, almost comically, a bit of noise of their own. Nicklaus drove poorly on the tenth, hitting a spectator and failing to take advantage of the fairway's precipitous downhill slope. Left with a four-iron to the green, he put it twenty-five feet from the hole and made that one, too. Behind him, Ballesteros bogeyed the ninth. Now, the Spaniard and the Australian were tied again. In two holes Nicklaus had gone from afterthought to three behind.

When he birdied the eleventh after a solid drive and eight-iron to twenty-two feet for his third straight birdie, Nicklaus was five under par with only two players to catch, Ballesteros and Norman. One of Augusta National's cardinal sins in Amen Corner is going for the pin on the right side of the twelfth green, the usual Sunday placement. The educated shot is straight over the bunker, to the middle of the shallow putting surface. Anything pushed right or hit by a gust of ghostly wind swirling out of nowhere inevitably finds the grass embankment and rolls back into Rae's Creek—with the notable exception of Fred Couples six years later, of course. Nicklaus aimed at the bunker but pulled his seven-iron left onto the back fringe. After leaving himself six feet for par, his putt hit a spike mark, deflected right, and missed. Bogey. Breathing room for Ballesteros and Norman. It had been a nice little run for Nicklaus. Great fun. But now it was over. Nothing more than a bit of spice in what looked to be a dramatic shoot-out between two of the game's current superstars.

Norman, however, was busy succumbing to the tenth hole yet again. He pulled his drive left, nicked some pine tree branches, and dropped into the fairway three hundred yards from the green. He would double-bogey the hole, the same score he'd had two days earlier when he four-putted it. Up ahead, Kite birdied the eleventh to go to six under par, a shot behind Ballesteros.

Nicklaus was hot leaving the twelfth green. Jack was famous for being not only the most prolific winner of major championships but also the most gracious loser of them. However, giving shots away, particularly under the gun, wasn't something he took well. Never did and never would. Getting beat was one thing. Beating himself was something altogether different. Having now pricked the balloon of hope he'd just inflated with three straight threes, Nicklaus knew there was no alternative but to release the hounds. Caution was going to get him nowhere. Not a natural right-to-left player, his tee shot on the dogleg-left thirteenth hugged the tree line. If it caught any part of a pine limb, the likely effect would be to kick the ball dead left deep into the woods, or, worse, drop it into the little creek that fronts the thirteenth green, runs down the left side of the hole, and empties into the larger Rae's Creek. His three-wood came within inches of a branch. "Dad, that's not good on a 24-year-old's heart," Jackie said. His father replied, "What about me? I'm 46."

The tee ball cleared the elbow of the little tributary and landed in just about the only flat, well, flattish, spot on the steeply canted fairway. Nicklaus's three-iron approach found the green, and he two-putted for a birdie to return to five under par. He was tied with Norman and Price; Jay Haas, who was already in the clubhouse; and Payne Stewart, who had just finished the other par five, the fifteenth, but would quickly drop a shot and fall out of the picture. Only Ballesteros and Kite were still ahead of Nicklaus at seven and six under par, respectively, but they had both par fives in hand. Nicklaus was thereabouts, for sure, but still very long odds.

While Nicklaus was making a delicate par at the fourteenth, chipping from the back fringe, both Ballesteros and Kite found the thirteenth fairway. Seve's six-iron to the green stopped eight feet from the hole. He tipped his visor to the crowd standing and sitting along the entire right side of the hole and shook Vicente's hand. When he made the putt for his second eagle of the day, Seve was certain he was power-walking off in the general direction of his third green jacket. Kite two-putted for his four on the thirteenth but still lost a shot to the Spaniard. Jack was now four strokes behind. Seve appeared in complete command, ready to hand Beman, the PGA Tour, and America, in general, the comeuppance they all so richly, in his mind, deserved. He would play the last five holes two over par.

Ballesteros's eagles notwithstanding, the most important one of the day was yet to come. Nicklaus was standing in the fairway at the top of the hill, looking down on the fifteenth green, two hundred yards from the hole. "How far do you think a three would go here?" the father asked the son. His four-iron never left the pin. It landed just short of the hole and rolled twelve feet past. By the time Nicklaus got to the fifteenth green, Ballesteros was looking at his birdie putt on the fourteenth. The Spaniard had a twenty-footer that could have iced the tournament, but it missed on the high side. Back on the fifteenth Nicklaus stroked the eagle putt. Jackie dropped into a crouch. When it went in, he leaped in the air, putting considerably more distance between himself and the ground than Mickelson would on the eighteenth green when he won his first Masters in 2004. Back up the hill, Watson watched it all, transfixed. In the pair behind him Ballesteros and Kite heard the unmistakable roar. Suddenly, Nicklaus was tied for second with Kite.

Emotion was beginning to seep into Nicklaus's eyes but not into his golf. The pin on the par-three sixteenth was on the left, near the pond, its customary Sunday spot. The severe slope of the green would feed anything to the right down toward it. Jack's five-iron landed to the right of the flag and spun down at the hole, missing it by a few inches and stopping within four feet. Watching the shot in the air Jackie said, "Be the right club." His father didn't bother to track its flight. He hadn't seen a drive land in years because he was so nearsighted, but from 175 yards it was more a matter of the small bowl in the section of the green where the pin was located that would obscure his view. "It is," Nicklaus replied as he bent over to pick up the tee. Jack has called those two words the cockiest comment he ever made on a golf course. That's probably true, though it wouldn't have been anywhere near the first time he'd thought it. For starters, a one-iron at Pebble Beach in 1972 comes to mind. "Oops, did I say that out loud?" was probably more like it.

The noise Nicklaus was generating was literally changing the game. Tommy Nakajima waited on the fifteenth to putt until Nicklaus walked to the sixteenth green, the applause was so thunderous. Watson rushed his eagle putt on fifteen, anticipating the noise that was to come on the sixteenth green. Ballesteros and Kite could only watch and listen, looking down from the fifteenth fairway above.

Nicklaus holed the putt on the sixteenth to get within a shot of Ballesteros. I was standing between the sixteenth green and the seventeenth tee as Nicklaus and Sandy Lyle made their way from one hole to the next. Perhaps because of the valley, perhaps because of the ramrod-straight Georgia pines, perhaps because history had turned off its hearing aid, one thing was certain: no group of people, polite patron or rowdy punter, has ever made such a bone-quaking racket, not in Super Bowls or heavyweight fights or World Series Game Sevens. I have never experienced anything to equal the intimacy of that sound. It was like being inside thunder.

The roars may have gone in Ballesteros's ears, but they exited through his hands. Kite, two behind his playing partner and one in back of Nicklaus, played first, putting his second shot on the fifteenth green. Ballesteros couldn't decide whether to hit a four or a five. He chose the four-iron and, from a slightly downhill lie, laid a slice of Georgia turf right over the ball. It wasn't that the shot didn't clear the pond in front of the green; it was so fat it barely reached it. There was a mixture of gasps and cheers in the crowd, mostly cheers, it seemed. "Then everything went wrong for me," Ballesteros said later. In truth everything had gone wrong for Seve the moment Jack clawed his way into his head. Ballesteros made bogey there and another at the seventeenth. Kite two-putted for birdie to get to minus eight but would par in. While Ballesteros was coming unraveled on the fifteenth, Nicklaus had driven it left on the seventeenth. He was struggling to keep the tears out of his eyes and trying to finish at the same time. There was golf yet to be played. His second shot from 125 yards left him a twelve-footer that Nicklaus knew would be influenced by Rae's Creek in the last twelve inches. I was standing on the small spectator mounds to the right of the green. He made it dead in the heart to take the lead at nine under par. The whole world seemed to rush up the hill toward the old white clubhouse. Usually forbidden, I promise you, there was running at the Masters that day.

Nicklaus hit three-wood off the eighteenth tee to avoid the fairway bunkers. His five-iron approach didn't reach the top level, leaving him a forty-footer. The pin was toward the back of the green, unusual but not unheard of for the eighteenth on Sunday. It had been back there when Ballesteros chipped in on his way to victory in 1983. Nicklaus's first putt, one of the best he hit all day, stopped just inches shy of going in. He marked so that Lyle could finish. After putting out, the father and son left the green with their arms around each other and not a dry eye in Augusta. Ken Venturi was sitting in the TV tower on the eighteenth green with Pat Summerall, tears streaming down his face.

With Kite unable to catch Nicklaus and Ballesteros going in the opposite direction, there was only one threat left on the golf course—Greg Norman. "People were counting me out with four or five holes to go," says Norman.

Nick Price is Zimbabwean and I'm an Australian, there aren't going to be a whole lot of people following us. We walk to the fourteenth tee and there may be 30 people and a raccoon and a possum sitting in the tree and I turned to Nick and I said, "Let's show these people we're still in this tournament." I birdied 14, 15, 16, 17. All of sudden we've come from four back to being tied for the lead. I remember walking down 15 when he (Nicklaus) made that putt on 17. There's gallery there now but there was never any gallery there before so, when I saw him pick up that putter, I went, "Oh, shit." You knew, right, you knew you had to do something because he was going to take it home from there. Jack is Jack.

Nicklaus watched the finish standing behind a couch in the Jones Cabin, too nervous to sit. Tied with him at nine under par after his four straight birdies, Norman was in the eighteenth fairway with a four-iron in his hands. It was plenty of club to get to the back tier. From an uphill lie, he came out of the shot and hung it out to the right. From the midst of the gallery sitting area, he pitched it to ten feet and missed. Nicklaus had won. In addition to everything else, it gave rise to one of Dan Jenkins's greatest lines. Writing for *Sports Illustrated*, he said, "Oh well, Greg Norman always has looked like the guy you send out to kill James Bond, not Jack Nicklaus."

Nicklaus called it the "December of my career." It was at least the Christmas. "I'm not as good as I was 10 or 15 years ago," he said. "I don't play as much competitive golf as I used to, but there are still some weeks when I'm as good as I ever was." His six Masters would equal Harry Vardon's six Open Championships, the only two professional golfers who ever lived to have won the same major title so often.

At the end of a major-championship Sunday, the media break camp like gypsies. It had been twenty-six-year-old Jim Nantz's first Masters for CBS. Near the cabins by the Par-3 Course, Ken Venturi pulled up beside him in his green golf cart. He told the younger man to jump in. "I'm going to predict that you may one day be the first man to call 50 Masters," he said to Nantz, "but I will tell you this: You will never live to see a day greater than this one at Augusta." On the other side of the clubhouse, like the witches in Macbeth, three photographers for a national sports magazine met in the parking lot to bag their film for the rush trip to New York. "Well," said the least experienced of the three, "there goes the cover." Getting the week's cover shot was the brass ring. The other two shooters, old hands at golf, looked at one another in disbelief. "What are you talking about?" one asked. After all, what could compare with Jack Nicklaus charging from behind to win an eighteenth professional major championship, his twentieth if you count the two U.S. Amateurs, at the age of forty-six? "Well," reasoned the less seasoned photographer, "Seve blew it." That he had. The coup de grâce had been a roar.

When Nicklaus walked into the media center following the green-jacket ceremony, he looked around for Tom McCollister but didn't see him. The Atlanta writer came into the interview room late. "Thanks, Tom," Nicklaus said when he saw him. "Glad I could help," McCollister replied. Guffaws bounced off the walls, making it nearly impossible to hear the rest of his reply. "Watson wants me to write about him next year," McCollister added. On the other side of the Atlantic at the age of fifty-nine, Watson would have the chance to out–gray beard the very man he'd watched make eagle from the hill above the fifteenth green that afternoon twenty-three years earlier.

Championship golf is a young man's game, but because it's not fast-twitch and muscle bound, it has as many last acts as Scotland has castles. And both come in all shapes and sizes. Kenny Perry, never a major champion, nearly won a Masters at forty-eight. Floyd was forty-seven when he dumped it in the pond at the eleventh. Gene

Littler was forty-seven when he lost to Lanny Wadkins in a playoff for the '77 PGA Championship after leading for three days and then shooting 41 on Pebble Beach's back nine on Sunday. Jimmy Demaret made runs at Augusta when he was forty-six and again at fifty-one. Old Tom Morris was top five in the Open Championship when he was sixty. Hogan was forty-seven when he nearly won the 1960 U.S. Open at Cherry Hills when three generations—Hogan, Palmer, and Nicklaus—intersected on the leader board. Seven years later Hogan had his miraculous 66 on Saturday at Augusta but followed it with 77 on Sunday. In the '84 PGA Championship at Shoal Creek, Gary Player, forty-eight, finished just behind the winner, Lee Trevino, who was himself forty-three. Sam Snead was sixty-two when he finished third behind Trevino in the '74 PGA. And so on and so on.

For sheer crushing disappointment, however, only Harry Vardon at Inverness in the 1920 U.S. Open can equal the angst of the aged experienced by Tom Watson at Turnberry in 2009. Seven years removed from losing to Ouimet at The Country Club, this time Vardon (now fifty) was facing a far sterner group of Americans, led by Walter Hagen. Through fifty-four holes, it was Vardon who was out in front, however, a stroke ahead of Jock Hutchison and Leo Diegel and two in front of his old traveling companion Ted Ray. Vardon went out in thirty-six and seemed in easy command. With seven holes to play he was five shots clear of the field. Just then a gale blew up off Lake Erie. Playing into the worst of it on the twelfth, it took Vardon four shots to reach the green, and he made six. He jabbed at a two-footer for par on the thirteenth and missed and three-putted the fourteenth, fifteenth, and sixteenth. It was a brutal, cruel unraveling. He played the last seven holes in seven over par and finished in a tie for second a shot behind Ray who, at forty-three, would be the oldest U.S. Open champion until Hale Irwin won in a playoff against Mike Donald at Medinah in 1990 at the age of forty-five. The fate visited on Watson in the tournament that would have tied him with Vardon as a six-time Open champion and Nicklaus as a six-time Masters champion was quicker but equally heartless.

A year shy of sixty, something mystical seemed to be happening when Watson shot the most familiar of scores in his opening round at Turnberry. His 65-65 there in 1977 beat Nicklaus's 65-66. They lapped the field as if Secretariat and American Pharoah could somehow have come down the home stretch at Belmont Park eyeball to eyeball and fetlock to fetlock. Another 65, Watson's opening round in 2009, left him just a stroke behind Miguel Ángel Jiménez. "There was something slightly spiritual about today," Watson allowed. He'd hit fifteen of eighteen greens in regulation, and he was putting from just off the surface on two of the ones he missed.

It was the seventh championship Watson had played on Turnberry's links, and he was Yoda-like, hitting fairways and avoiding bunkers. For four days Old Tom would roam the Turnberry links with his arms clasped at the small of his back, surveying the distant horizon like an admiral on the weather deck of the HMS *Resurrection*. He'd stride forward, leaning into the wind off the Firth of Clyde, his hands thrust deep into his pockets as if they were digging down for the warmth of old memories. He would drive the ball magnificently and right himself whenever he appeared unsteady, saved by the club that had betrayed him in his late thirties. He ran in enormous putts, so long they seemed to reach all the way back to Birkdale, Carnoustie, Muirfield, Troon, or even as far away as Pebble Beach, and he made the little ones he needed, too. All but one.

The weather for the first round was more like the Caribbean than the coast of Scotland. Turnberry would never be more accommodating. The forty-six-year-old Jiménez, a.k.a. the Mechanic, became the first ponytail to lead a major since Mel Gibson won the Revolutionary War in *The Patriot*. A wine connoisseur who had a practice-ground stretching routine resembling a cross between an exotic dancer on a pole and the pregame Haka of New Zealand's All Blacks, Jiménez said he was channeling his ailing countryman Seve Ballesteros and was effusive in his praise for Watson. "He was a legend before. He was a legend today. And he will be a legend tomorrow. We have to feel proud to play with him," said the cigar-smoking Spaniard.

If the opening round was a day at the beach, they knew they were in Scotland on Friday. What would you expect of a place whose version of Doppler radar is whether you can see the Ailsa Craig, that big, curling stone in the Firth of Clyde? (If you can't see it, it's raining; if you can, it's going to rain.) It wasn't the worst day of weather they've ever had on the Ayrshire coast, but it was sufficient to do what links golf is supposed to do, which is to utterly expose everyone who's almosting it, including Tiger Woods, the world number one who, unknown to everyone, including himself, was on a collision course with a fire hydrant and an irate Nordic blonde. Woods had laid down a marker in advance of the first three majors, completing the immortal-host Slam by winning at Bay Hill (Arnold), Memorial (Jack), and Congressional (himself). At Turnberry he tried to be conservative, but his swing wouldn't cooperate. He flared his bad shots right; played a six-hole stretch seven over par, including a lost ball; and couldn't save himself with his short game. It added up to 71-74 and firing up the King Lear. This was the second straight major Woods left his instructor, Hank Haney, at home, and the expiration date on the relationship was in sight.

At the end of the day the two leaders, at five under par, were American Steve Marino, who played in the worst of the morning conditions and required just twenty-two putts for his eighteen holes, and Watson, who went around in the worst of the afternoon weather and shot 70 with an incoming nine of 32. It could easily have come unraveled for Watson going out. He bogeyed four straight, beginning at the fourth. As Italian sixteen-year-old Matteo Manessaro, the fifty-nine-year-old Watson, and Sergio Garcia walked down the eighth fairway, Garcia gave Watson a little pat and said, "C'mon, old man!" The old man responded. "Well, that was nice of Sergio to give me a little pep-talk there," Watson said. "No, it was. He was making a joke of it, but I said, 'Well, I feel like an old man.' I played two really good shots at No. 8 and then I played two good shots at No. 9 and made a putt, turned my round around."

Watson finished it off with a sigh and a flourish. In the eighteenth fairway he and his caddie, Neil Oxman, talked about Watson's longtime caddie, Bruce Edwards, who had died of ALS, Lou Gehrig's disease, four years earlier. All three had been the best of friends. "I think Bruce is with us today," Oxman said. Neither Oxman nor Watson could hold back tears. Watson's last stroke of the day was a fifty-footer that went dead in the heart of the cup. He kicked his right leg, the hip with the original equipment, high and looked up at the sky. One thing was already certain, Watson was going to be low artificial hip. His left one had been operated on the previous October. He finished the day right where he started, five under. Watson had been trading text messages with Barbara Nicklaus during the week. Before the tournament started, she wished him luck. He replied, saying they were missed. Jack had waved farewell to the Open Championship from the Swilcan Bridge four years before, playing alongside Watson. After the second round she sent another text rooting him on.

The Saturday and Sunday winds were Turnberry's most diabolical. Blowing in off the sea, eleven holes played, to varying degrees, with a treacherous crosswind, shrinking the fairways and massively expanding the threat of the bunkers and the thick fescue. After falling behind briefly on Saturday, Old Tom holed a massive putt on the sixteenth for the second consecutive day, then reached the seventeenth in two and two-putted for the birdie that put him alone at the top of the board at four under par. He was joined in red figures by Australian Matthew Goggin; Brit Ross Fisher, whose wife in London was expecting at any minute; Lee Westwood; Retief Goosen; and the balding Americans Stewart Cink and Jim Furyk. There was the hint of history in the air and the fear it might all end badly.

"It was awesome playing with Tom," Marino said after the third round. "I told him he could be the King of Scotland. These people love him. It was super special to watch him and, you know, there's a reason he has won five claret jugs."

Tour pros don't watch golf on television. Maybe a few moments of a major championship here or there. Perhaps a Ryder Cup. They've been there, done that, have the silver in the trophy case. But Watson's run had even gotten Jack Nicklaus to put down his tennis racket and pick up the remote. "If Tom plays smart golf tomorrow, he's the favorite," Jack said. "And I don't anticipate him playing anything but smart golf. We all have nerves, but your nerve needs to overcome your nerves. That means you have to be nervy enough to do the things you have to do to overcome nerves. That's what competition is all about. Tom does a good job at that." Especially at Turnberry. Who would know that better than Nicklaus?

"For some reason today I just didn't feel real nervous out there," Watson said after the third round. "I felt, I guess, serene. And it was a day that even though I messed up a couple of times, I didn't let that bother me. It's just part of the game and I made up for it coming in. I don't know what's going to happen but I do know one thing, I feel good about what I did today. I feel good about my game plan. And, who knows, it might happen."

The game plan was to allow himself three bogeys and make up for them with three birdies. If he had done it, he would have won. There was one bogey too many. Over the final nine holes Sunday afternoon, the planets seemed to be jockeying into position for the fifty-nine-year-old Watson, who was turning the unthinkable into the probable before our very eyes. Playing steadily, but without the flashes of brilliance that characterized the first three days, Watson watched his pursuers fly away like a flock of marshmallow chicks. The English trio of the expectant father Fisher, twenty-one-year-old Chris Wood, and the sorrowful Westwood all fired and fell back, the worst being Westwood, who three-putted the last to miss the Watson-Cink playoff by a single shot, the same margin he missed by the previous year in the U.S. Open at Torrey Pines when Woods beat Rocco Mediate with a broken leg and a torn ACL. Goosen, who's been struck by lightning once and the U.S. Open twice, couldn't make a putt. Goggin, the Tasmanian Devil, hung around until three straight bogeys on the back finished him off. Even Cink, who early in the week took to his favorite form of self-expression, Twitter, to complain of having swine flu, would birdie, then bogey, birdie, then bogey. The claret jug seemed to be Watson's for the taking.

At the last Cink hit a wonderful nine-iron that stopped twelve feet from the hole and made the putt, closing within a shot of Watson, who had birdied the par-five seventeenth to reach three under par. Watson positioned his drive perfectly off the eighteenth. All week he'd been clever about getting the ball in play. His eight-iron second was just as perfectly struck. "I hit the shot I meant to and when it was in the air I said, 'I like it.' And then all of a sudden it goes over the green," he said. He elected to putt the ball from a tough lie instead of chipping it, and it screamed past the hole. It was only eight feet, but it might as well have been a thousand yards. There was no way the ghost of Harry Vardon was going to let that ball go in. Watson put a horrible stroke on it, the putt never had a chance, and all the hopes of all of Scotland couldn't put him back together again.

Watson played so poorly in the four-hole aggregate playoff, he would have lost to a caber tosser. His legs were gone. The illusion of a man about to close out his sixth decade of life by winning a sixth Open Championship aged before everyone's eyes; in the end, Watson looked as old as the Ailsa Craig, and Cink, an Alabama native and Georgia Tech grad known more for his barbecue recipes than his trophies, was the antihero for a day. After a double bogey at the seventeenth when he drove it in the hay, and in the face of Cink's rock-solid birdie-birdie playoff finish, all that remained for Watson was one last funereal march up the eighteenth, a place where before he'd known only festivals.

After it was all over, the most poignant message came from Nicklaus. It was the first text message Jack had ever sent in his life after watching the first full eighteen holes of golf on television he'd ever watched in his life. He told Tom he'd hit two great shots and made the right choice from behind the green. The putt just didn't go in. The greatest player in the game was applying the kindest salve he could—you didn't make a mistake; you just didn't win.

In the Masters forty-eight-year-old Kenny Perry began the year of the antistory when he finished bogey-bogey and lost. Lucas Glover edged the people's choice, Phil Mickelson, in the U.S. Open, the major he would place second in six times. Turnberry, however, was a broken heart too far. Cink's previous closest call in a major had come in the U.S. Open at Southern Hills in '01. In a hurry to get out of Retief Goosen's way on the seventy-second hole, he missed a tiddler that, when Goosen stab-pushed his, kept Cink out of that eighteen-hole playoff. It was both understandable and inexcusable at one and the same time. With the help of sports psychologist Dr. Morris Pickens, Cink devised a putting routine to go with his recent return to the standard-length putter. Pickens's admonition for the week was "Keep playing Turnberry, keep playing Turnberry." It proved prescient. When Cink birdied the last, it seemed it would only secure second, but he never stopped playing until he'd run out of holes and Watson, as it turned out, had run out of gas.

When Watson sat down at the interviewer's table in the media center, he looked around and said, "This ain't a funeral, you know." But it was.

"It would have been a hell of a story, wouldn't it?" Watson said.

It wasn't to be. And, yes, it's a great disappointment. It tears at your gut, as it always has torn at my gut. It's not easy to take. The playoff was just one bad shot after another and Stewart did what he had to do to win. I didn't give him much competition in the playoff. The one memory? Well, I think coming up the eighteenth hole again. Those memories are hard to forget. Coming up in the amphitheater of the crowd and having the crowd cheering you on like they do here for me. As I said, the feeling is mutual. And that warmth makes you feel human. It makes you feel so good.

This was the place, more than any other, where Watson and Nicklaus made "golf" and "rivalry" as inextricably linked as shepherds and pie, mince and tatties. Sometimes, the stories don't end well. This time around they were there to commiserate with one another. It wasn't the Duel in the Sun. Time, it turned out, was a lot tougher than Jack Nicklaus. Old Tom missed the early-bird special on claret jugs when he bogeyed the last hole after two wondrous shots, and Stewart Cink was as happy as Robert the Bruce to drive a stake through the heart of history.

Watson had won his five Open Championships with the late Alfie Files on the bag, but it was Oxman who was beside him when the extraordinary nearly happened at Turnberry. A cofounder of the Campaign Group, Inc., in Philadelphia, Oxman creates radio and television ads for Democratic candidates or, more often now, the multitude of sympathetic independent committees that have proliferated since the Supreme Court's *Citizen's United* decision. Oxman once charitably described his staunchly conservative golf boss to the *Philadelphia Inquirer* as a "Heinz-Rockefeller Republican. . . . [O]n some issues he's conservative, on some he's moderate."

Oxman began caddying part-time on the PGA Tour in 1972, Watson's first full season after graduating from Stanford University. One was headed for stardom, the other for law school. Oxman, never much better than a bogey golfer, grew up in Philadelphia and caddied for his father, Morris, a World War II veteran everyone knew as Pip, who was the co-owner of a ladies-hat manufacturing company. Neil was seventeen when his father died, and he turned to caddying to put himself first through Villanova University and then Duquesne University Law School. He traveled the tour in a '66 Chevelle Malibu covered in gray primer paint, having purchased the car from a double cliché—two little old ladies—for $150 and $9 in sales tax. Oxman went to law school because someone told him if he wanted to work in politics, he should.

Sometimes the art of politics and the art of golf can seem remarkably similar. "What we do is very adversarial," Oxman says of his political life. "Somebody has an office and you're trying to take it from them, or you have an office and someone is trying to take it from you, or it's open and you're both playing king of the hill. The whole thing is a struggle and a fight."

Not all experiences are happy ones, like that July day in 2009. After a dreamlike week and a nightmare playoff, Oxman drove all night from Scotland to London for the Senior British Open the next week. It was impossible not to think about what had happened. Back at the Turnberry Hotel, Watson couldn't sleep, either, kept awake by the howling dogs of what might have been.

"In 1984 we did Dee Huddleston who lost to Mitch McConnell by 5,184 votes out of 1,284,811. That's over 30 years ago," Oxman says. "We had a 20 point lead and a guy in the campaign would not let us continue to run negative ads in the last three weeks, saying this election's over. The pollster and I couldn't convince the guy otherwise. Mitch McConnell should never have been a United States Senator—he might have been at some point—but he should not have won that Senate race in 1984. I'm still not over it. I'm not kidding. I'm still not over '09 and I'm still not over that."

Oxman's windowless Philadelphia office is on the third floor of a town house originally owned by the Breyers ice cream family. One wall is covered by pink sticky notes with election results. There's Annie Lebovitz's photo of John Belushi and flags from the eighteenth hole of Watson's Senior British Open victories at Royal Aberdeen in '05 and Turnberry in '03, the caddie's victory pelts. He has a portrait of General James Longstreet, a figure he half-jokingly says he was in a previous life. And there's the picture of Nicklaus's farewell in '05 when Jack called his playing partners and their caddies up on the Swilcan Bridge to join him. Moments before on the seventeenth green, Nicklaus had missed a birdie putt. Knowing he was going to miss the cut, he walked to the back of the green and stood next to Oxman. "We were waiting for Luke Donald to putt and he said to me, 'Ox, that's my last shot ever as a real golfer. My next one is my first as a ceremonial golfer.' He wasn't saying it to be dramatic," Oxman says. "He just sort of said it and I just happened to be next to him."

Watson cried at the bridge as Nicklaus stood there, and he cried harder walking up the eighteenth alongside his old friend and old foe. Watson still chokes up when he talks about it. "The crowd gave Jack his due as the greatest player who ever lived," Watson says. "From the first hole through the thirty-sixth hole, he got a standing ovation every stand he went by. And it was genuine, from the heart. It was a privilege to be paired with him."

Once, when Nicklaus and Watson sat down to relive their Duel in the Sun at Turnberry for a television show, Nicklaus claimed he couldn't remember much about it, just that he'd lost. Watson put his arm around him and jokingly said, "That's okay, Jack. I remember every shot." After the '09 Open Championship ended Watson said, "This would have been a great memory. Now, it's going to be like Jack. I'll never remember what the hell club I hit anytime during the whole tournament."

But no one else would ever forget.

# 12

## Generation Next

The open mouth of a Hoover washing machine is as good a place to start as any. On a piece of old videotape nine-year-old Rory McIlroy can be seen pitching golf balls into one on a television talk show set, something he'd been doing in his home in Holywood, Northern Ireland, since the time he was roughly the height of the machine itself. He was a boy with recognizable gifts, and his parents, Gerry and Rosie, were clever enough to recognize them. In order to finance their only child's golfing ambitions, Gerry worked three jobs, cleaning the toilets, locker rooms, and the bar in the morning at the local rugby club; then pulling pints at the Holywood GC in the afternoons; and, finally, working the evening shift as the barman back at the sports club. Rosie worked the night shift at the local 3M plant. Gerry had grown up in public housing in Belfast. Rosie, whose father, Danny, drove an ice cream truck, had her first factory job at sixteen.

Rory enjoyed all the successes of your run-of-the-mill boy golfing genius. Played in the World Amateur Team Championship at sixteen. Top-ranked amateur in the world at seventeen. Silver medal for low amateur in the Open Championship at Carnoustie at seventeen. He turned pro and won enough fast enough to put a Ferrari in the garage in the big house by the time he was twenty. The story of the championship player, however, begins on the tenth hole of Augusta National in 2011 roughly a month before his twenty-second birthday.

Taking a four-shot lead into the final round, McIlroy broke apart like a meteor careening through Earth's atmosphere, struggling on the front nine and then burning up on the back, making a triple bogey on the tenth when he caromed his tee shot off a pine bough and into the luxury white brick cabins on the left, very near the one Jordan Spieth would stay in on his first trip to Augusta National a couple of years later. It was, literally and figuratively, downhill from there. Stunned, shaken and stirred, the phenom played the tenth, eleventh, and twelfth a combined six over par and finished with an 80, the same score he posted the year before in the second round at St. Andrews after opening with a record-tying 63 on the Old Course.

McIlroy played the first two days of that Masters with a twenty-two-year-old American, Rickie Fowler, and twenty-three-year-old Australian Jason Day, a veritable antique by comparison. Augusta National had egg salad older than any of them. Bottles of wine so youthfully impertinent couldn't make it into the club's celebrated cellar. In two days the brat pack was a combined twenty-three under par. McIlroy's serviceable 69 on Friday got him to ten under par, good for a two-shot lead over Day. Staying in a house off Berckman's Road with some Belfast buddies and displaying a form that could retard the cause of Irish quarterbacking for generations, McIlroy and his friends killed time throwing a football around in the street until they were chased off by a little old southern lady with an aversion to high spirits.

After McIlroy threw the gates open Sunday, it seemed like half the golfing world scrambled through. Ángel Cabrera was ten under after a birdie on the eighth. Geoff Ogilvy birdied the twelfth through the sixteenth holes to get himself to ten under. Adam Scott was ten under through the eleventh. Luke Donald double-bogeyed the twelfth, then birdied the fourteenth, fifteenth, and sixteenth to get to ten under. Bo Van Pelt eagled the fifteenth to get to, once again, ten under. Day was ten under through thirteen, and K. J. Choi was ten under with two to play. The four corners of Augusta National were a rolling cacophony. An Argentine. A South African. Three Aussies. A Korean. An Englishman. Heck, even a couple of Americans. The roars came from every direction. Ogilvy here. Cabrera down there. Scott in the valley. Day on the hill. Choi in the corner. Donald hitting a bank shot off the pin at the eighteenth and then chipping in. Ultimately, Charl Schwartzel birdied the last four to snatch the jacket off the shoulders of Aussies Scott and Day. Sharing a private jet Sunday night with the lead loser, Schwartzel wore the jacket, while McIlroy, laid bare on the golf course, was clothed only in the graciousness he'd shown after beating himself.

"It's so goddamn hard to win out there. I don't care what decade you want to go back to. It was hard to watch him, that last round," said Tom Weiskopf, someone who knew a little about Masters heartbreak, of McIlroy. "I always look at a young guy like that, that's very talented, the next time he may win but he may not again, too. It's just that difficult." McIlroy made it look easy, and fast.

In the time it took to change spring to summer, with a birthday party and a trip to Haiti for UNICEF in between, McIlroy matured into the portrait of the champion as a young artist, winning the U.S. Open in a walkover, dropping records behind him like bread crumbs marking the trail to the future. Unpretentious, gifted, confidently humble, swaggeringly modest, McIlroy bounced across the soggy fairways of Congressional CC. His seventy-two-hole total of 268 was the lowest ever by four shots. His sixteen-under-par total broke the previous mark versus par, set by Tiger Woods at Pebble Beach, also by four. He was the youngest Open champion since Robert Tyre Jones in 1923. He hit more greens in regulation than anyone in a U.S. Open, for as long as someone had kept track of such things. His eleven-under par on the par fours broke that previous mark by a mere seven shots. He had the lowest fifty-four-hole score in Open history. He became the only player to reach thirteen under par, fourteen under par, fifteen under par, sixteen under par, or seventeen under par in a U.S. Open. He had the lowest thirty-six-hole total ever and was thought to be the youngest thirty-six-hole leader since Walter Hagen in 1914.

In April at Augusta Graeme McDowell, the 2010 U.S. Open champion from Northern Ireland who is as close to an older brother as McIlroy has, sent him a text message: "I love you." At the time McIlroy joked it might be the drink talking. G-Mac left another note in Rory's Congressional locker. The words were different, but the meaning was the same. "Nothing this kid does surprises me," said McDowell when it was all finished. "This guy is the best I've ever seen, simple as that. He's great for golf. He's a breath of fresh air for the game and perhaps we're ready for golf's next superstar and maybe Rory is it."

As McIlroy was walking to the eighteenth tee with an eight-shot lead Sunday evening, Lee Westwood was walking off it. As they got closer to one another, Westwood, a nominee for the crown of "Best European Not to Win a Major," broke into a broad grin. McIlroy looked down, smiling, deeply proud but deferential to an older friend he knew wanted a big title every bit as badly as he did, maybe more so. They exchanged a light fist bump as they passed. Two steps farther on Westwood gave McIlroy's caddie, J. P. Fitzgerald, a whacking high five.

At Augusta National the final walk on the eighteenth is dramatically uphill. In April, when he got to the top, instead of claiming a green jacket, McIlroy wrapped himself in dignity in defeat. At Congressional his walk at the last was dramatically downhill to his first major victory, what many believed to be his destiny. In a Jim Craig–Olympic-hockey-style moment, he scanned the crowd looking for his father. "I knew he was going to be somewhere close," says McIlroy. "I just spotted him before I hit my first putt. And then when I put it up to whatever it was, a foot or whatever, I looked to him and gave him a little smile, a little grin."

On Friday when McIlroy hit wedge to the rear of the eighth green, allowing the ball to funnel back down the slope and into the cup, he threw his head back, his arms open, and beamed at the heavens. The records mounted as the week wore on. He was the fastest to double digits under par in the history of the U.S. Open. He got there at a younger age than Gil Morgan, Ricky Barnes, Jim Furyk, or Tiger Woods. McIlroy hit seventeen of eighteen greens in Thursday's 65 and fifteen more in Friday's 66, tying Woods for the largest thirty-six-hole lead in the 111 years of the championship. Instead of throwing a football with the lads, he killed Saturday morning watching *Batman*, then went all *Dark Knight* on them Saturday afternoon with a near-flawless 68. He'd held at least a portion of the lead at some point in each of the previous four major championships and went into Sunday of the U.S. Open eight shots clear. Unlike Augusta, disaster was not on the menu. Day ultimately won the B flight, adding second in the U.S. Open to his T2 in the Masters.

If the wisdom of Weiskopf was rendered moot almost immediately by McIlroy, not so Jason Day. It took four years of frustration dealing with injury and self-doubt for the Australian to break through in a major championship. When he did he set the record for the lowest score ever shot in a major with his twenty-under-par performance at Whistling Straits in Wisconsin in the PGA Championship of 2015. If McIlroy had come from a humble home, Day had turned away from nothing short of juvenile delinquency. He lost his father, Alvin, to stomach cancer when he was just twelve years old, a grief that turned rebellion into the recklessness of drinking and fighting. The family was poor, boiling water for hot showers. His mother, Dening, worked two jobs and mortgaged anything of value to send Jason to Kooralbyn International School. It was there he met Colin Swatton, who would become his golf coach, his disciplinarian, his caddie, his older brother, his surrogate father. After he won the PGA Tour's Match Play Championship in Tucson in the winter of 2014, Day touched on that past. "I think I finally realized—I'm going to be honest here, I came from a very poor family—so, it wasn't winning that was on my mind when I first came out on the PGA Tour. It was money. I wanted to play for money, because I'd never had it before. Winning takes care of everything. And it's not about the money anymore. I just want to play golf, golf that I love, and win trophies." There were more close calls, including the Open Championship at St. Andrews just weeks before Whistling Straits, but when the Wannamaker Trophy came, it came with tears for all that had gone before.

McIlroy was slow to back up his record-setting performance at Congressional, but when he did, it was equally dramatic. With a near-flawless final round of 66, he added an overpowering PGA Championship title on a long, wet Kiawah Island Ocean Course to his overpowering U.S. Open on long, wet Congressional, propelling himself to number one in the World Golf Rankings and halfway to the career Slam, joining Jack Nicklaus, Seve Ballesteros, and Tiger Woods as the only modern-era players (Jordan Spieth would join them in short order) to have won two major championships before their twenty-fourth birthdays.

Having survived a second round where the wind blew so hard off the Atlantic Ocean Walter Hagen wouldn't have bothered to get out of his Pierce-Arrow, McIlroy built a three-shot lead going into Sunday. Taking a tip from Nicklaus, he set himself the goal of playing all four rounds in the 6os. "I got to 12 (under) and stood on the 18th tee and was seven ahead," said McIlroy, who then turned to his caddie, Fitzgerald, and told him he was going to win this major by eight, too.

After yet another perfectly placed, massive drive on a golf course meant to be so visually intimidating that the grip of a driver feels like a live hand grenade in a player's fingers, when McIlroy approached the green the crowd closed in behind him in the late-afternoon light. He broke into a wide grin when he saw his father standing by the scaffolding bridge that led from the green to the clubhouse. He made the twenty-footer from the front edge, of course, then stood beside his golf bag, bent over like an Olympic sprinter catching his breath. He straightened up and put his head back to look at the sky, reprising the picture of joy after his eagle from the eighth fairway at Congressional. He walked toward his father with his head down, clutching double handfuls of his own curly dark hair, on his way to another level in the game. A measure of McIlroy's complete dominance was that the ultimate runner-up, David Lynn, was never even a hint of a factor. He didn't allow so much as a whiff of weakness to float off on what had become a gentle breeze, playing each nine three under par, scrambling magnificently when he needed to, closing the tournament as impeccably as he'd opened it, with a bogey-free round.

"The thing he's done is he's lapped the field twice," said three-time major champion Padraig Harrington, another Irishman. "It says when he plays well, he's better than everybody else. There's been ups and downs since his last major win because of the pressure and the expectations and the hype. Now that he's delivered again, it will be a lot easier for him going forward."

If there was a knock on McIlroy—and there was—it was that perhaps he lacked the fire in his belly. Being half of Wozzilroy, one of the tabloid titles for the celebrity union of Danish tennis star Caroline Wozniacki and the youthful Irish golfer, seemed more interesting to him than a quest for greatness. Earlier in the year McIlroy, himself, said he'd taken his eye off the ball. And if there was a knock on his record, it was that he didn't win as often as a talent mentioned in the same breath with Tiger Woods ought. McIlroy, it seemed, enjoyed a life outside golf, a life that got a little messy.

The Ocean Course was followed by troubled waters. McIlroy changed equipment, and struggled. He hired and fired and sued agents, went to court, settled, and struggled. He sent out Wozzilroy wedding invitations and, before the ink was dry, RSVPed his own regrets. Despite a growing history of fast starts and Friday falters, at Hoylake in the 2014 Open Championship he seemed at ease again. "I don't know if I can describe it. It's just I feel like I have an inner peace on the golf course," he said. "I wish I could get into it more often."

McIlroy's instructor since his boyhood, Michael Bannon, remained an anchor in the tumult. "You're looking at somebody who's just got his game back and is working hard at it all the time. That's what I see," said Bannon. They began preparing for Hoylake by working on all the fiddly shots around the greens. They discussed a bit of course management, Gaelic style. "One thing I did say to Rory was to make sure when he hit the ball to make it go forward, you know," said Bannon with a pixie smile. "That was the big thing we worked on." The Irish translation: stay out of the bunkers and the gorse.

Before the 2014 Masters McIlroy said, "It's almost like golf is waiting for someone to stamp their authority on the game and be that dominant player. I hope it's me." After Hoylake it was. The year's two majors prior to the Open Championship had been won in dominating performances by Bubba Watson and Martin

Kaymer. It was a second major title for each, and both had been through dormant stretches. Watson smote Augusta National with his pink driver. Kaymer coldly dissected Pinehurst's reconstituted native areas after Ben Crenshaw and Bill Coore restored them to Donald Ross's No. 2 Course.

If Watson was something of an enigma, it wasn't a particularly good one. He'd grown up in the Florida Panhandle. His father, Gerry, was a Green Beret in Vietnam and carried the scars, emotional and physical, to prove it. The boy's golf swing was homemade, dug out of the sandy soil of a town once called Scratch Ankle. The son hit the ball enormous distances. He verbally abused his caddie. He could curve shots like no other player in the world. He won his first Masters in 2012 when he was thirty-three in a playoff on the strength of a recovery shot from so far back in the dark woods on Augusta's tenth that the marshals might as well have been gnomes and trolls. Even Louis Oosthuizen, whose nickname is Shrek, knew it was the best shot he saw all day, and he'd made a double eagle on the second. It was off the pine needles and leaves, under the limbs, through the patrons, around the TV tower, up in the air, 135 to carry, 40 yards of hook, kick right, two putts to win. "I'm used to the woods. I saw the gap. I got there. I saw it was a perfect draw, a perfect hook," Watson said in his rapid-fire cadence, the iambic pentameter of his self-diagnosed ADD. "I hit my 52-degree, my gap wedge, hooked it about 40 yards, hit about 15 feet off the ground until it got under the tree and then it started rising. Pretty easy."

Bubba bludgeoned Augusta National for an encore two years later. "There's no one else that can really play the way he does," said Rickie Fowler, a friend though Watson was ten years his senior. After winning in 2012 Watson confessed to a green-cloth and brass-button hangover, unable to crack the top twenty-five in a major in 2013. At times he could run as hot as a double-bogey vindaloo. "I can tell you, last year was a rough year with the pressure of trying to prove yourself," said his caddie, Ted Scott, after Watson won a second Masters in three years.

For his second act Watson flew it over bunkers, slung it around doglegs, and scooped up his adopted son, Caleb, on the eighteenth green, turning Augusta National into Bubbaland, a personal playground the boy from Baghdad seemed born to romp across. Sunday opened with Watson tied with Jordan Spieth, a twenty-year-old Masters rookie from Texas. Through seven the kid from Dallas was at minus eight and two ahead of Watson. Fortunes flipped in two holes when Watson went birdie-birdie on the par-five eighth and the par-four ninth and Spieth went bogey-bogey. The back nine was pure Bubba. He hit it so far around the corner on the thirteenth that, despite clipping a pine tree or two, all he had left into the green was sand wedge. "When he had wedge into 13 I said OK, well, this is pretty ridiculous," said Spieth. "So, hat's off to him." Watson won by three.

In June 2014 Kaymer completed the Hallmark Calendar Slam by adding a runaway eight-shot U.S. Open victory on Father's Day to the Mother's Day Players Championship he had won in May. For four days Kaymer played chess with the great architect Donald Ross, relying on an aggressive opening gambit of back-to-back 65s, the best opening thirty-six holes in the 114-year history of the championship, then patiently trading pawns with the field, missing in the right spots, keeping disaster at a swale's length. In the process he linked the sand hills of North Carolina to the sand dunes of Lake Michigan, where he claimed his first American major in the 2010 PGA at Whistling Straits in the play-off Bubba Watson lost and Dustin Johnson missed by grounding his club in a bunker that moments before had been standing-room only for about a thousand spectators. Six months shy of his thirtieth birthday, it gave the greatest German golfer never to have had the yips two majors and a major-minor, a triptych of titles owned by Jack Nicklaus, Lee Trevino, Ray Floyd, Tiger Woods, and Kaymer.

Going into Sunday's final round with a five-shot lead, Kaymer did one of the hardest things there is to do in golf: he increased it. "When you lead such a big tournament with five shots, it's very, very difficult to keep going," said Kaymer. "A lot of people can say I want to keep going, I want to play aggressive. But then somehow you hold back. You have to believe. You have to play brave. If you hit a bad shot, you hit a bad shot. But that's the way you want to play golf, or at least the way I want to play golf."

It was a job made considerably easier when, among Kaymer's five chasers in red figures going into Sunday, only Erik Compton, courageously playing tournament golf six years removed from a second heart transplant, could equal par on the outgoing nine. He would finish a distant second, tied with Fowler, eight behind. While the 2010 PGA at Whistling Straits is remembered as much for the guy who missed the playoff as it is for the guy who won it, Kaymer went to the Masters in 2011 as the world number one but left it despondent, missing the cut for the fourth straight time, and convinced he couldn't play Augusta National with his natural left-to-right ball flight. It wasn't that he wanted to overhaul his swing as much as he craved a full arsenal of shots. He put himself in the hands of his longtime instructor, Gunter Kessler, and set about gathering them, immediately going into a slump that elicited howls of "What was he thinking?" Kaymer understood the process would take time, but he couldn't put everyone else's expectations on hold. "I knew that I would struggle a little bit for a while," he said. "Getting so much attention and then all of a sudden, you know, you don't win again. So why is that? So why do you change? And it's annoying." Pinehurst No. 2 was the payoff.

At Hoylake in '14 McIlroy stamped a little of his own authority on the game, showing a toughness down the stretch his critics believed was the one club he didn't have in his bag. After delivering a finishing kick on the old racetrack at Royal Liverpool that staked him to a six-shot lead after fifty-four holes, McIlroy showed his mettle Sunday, staring down the pack of wolves nipping at his heels with 65s and 66s and 67s that he knew would do him no harm without his help. McIlroy had pummeled Hoylake for three days and kept his bottle on the last one to win the Open Championship by two over Sergio Garcia and Rickie Fowler. Rory's father, Gerry, along with some pals, had placed a series of three wagers with Ladbrokes that his boy would win the Open Championship by the time he was twenty-five. Since the first one was made when Rory was fifteen, the bets had some attractive, if diminishing, odds. It wasn't the first time a Hoylake side bet paid off. Bobby Cruickshank got 50–1 on Bob Jones to run the tables in 1930, including the Open there.

The victory put the twenty-five-year-old Irishman a notch ahead in history's ledger, adding the claret jug to his eight-shot victories in the U.S. Open at Congressional and the PGA at Kiawah Island, and gained him entry into the select club of players who had completed three legs of the modern career Grand Slam. "I've always been comfortable from tee to green at Augusta," said McIlroy of the one that got away. Had it not been for his 80 that day three years before, McIlroy might already have his Slam. When Rickie Fowler rallied to tie him on Saturday at Hoylake, McIlroy exploded at the finish with a pair of eagles in three holes. When Sergio Garcia went out in five under par through ten holes on Sunday, McIlroy held steady. It was Garcia who finally blinked, leaving his ball in the bunker on the par-three fifteenth.

After Garcia's demoralizing mistake, McIlroy had a three-shot lead with three holes to play and two of them the par fives, the sixteenth and eighteenth, that he'd played in six under par through three rounds. Barring an out-of-bounds disaster—and Hoylake had them—he wasn't going to be caught, particularly with the luxury of having iron in his hands on the seventeenth and eighteenth tees. The more pressing question for McIlroy was the same one facing Watson and Kaymer. They've achieved escape velocity, separating themselves from their peers, but could they continue to cruise at altitude?

"I've really found my passion again for golf," McIlroy said. "Not that it ever dwindled, but it's what I think about when I get up in the morning. It's what I think about when I go to bed. Even though there's still one major left this year that I want to desperately try and win, I'm looking forward to next April and trying to complete the career grand slam." It didn't much matter that a few weeks later the PGA Championship finished in the dark because, by then, it had become clear McIlroy was golf's shining light. If he had managed to stay out front at Hoylake when it came to the PGA Championship at Valhalla, he would have to come from behind. McIlroy took a narrow one-shot lead into the final round, but after playing the first nine one over par, he headed for the back two behind. It would grow to three standing in the fairway of the par-five tenth when Rickie Fowler made a thirty-footer for birdie up ahead.

McIlroy responded with three-wood from 281 yards that got the right bounce and rolled to within seven feet of the hole. "The ball flight was probably around 30 feet lower than I intended. And the line of the shot was probably around 15 yards left of where I intended," he said. "It was lucky, it really was. You need a little bit of luck in major championships to win and that was my lucky break. I didn't hit a very good shot there but it worked out well and I made eagle from it."

It lifted him back into contention a shot behind Fowler and the forty-four-year-old Mickelson, who birdied the eleventh. By the time Fowler, Mickelson, McIlroy, and his Swedish playing partner, Henrik Stenson, had all gotten through the thirteenth, there was a four-way tie at fifteen under par. Fowler and Stenson both bogeyed the fourteenth. Mickelson bogeyed the sixteenth. McIlroy hit a nine-iron from a fairway bunker to ten feet on the seventeenth for the birdie that would give him a two-shot advantage going into the PGA Championship's first night game, played in its entirety on the par-five eighteenth.

There had been a two-hour weather delay Sunday, and with late tee times designed to push television viewing as late as possible into prime time, the players were running out of light. McIlroy scrambled to hit a drive at the eighteenth before either Fowler or Mickelson had played their second and very nearly hit it into the hazard on the right. The final two pairs were scurrying to finish. Mickelson and Fowler didn't know McIlroy was going to play his second to the green before they'd finished the hole but then stepped aside while he played up. Each still had a potentially game-changing eagle attempt. Fowler wound up three-putting from fifty feet. Mickelson nearly holed his chip but settled for a birdie that closed the gap to one. It was a chaotic denouement catering to showbiz instead of championship golf. McIlroy's second was in the greenside bunker, and he blasted out and two-putted for his fourth major championship, joining Walter Hagen, Nick Price, Tiger Woods, and Padraig Harrington as the players who had captured the last two major championships of the season. "I really gutted it out today," McIlroy said. "Look, I'm playing some great golf at the minute and I want to keep this run going as long as I can, and hopefully I'm in just as good form heading into Augusta next year and have a chance to win the career Grand Slam. If that happens, then we'll turn our attention to Chambers Bay and I'll try and get the job done there." The first Reign of Rory—for the throne is always in danger of a palace coup of one sort or another—turned out to be a shorter one than Edward VIII's, though he didn't exactly abdicate. He did, however, put himself on the bench for a significant part of 2015 after suffering an ankle injury playing football (European style) with his mates.

After coming so close in 2014, the young Texan Jordan Spieth figured Augusta National owed him one. He took two.

If McIlroy was your basic Irish prodigy, Spieth was the Lone Star version. He won two USGA junior titles, was on the leader board of the PGA Tour's Byron Nelson Championship when he was in high school, and won an NCAA team championship in his only year at the University of Texas. He grew up in a middle-class Dallas neighborhood of brick ranches where the streets are named for Disney characters, the place where dreams come true. Jordan's parents, Shawn and Chris, were among two hundred or so in a high school graduating class in a small town in Pennsylvania. Shawn went to Clemson University to play baseball but transferred after a year to Lehigh University, where he pitched and played first base and center field. Chris was a power forward with a sharp pair of elbows across the river at Moravian College.

He got his first job with Alcoa and later a master's of business administration. She was a computer engineer and worked for Neiman Marcus for seventeen years. Their middle child, Steven, is six-feet-six and played shooting guard at Brown University. Jordan is six-feet-one. "The last time I played him one-on-one, I beat him," says Jordan. "I knew it was the luckiest I could ever be so I said, 'I'm never playing you again.'" And he didn't. Spieth learned his golf at Brookhaven CC, a middle-class club in Dallas where they let kids be kids. Jimmy Johnson, Steve Stricker's longtime caddie, played at the same golf course where Spieth sharpened his game. "He doesn't like to lose," says Johnson. "That's about the biggest compliment I can give to him—he just doesn't like to lose."

The Spieths' third child, Ellie, seven years younger than Jordan, was born with neurological challenges the cause of which has never been fully understood. "She's what keeps our family grounded," says Jordan. "She's by far the funniest person in our family, by far." Steven's basketball games were easier for Ellie to attend than Jordan's golf tournaments because, as Shawn, says, "you just never know when she's going to want to talk or yell Jordan's name."

Both Jordan and Steven attended the Jesuit College Preparatory School of Dallas, where after Ellie was born Chris worked part-time to defray tuition costs. Seniors there spend part of every Wednesday doing community service. Jordan asked if he could work at Ellie's school, the Vanguard Preparatory School, where most of the children have mood disorders or are somewhere on the autistic spectrum. Ellie's classroom had three small tables surrounded by small chairs, art projects on one wall, the alphabet on another. Kevin Goodnight was Ellie's teacher then. "I'm a huge golfer," he says, "but we never got to talk shop. Jordan would come in and he would instantly go to work with these kids. If we were doing math, he would find someone who needed help. You doing okay? Are you okay? Until he found someone. We had a boy who could not shoot a basket. He would throw the basketball up and it would go backwards over his head. It would go everywhere except at the basketball goal. Jordan worked with this boy and worked with him. The kid finally made a basket. Oh, he just went nuts and the whole playground erupted."

When Chris was four her mother, Ginny, collapsed on the kitchen floor, stricken with a brain aneurysm. She survived. Chris's father, Bob Julius, was an electrical engineer at Bethlehem Steel. At first Chris and her five siblings were split up, sent to other families to live. Eventually, Bob was able to gather everyone back together. Ginny was handicapped the remainder of her life, severely so as time passed. Bob took care of her for forty-four years. All of Jordan's life he'd watched people he loved taking care of other people he loved. It was that voice, whispering the things that actually matter in his ear, that made him universally liked among his peers.

Spieth fell in love with Augusta National's greens the first time he saw them. To him, putting wasn't a mechanical exercise but an artistic one—something he'd learned from watching another Texan, Ben Crenshaw—and there is no better canvas than Augusta. McIlroy played his golf from the teeing ground out. If he had his driver under control, he was close to unstoppable. Spieth played the golf course from the green back, plotting his path to produce the putt he wanted. It was no mistake that in his breakout 2015 season, Spieth was the deadliest putter in memory from twenty to twenty-five feet. At least the deadliest since Tiger Woods. He knew which side of the hole he wanted to be on and was hitting his irons well enough to execute.

His Texas roots helped him in his first Masters when he nearly out–General Lee'd Bubba Watson, relying on Crenshaw and Crenshaw's longtime Augusta caddie, Carl Jackson. "I have a lot of respect for this golf course," said Spieth. "I told Michael (his caddie Michael Greller) I was going to buy a t-shirt for him that says, 'Carl Says,' because he keeps saying that to me out there." Before becoming Spieth's caddie Greller had been a sixth grade teacher at Narrows View Intermediate School in University Place, Washington. He began caddying as a summer job at Chambers Bay, the course where Spieth would follow up his record-setting 2015 Masters victory with a U.S. Open title.

If McIlroy was blessed to have Michael Bannon from a young age, Spieth was equally lucky to find Cameron McCormick. Just before his thirteenth birthday, he and his father, Shawn, decided it was time for more formal instruction than anything he was getting at Brookhaven. McCormick was at nearby Brook Hollow GC, one of President George W. Bush's hangouts. A transplanted Australian, McCormick came to America to play college golf; got a foot in the door at Butler Community College in El Dorado, Kansas; and eventually transferred to Texas Tech. After graduation he returned to Australia to try to play but didn't have much luck. He gave the mini tours a whirl in Florida and quickly ran out of money. Having majored in international business, he was about to set golf aside for commerce when he got an assistant's job at the Lakes at Castle Hills GC, then another post at Dallas CC, and, finally, a teaching spot at Brook Hollow, where the Spieths found him.

"I had a big loop in my swing, a very weak grip, misaligned, shoulders open and hit kind of push draws," said Spieth. "I went to Cam and he asked me what my goals were. I said I want to be the best player in the world someday. He said okay, then we're going to have to make some changes and it's going to be difficult. It's probably going to take a little while and you may not play your best golf for a while. I just went to the range and I'd hit bags of balls, a bunch of 7-irons, and they wouldn't go higher than this off the ground." Spieth held his arm out to his side to demonstrate. Something of a Butch Harmon in Sean Foley clothing, McCormick is a student of biomechanics, relies on TrackMan for feedback, is interested in the intellectual and psychological aspects of the game, and considers himself more overall coach than swing instructor. His intent was to refine Spieth, not define him. "It was fascinating to see. A kid of immense skill, you don't want to screw him up but, still, he was very one-dimensional. I'd only been teaching for five years at that point and this was the most talented man I'd ever come across," says McCormick. "Over time it's always been about softening the excessiveness of his tendencies while still enabling the athlete to produce the outcomes that he wants to produce."

What the athlete produced was a major championship season just short of another Texan, Ben Hogan.

Spieth had the best seat in the house to witness Bubba Watson's dismantling of Augusta National in 2014. The pet theory of the moment was that the MacKenzie & Jones course, pinched in with tree plantings and tickled with light rough, had become a patsy for left-handed power players—Phil Mickelson and Bubba Watson, to be precise. The high power fade of a lefty was the new gold standard, the most advantageous way to attack the golf course. An entire generation of players saw Tiger Woods do things they couldn't do, and in response, their chins dropped to their chests. Jordan Spieth saw Bubba Watson play the thirteenth hole at Augusta National with a driver and a sand iron. But when Watson won his second green jacket with an eight-under-par total, Spieth's reaction was, "Okay, fine. How do I get to nine?"

The mistakes Spieth had made on the eighth and ninth holes as a Masters rookie, and later on the twelfth, simply couldn't be repeated. Spieth and Greller went back to Crenshaw and Jackson. They doubled down on Spieth's affinity for the greens, and the results were as dominating a performance as Augusta had ever seen. His only brush with vulnerability came when he finished his Saturday round with a double bogey on the seventeenth and a salty up-and-down with a delicate flop shot from the right of the eighteenth to a tight pin. When it was done and dusted, Spieth had shot 270, eighteen under par, to tie Woods's scoring record set in 1997. He was the first wire-to-wire winner of the Masters since Raymond Floyd five-wooded the place into submission in 1976. He set the fifty-four-hole and thirty-six-hole scoring records. Only Woods won a Masters at a younger age. He made more birdies in four rounds than anyone who had ever played in the tournament.

Golf, and Augusta National, had seen its share of dominant players, golfers who were capable of overpowering not just that golf course, but any golf course. When Bob Jones said that Nicklaus played a game with which he wasn't familiar, it was a tip of the cap to his power with woods and long irons. Woods displayed a power game few could imagine and none of his peers could duplicate. In the age of rocket balls, driver heads the size of cabbages, computer-monitored launch angles, and ball flights that carried farther than Orville and Wilbur did at Kitty Hawk, suddenly there was a player, Spieth, who could be dominant by what seemed like sleight of hand. Sure, he made a lot of putts. Who wins who doesn't? This, however, was something altogether different. It was the ultimate backhanded compliment, acknowledging how good Spieth was without being able to define what made him that way. How does he do it? Hell, if I knew, I'd do it too, they all said.

The question no one could quite wrap their arms around was simply, what makes this guy so damn good?

Later in the Summer of Spieth, after Zach Johnson had won the Open Championship for his second career major and Spieth had missed his quest for the calendar Grand Slam (and the playoff at St. Andrews) by a shot, the '07 Masters champion did as good a job of explaining golf's newest, youngest star as anyone. "I get that every aspect of his game, it doesn't look flashy—this, that and the other—but everything is really good. And he's a great putter," said Johnson.

> But I think what sets him apart, at least in my opinion, is the intangibles. If I knew what they were, I'd try to implement them, but it's like an innate ability to just get it done. You're just like, man, you think he's out of it and all of a sudden he surfaces again. He's gritty. He likes to grind. Seems to me he kind of likes when his back is against the wall. I think there's a little bit of tension and pressure, to some degree, that guys have when you're supposed to rise to the top. For whatever reason, that doesn't bother him a bit. It's impressive.

Spieth shot 64-66-70-70 to wreak his revenge on Augusta National, and his season was only getting started. All the talk going into the Masters was of McIlroy's quest for the career Slam. All the talk coming out of it was Spieth. The U.S. Open was headed to Chambers Bay, the golf course where Spieth's caddie, Michael Greller, not only worked but had been married. In the Masters McIlroy shot a final-round 66 to finish six behind Spieth. At Chambers Bay he shot a final-round 66 to finish five behind Spieth. By the time they left the Pacific Northwest, the calendar Grand Slam had gone from darn near inconceivable to achievable.

Rarely had national championship golf been played in the Pacific Northwest. The PGA Championship was held at the Portland GC in 1946 and again at Sahalee CC outside Seattle in 1998. The U.S. Open had never been in that part of the world, an oversight the USGA hoped to rectify by adding Chambers Bay to its rotation. The blue blazers had developed a case of puppy love with the romantic notion of a links-style, entirely fescue-grass golf course—tees, fairways, and greens—as if Puget Sound was the Irish Sea. Unfortunately for the condition of the greens, it's not. The result was an agronomic nightmare of Poa annua (which grows in every West Coast course) and fescue. On perhaps the worst playing surfaces since the advent of the lawn mower, the greens were close to unplayable, eventually reduced to little more than dirt. This was not the product of poor work by a grounds staff but, rather, the backwash of a bad idea. Spieth's victory there was all the more remarkable because, if he wasn't the best putter in the world, he was certainly the hottest. It was like playing a championship with his best weapon tied behind his back.

Of course, everyone plays the same course. But bad greens tend to negate the advantage of the best putters because no one makes much of anything. Right up until the point when it counts, that is. Spieth went into the final round at Chambers Bay tied with Dustin Johnson, South African Brandon Grace, and Jason Day, who had been knocked to the ground on the ninth hole (his eighteenth) of the second round with benign positional vertigo, the aftereffects of which continued to bother him Saturday when he shot 68 to tie for the lead. Johnson, one of the longest hitters in golf, seemed to take control of the tournament, building a two-shot lead over Spieth and Grace after Sunday's first nine holes. Day struggled from the outset and shot a dispiriting 74. Johnson bogeyed three of his first four holes on the back nine and fell two shots behind Grace and Spieth. Grace, a stocky, little-known commodity in the United States who nonetheless had won six times on the European Tour, dropped out when he sent his tee shot on the short sixteenth out to the right, skipping onto the Burlington Northern Sante Fe railroad tracks—a links echo of the trains running along the eleventh hole at Royal Troon. When Spieth birdied the same hole with a twenty-five-footer, he had a three-shot lead with three to play. It wouldn't last.

A drive into the rough followed by a poor six-iron ("That was as far off line as I've hit a 6-iron in a long time," said Spieth) led to a double bogey at the seventeenth, dropping him to minus four. He put his head on Greller's shoulder. Had he lost the U.S. Open? Up ahead, Louis Oosthuizen birdied the reachable par five eighteenth for a remarkable sixth birdie in seven holes to post four under par. Johnson would birdie the seventeenth to make it three at minus four. Spieth, playing ahead of Johnson, drove into the eighteenth fairway. He had 250 to the front of the green and 282 to the pin. His three-wood faded slightly right, rolled across the green's NASCAR-like embankment, and stayed on the top shelf. He two-putted for birdie and the lead. If Spieth played the eighteenth beautifully, tee to green, Johnson was just short of perfection. He hit a massive drive and a five-iron to twelve feet. Unfortunately, it was twelve icy feet above the hole. Barely touching his putt, it rolled four feet past. The comebacker missed, or, as Johnson later described it, alluding to the greens, "bounced out."

Johnson was just a few days shy of his thirty-first birthday. Coming off the course he was met by his girlfriend, Paulina Gretzky (the daughter of hockey Hall of Famer Wayne), who was holding their infant son, Tatum. The party girl and the party guy. Though he'd supposedly been suspended in the past for what were reported by at least one news outlet to be failed drug tests—the tour didn't acknowledge such things—if the question was who was the best athlete in golf, Johnson's name was the answer you almost always got. He was six-feet-four and 190 with the oily gait of a jungle cat and routinely hit his drives three-hundred-plus yards, four hundred on the hard turf of Chambers Bay. Johnson had overcome more difficult things than losing. In his middle teens it would be fair to characterize him as at risk. His father was a golf professional who lost his job. His parents divorced. Johnson was involved in minor crimes that escalated out of control. A young adult intimidated Johnson and a small gang of friends into committing burglaries. That person, Steven Gillian, is serving a life sentence in a psychiatric prison in South Carolina for an execution-style murder. He had forced Johnson to buy him the ammunition. There is no equivalence between the crime Gillian committed and the mistakes Johnson made, nor should anyone have to be reminded endlessly of the ill-advised things one did at sixteen. It's enough that those universes touched, even briefly. Golf helped get Johnson out. He was rescued by his grandmother Carole Jones and by the man who was, at the time, the golf coach at Coastal Carolina University, Allen Terrell. "It could have gone a lot of different ways," says Johnson. "I had some help from some good people and ended up picking the right path." Chambers Bay was the third major he'd been in a position to win but hadn't. In 2010 he'd taken a three-shot lead into the final round of the U.S. Open at Pebble Beach, came unraveled on the second hole, and shot 82. That year in the PGA at Whistling Straits, he had what looked like a putt to win on the eighteenth green except he'd grounded his club in the bunker that didn't look like one. Johnson had been putting things behind him his whole life. Chambers Bay would have to be one more.

Spieth's roller coaster was altogether different. He thought he'd won it. Then he thought he hadn't. "And then, after DJ hit his second shot in, I thought, 'Shoot, I many have lost this tournament," he said. And then, quick as a three-putt, he'd won it again. "I've never experienced a feeling like this. Just kind of total shock," he said. He had confronted two of the biggest hitters in golf, Johnson and Watson. He'd seen what Bubba could do to Augusta National, then came back a year later to take the jacket off his shoulders. At Chambers Bay he hung around long enough for Dustin Johnson to take himself out. In the process Spieth became the youngest U.S. Open winner since Bob Jones in 1923. He was the sixth player to win both the Masters and the U.S. Open in the same year—Craig Wood, Ben Hogan (twice), Arnold Palmer, Jack Nicklaus, and Tiger Woods. And his birdie at the last was the first seventy-second-hole birdie to win an Open since Jones in 1926.

The Slam was alive. But before Spieth got to St. Andrews he had a stop to make. Silvis, Illinois. Rather than go to Scotland early to scout the Old Course, Spieth would honor his commitment to play in Zach Johnson's charity event and in the John Deere Classic, the site of his first PGA Tour victory. "So, the U.S. Open came along and I'm thinking, well, I don't know, he's still committed, right? I'm assuming Clair Peterson at the John Deere was kind of thinking the same thing," said Zach. "Clair and I were texting one day and I'm like, you know, he's a great kid. He's a phenomenal player. He's an even better kid. If he and his team feel it's necessary to not play I totally get it. I wouldn't be surprised either way and Clair wouldn't have been either. What he did honoring his commitment is beyond classy and just goes to show, once again, how much he truly gets it. He didn't have to do it." Oh, and by the way, he won.

Hogan won his third straight major at Carnoustie in '53. Palmer finished a shot behind Kel Nagle in '60 at St. Andrews when he had his shot at it. Nicklaus and Woods both came acropper at Muirfield, Nicklaus losing to Lee Trevino in '72 and Woods getting blown out of his shoes on Saturday and finishing six shots out of the playoff won by Ernie Els in '02. It was Spieth's turn in the barrel, and the barrel was the home of golf, and he would lose to the man whose charity tournament he'd graciously attended the week before.

It had been eight years since Zach Johnson, now thirty-nine, had won the Masters. He'd beaten Tiger Woods, Retief Goosen, and another South African, Rory Sabbatini, by two shots on a cold and windy Augusta National by never going for a par five in two, wedging them to death instead. It was the first time in his professional career that Woods had held the lead in a major on the last day and lost. Describing himself in 2007 as just a regular guy from Cedar Rapids, Iowa, Johnson was anything but. At five-feet-eleven, on a particularly uplifting day, and 160 pounds if he was draped in chain mail, Johnson was neither an imposing physical specimen nor a long hitter. He was a deft putter, using an unusual stance with his eyes inside the ball, and particularly dangerous with short irons in his hands. Pound for pound, Johnson was the toughest player on the tour. In a rare Monday finish caused by wind delays, Johnson tied with Louis Oosthuizen, who had won the previous Open Championship at St. Andrews, and Australian Marc Leishman, who'd been playing with Adam Scott when Scott became the first Australian to win the Masters, all at fifteen under par. Jason Day left a putt that would have earned him a spot in the playoff agonizingly short on the tiny eighteenth, but it was Spieth's near miss that was the headliner.

Despite a four-putt double bogey on the eighth hole, Spieth made yet another long birdie putt on the sixteenth to reach fifteen under par. He couldn't hold it at the seventeenth, no disgrace on the moiling Road Hole, and needed a birdie three on the short eighteenth to earn a spot in the playoff. It was a score both Oosthuizen and Johnson had produced, the latter sending Johnson's caddie, Damon Green—a good-enough player himself to make some noise in a U.S. Senior Open—into an abbreviated version of his celebratory "chicken dance." Spieth hit his drive on the eighteenth well left of his intended target, the clock on the R&A. No real damage was done, since St. Andrews's first and eighteenth fairways combine to make the widest target in all of golf. It did, however, leave him with an awkward yardage to the pin. His wedge finished in the Valley Sin, "the gulley" as he Texified it later, from where he failed to make three. It had been a gallant run at three majors in a row. The defending Open champion, McIlroy, had missed it all. His left foot was in a walking boot after rupturing a ligament playing soccer with friends. It was the first time the defender hadn't played in the Open Championship since Ben Hogan decided not to come back in 1954.

Even more unusual was Spieth's waiting on the steps of the Royal and Ancient with his caddie, Greller, as the threesome went out for their four-hole playoff won by Johnson when he started birdie-birdie on the first and second holes. When his victorious friend walked by, Spieth warmly congratulated him. Later, they flew back to the States on the same plane with several other players, drinking from the claret jug. "Jordan, he's a good friend," Johnson said later. "He embraced it. He was genuinely happy for me."

Not that Spieth was content to lose. "We wanted to work hard and give ourselves a chance and I felt like, if we did that, we could pull it off," he said. "Unlike the first two majors, I had a chance to win and I didn't pull it off. And that was the hardest part to get over, for me. I knew the history of it. I knew what we possibly could have done but, at the same time, my frustration was only that we were tied for the lead with two holes to go and we didn't close it out. You don't get many opportunities to contend in a major, in an Open Championship at St. Andrews, in your life."

At Whistling Straits in the PGA, Spieth reprised the role he'd played opposite Bubba Watson in the 2014 Masters. This time it was Jason Day who put on a driving exhibition. After coming up inches short at St. Andrews, Day seemed to turn a corner when he won the next week in the Canadian Open. He proved unstoppable in Wisconsin. Playing with Spieth on Sunday, Day took a three-shot lead into the final round, shot 67, and was never challenged.

"I was amazed that he kept pulling driver and kept hitting it in the tight zones," said Spieth. "I probably would have hit 3-wood in that scenario just to keep it in play. He proved me wrong. Each time he stood and took it back, I had hope. And each time after it came off the face, the hope was lost." After a massive tee shot on the par-five eleventh, when Spieth saw how far Day had driven it past him, he turned to the Australian and shouted at him, "Holy shit, you've got to be kidding me!"

Spieth embraced the tearful Day on the eighteenth green with the same esteem and respect he'd shown for Johnson weeks before in St. Andrews. Even in defeat he would ascend to number one in the world, the dream he'd told Cameron McCormick about as a teenager. It was a perch he'd fall off quickly, replaced by Day, and return to almost as fast when he won the FedEx Cup. Conventional wisdom held that McIlroy, Spieth, and Day would be passing that mathematical honor back and forth for years the way kids used to trade baseball cards. Here were three players who possessed outsized ability and candid honesty, from modest backgrounds and different corners of the globe, who showed an appreciation for achievement, be it their own or someone else's. They were humble in victory, dignified in defeat, and formidable in competition. The torch had passed into generous hands. And more were on the way.